MW00694660

MY EIGHT DADS

MY EIGHT DADS

*"My Mom marries 'em
and I bury 'em!"*

A memoir

Mark Kirby

atmosphere press

Copyright © 2021 Mark Kirby

Published by Atmosphere Press

Cover design by Jeff Dryer

Thanks to Sarah Simon for her editorial
assistance in drafting this manuscript.

Warning: this book contains adult themes
of sexual abuse and alcohol abuse.

No part of this book may be reproduced
except in brief quotations and in reviews
without permission from the publisher.

My Eight Dads
2021, Mark Kirby

atmospherepress.com

My ONE and Only?

I was diagnosed last March with a stage four variety of *it*. I couldn't even say the word out loud, it scared me so damn much. It is a terrifying experience, really. Two triggers back-to-back and I am a four-year-old boy again, trembling in fear.

I can remember *it* like yesterday really. *It's* hard to forget. *It* will traumatize you for a lifetime. Every time he took out the wine in *that* big glass jug from the GE refrigerator, I knew our *little* twisted, secretive ritual on the family beige cloth couch was about to begin. I could *smell* his odorous breath. The smell of Marlboro 100s and wine mixed together. He wore a heavy dose of *Old Spice* cologne. He was desperately trying to *mask* his *sweat* from a hard day of work at the office. It *never* totally worked. He *stunk*. My alcoholic stepdad. It was like *he* was covering up a *crime* scene. And I his *victim*. The *wine*, his escape from what *he* was about to do to me. I *loathed* that *smell*.

I can still remember the name of *it*. *Carlos Rossi, Vin Rose*. Red wine, like *blood*. My *blood*. It was as if I was being *sacrificed* to him once again by my mom. He the *beast*. I his *prey*. He would take a huge tap off the enormous jug and *belch*. He was really a disgusting pig. I was always forced to reciprocate. It was our *little secret*.

Just *him* and me. I drank his *blood* time and time again. Gagging at least once on every occasion. The wine was *our* sacrament he would say. He could never get enough of *me*. Our own little ceremony. Light headed, woozy. I knew *it* was coming next. The Father and his only begotten son were about ready to take it to the *next* level.

Do I feel guilty? What do you think? I'm still *angry* at my mom for not doing *her* job to this very day. Couldn't she *smell* the wine on my breath each time she tucked me in at night?

I would need my *jaded* sense of humor more than ever now as I *believe* God was testing my inner strength and resiliency for a second time much later on in my life. Or, could it be, God was *punishing* me? I was a participant in *all* of *it*. Willing? Nah. Certainly, not *FREE* will. I was just an *innocent* little kid. Minding my own business. Thinking about which toy I would play with next. I believed in *him* implicitly as my protector. I *trusted* him. Big mistake. I wanted *love* from my dad. But not that *kind* of love.

This *monster* would affect every relationship I had with adult males throughout my entire life. *Trust* me on that. Teachers, coaches, teammates, fraternity brothers, male supervisors and colleagues in the workplace. I would always be *skeptical* of their intentions. Would never let *them* get too *close* to me.

Could I have done more to help those *other* little boys? Probably so? Those pictures still *haunt* me in my sleep. Those damned *pictures*. His little *trophies*. My *horrific* memories. Naked boys *stripped* of their innocence. Just like I was.

Maybe this *book* could help me make sense of the senseless? Bring some semblance of order to the *chaos* that was my childhood. Bring closure to *those* chapters in my life I wanted to let go of. My way of making *peace* with myself. And with God, before I *leave* this earth. This was my *hope?* My *fervent* prayer. I wanted to move forward with my life. What was *left* of it anyway.

I *confess.* Masking my *pain* with humor was always my way of *dealing* with *it* as a kid growing up. I never wanted the other kids to know my *secret.* I was *petrified.* I would have been *shunn*ed for sure by my peers if *it* got out. I was only thinking of myself. My self-preservation. Surviving in the hostile world we called *family* when I was growing up.

This was serious stuff now. Life threatening. A *pivotal* point in my life. My *malignancy* had retriggered my *past.* Me versus the *unseen* enemy. It was as *simple* as that. And yet so complex for me to *sort* through as an adult, now in my late fifties. Layers upon *layers* of memories that needed to be *unpacked* here. *It had pushed* what was *buried* deep inside of *me* to the surface now. I would need to *battle* with all my *might* just to survive *it* one more time.

It was time for me to move on with my life. Make *peace* with my *maker.*

In February, right after a day of teaching economics to seniors in my high school, I had a pulmonary embolism, a blood clot, that went to straight to my lung. I went to the emergency room, with a sharp pain in my rib section and I was having trouble breathing. It felt like someone had taken an aluminum baseball bat and *smacked* me right in my rib cage. Two days prior, I had been spitting up some blood, but foolishly did not give it much thought. I could have easily died that day. The doctors could not figure out where the blood clot had come from.

After they ran some tests, my wife and I sat in the

doctor's office. Those clots often travel up from your legs, they said, usually after sitting for long stretches of time. But after getting an ultrasound, the doctors found no evidence of that.

My wife had noticed I frequently urinated. She asked the doctor, "What about his prostate, can we check that?"

"We can get a blood test now, today, to check his PSA level."

Why I never got this simple blood test before, I will never know. I think deep down, the four-year-old boy inside of me was petrified of getting a rectal exam. I had always associated *it* with the dreaded rubber gloves. The thought of someone invading my privacy in this way *again*—as I said, petrifying. Paralyzing.

I got my PSA blood test results back and my level was at a whopping 122. A normal PSA level for most men is between 1 and 2. I was behind the eight ball and in deep trouble. In the procedures to follow, I found myself thrust feet-first into what I would refer to as the *booby hatch*. An MRI would help us get a better look at *it*, up close and personal, with imaging-enhancing dye injected into my vein, vomiting rainbows throughout my body. I could not ingest enough valium that day to calm my nerves. This test was as scary as anything I had ever faced in my life up to this point. Why? Because of *what*, because of *it*.

The medical technician pushed me afloat, wading into the dark, noisy, and confining chamber. There wasn't water, but there sure were waves—suffocating, asphyxiating. Waves that carried me toward thoughts of my *real* father, resenting him for bringing me into this cold, cruel world, for abandoning me at a young age as I was left to row around on my own.

(1)

I was born with the last name "Barnes." Marilyn, my mom, was only nineteen when she got pregnant. Sheldon "Skip" Barnes was two years older. They were just a couple of kids who knew each other from high school. They probably hung out at the malt shop, went to sock hops and held hands. They went only as far as playing a little back seat bingo at lover's lane. We called it *parking* when I was a teen in the seventies.

My mom had followed Skip down to school at Pepperdine University to finish his final year of college. One day they decided it might be neat to get married. It was as simple and thought out as that. Back in 1959, if you wanted to sleep with someone, you felt family and societal pressure to marry first. You certainly did not live together, nor test drive the car before buying it; instead, you arranged an elaborate church wedding with a large guest list and joined two families together in a "dignified" and "proper" way. After the wedding and large reception and all the fanfare and hoopla that goes along with that one special day in a girl's life, you got to the sex.

So, I began my journey as the sperm that got away— probably on two virgins fumbling, bumbling, stumbling on a wedding night. From that moment forward, I would always be a survivor: the little sperm that could, swimming my way upstream against the very strong current of life. Dandy mental image, right?

There is a lot of blame to go around on failed marriage number one, but considering the time period, the age, the immaturity—it is a wonder that this marriage lasted longer than two years (two years and three days, to be exact). My mom was homesick, missed her parents; my dad was a total mama's boy. Any slight problem with his wife, and he would call on mama for a nice cry. Mama would take young Skip's side, a familiar fire would ignite, and the storm would consume their tiny one-bedroom apartment. Flames licking the ears of neighbors from miles around.

(2)

My only recollection of my real dad goes something like this:

I am about two-and-a-half years of age, my pants soaked and Flintstone underwear pulled down around my boney knees. Is it on the adult potty upright and still, like a man in an electric chair, waiting? I am motionless with fear. I anticipate punishment.

Skip enters the bathroom, frothing at the mouth. He begins to *shake* me. I am not talking about a "wake up, son, it's time to get up" shake—no, he is shaking the snot out of me like someone who is grabbing and manhandling a candy machine that has failed to dispense treasured peanut M&Ms. Why was he shaking me so hard? I tried my best to get to the potty, but between my hurried walk from bedroom to bathroom, I had little time to undo the button on my pants, unzip my zipper, pull down my underwear and pants, climb onto the potty and go. Too much for me to do in too little of a time frame, so I just stopped mid-journey and relieved my bladder without taking anything off. Sweet relief.

Skip did not see it that way and, upon feeling my wet parts, swooped me up under his arm, delivered me to the bathroom, *ripped* down my pants and placed me firmly on the toilet.

"Why in the hell did you *piss* in your pants?" asked Skip, screaming at the top of his lungs, face beet-red.

No answer. Small cries.

"What in the hell is your problem, son? Don't you get it? You are a big boy now, and big boys *piss* in the potty. You are wasting my time here, young man. Next time you *piss* in your pants, I am getting out the belt. For now, you can't get up until you have gone the big-boy way."

Still no answer. Crying turns into sobbing.

I sat and I sat and I sat on the potty for what seemed like an hour or two, until I finally went again, a little trickle of pee hitting the water and creating a ripple below. After inspecting the crime scene, Skip summoned my mom to retrieve me and I was "tidied up" and "put to bed without supper." Skip's orders.

This is the only father-and-son bonding moment I remember. Nothing comes back regarding a trip to the zoo, a Saturday matinee at the movie theater, a trip to the ice-cream parlor, a ride on the merry-go-round at the fair, a simple walk in the park or playing catch. I remember anger, yelling, cursing, intimidation, and resentment toward me for interfering with his young life. Skip was not hardwired, or ready, for the messiness of fatherhood. He couldn't even potty train his own kid without ripping him apart.

(3)

My mom's recollection of my real dad (after drinking a few gin and tonics):

Skip Barnes—handsome, young, up-and-coming business executive, newly married with a young son, and a new job as an accountant for a local chain of car dealerships. He arrived home each night around six. Skip was indeed the king of his castle in his own egocentric mind, and he walked up the flight of stairs like a man on a mission, ready to check the daily efforts and "hard work" of his devoted wife. He walked into his one-bedroom castle, briskly inspecting the crime scene for clues as to "what his lazy wife had been up to all day while he was away at work." Another: "The cat's away, the mouse will play." He entertained himself with these sayings, picking up every small item in the room (ashtrays, candy dishes, vases, etc.) for evidence of a lack of dusting from his "good-for-nothing wife."

Next, on to the kitchen, where Skip would slip on his rubber gloves, one by one and ever so slowly, beaming eyes like an evil proctologist at work—and remove "said garbage from said kitchen garbage can." You see, Skip's young wife was putting on some extra pounds and he didn't want her to "get any fatter on his watch." He had a snack drawer full of treasures that included chips, Cracker Jacks, pepperoni sticks, licorice and Jujuy Fruits, and she was never ever to touch his booty of loot. Evidence of snack wrappers would not sit well with the young executive, oh no.

Lastly, Skip would slowly approach the television set, whispering in a hoarse voice, "I got you now bitch, I got you now." He proceeded to rub the TV down with the palms of his hand, as if applying tanning oil to someone's back on a beach. He was checking to see if the TV was warm. If *she* had been watching it again while he was away after a hard day's work, there would be hell to pay. You see, "television watching is for breadwinners," according to Skip, and his wife was by no means a breadwinner in *his* house. No, she was a mere servant to Skip's every need at home. My mom, of course, was miserable with this routine and hated being victim to Skip's mental abuse every day. She kept this frustration to herself until all hell broke loose.

Skip had a temper, and he was always used to getting his way; his mom had seen to that since he was a toddler, and from time to time he would explode if things did not meet his standards. For the first year of his marriage, he would shove or push his wife, spank, or shake his young son, but he never hit either of them—until one day, when he backhanded his wife to the face after she questioned him. Skip never liked to be questioned by anyone at work or at home! It was always "his way or the highway." This display of physical aggression to his young wife would cause his immediate fall from grace.

A call to my protective grandparents would get the wheels in motion. Mom and I moved out in the middle of the day, caught a flight back to Washington. Divorce papers were served and marriage number one would abruptly end. I was a fatherless child at age two. I would bury my very limited recollections of Skip Barnes, my real dad, in the back of my mind until 1985.

No one in my family ever talked about him when I was growing up. It was as if everyone was ashamed of marriage/mistake number one. In fact, my mom hid all photos of Skip when I was a kid. I always lived among *secrets* as a young boy I always assumed Dad number two was my real dad growing up. This would bring both pain and relief when I found out as a teen that my next dad was *not* my biological father, even though I shared his last name. I would learn at a very young age: As an underdog, I would have to fight that much harder just to *survive* in this world.

(4)

I only met Skip once after. I actually worked for him for about three months down in Pasadena, California. My mom had contacted Skip by phone and said that it might be nice for him to connect with me, as I was getting married in October. She was worried about me and I am sure she thought I was too immature to get married. This one time in her life, her intuition was spot on. I was about as ready to get married as the Beatles were ready to get back together for a reunion tour in the eighties. It was an ill-conceived idea, and the person who would really suffer would be my young wife. She would patiently have to wait it out for many years until I finally grew up.

I met Skip for dinner, and he encouraged me to "come on down to LA," working for him at one of his moving and storage warehouses. I was unhappy selling insurance, but I thought this might be the big break I needed. I was hoping, wishing, praying my rich dad had come back into my life to *save* the day. I really wanted and needed a dad in my life. I thought good old Skip was going to be that person for me. I ached for a role model, a mentor—a wise older male adult who would guide me through the rest of my twenties and beyond. I have been searching for that man all my life.

I moved down to the Los Angeles area in July after getting engaged to Barb, a nurse in the Salem area. We had been dating for one month. She would continue to stay up in Oregon with her family and work. I was to get living arrangements settled in California. We would drive down together and move into our new apartment after our wedding in Oregon.

I was in love with Barb, and we both wanted to get married. The pressure of her being pregnant was not even a factor in our decision, really. We were both twenty-five, but I was not as mature and level headed as my wife; she had already settled on her career and I had absolutely no clue as to what I wanted to do.

In LA, Skip allowed me to stay at his small apartment until my wife moved down. I would sleep on the couch. Skip assigned me to one of his moving and storage warehouses near the University of Southern California, or USC, in a sketchy area of the city. It was a two-hour drive to work each day, nightmare traffic. I was given the title of Assistant Manager, but did all the dirty work the manager did not want to do. I moved boxes, drove the delivery truck, swept the warehouse, cleaned the restrooms, all among other managerial tasks assigned by my direct supervisor. I was only making minimum wage, much less than I had been making selling insurance in Oregon. Skip made it sound like I was going to be making much more when we had dinner together in Oregon. The move to LA was definitely a trade-down and I would soon realize I had made a *big* mistake.

As a businessman, Skip Barnes was a tenacious bulldog. After divorcing my mom, he remarried and had my two half-sisters, whom I met only once on a weekend trip to Palm Springs with my wife. Shortly after getting remarried, Skip devoted his full attention to climbing the corporate ladder; he got a job as an accountant for a national moving company and eventually worked his way up to the prestigious position of president and CEO. His second wife tended to the house and kids. In the late seventies, he took his money and purchased a moving franchise of his own in the LA area, which had a corporate office in Pasadena and several warehouses dotting out from there. He would later make millions in the lucrative self-storage business that swept the US landscape in the late eighties and nineties.

Skip was all set up, and his professional dreams had been fully realized. For the first time in his life, he had a substantial amount of money—tens of millions of dollars to be exact. But Skip let his testosterone be the guide and had an affair with his executive secretary. This did not end well for poor old Skip, as it is never wise to mix business with pleasure. In a few short months, Skip's wife was living in their once-shared spacious Malibu home overlooking the Pacific Ocean. Skip was now sharing a modest two-bedroom apartment with his secretary in the low-rent area of Alhambra and paying alimony and child support to his ex-wife.

This is when I arrived on the scene and got my first look at my dad—the businessman, the entrepreneur in action. Skip was now a disgruntled man, suffering from a mid-life crisis. I think he knew deep down that he had blown it. After all, he got caught with his pants down in a moment of temporary insanity and lust. He knew he was an idiot—a spoiled child, really, just like my mom had warned me over a few Tanqueray and tonics when I approached her as an inquisitive young boy, wanting to know what my real father was like.

At work, he was more of a tyrant than he was at home. For all of the success Skip had as a businessman, he was not really much of a people person. I wondered how Skip could be so downright clueless in terms of his people skills. His employees hated him. As I hung out in the warehouse with "the grunts," as Skip referred to them, I got a daily earful of disparaging remarks about my long-lost dad.

"Your dad is a fucking Little Hitler, man."

"More like Napoleon, dude, his hand is up by his vest holding on to his damn wallet."

"He's got small-man's syndrome and I betcha he's got a little dick."

Everyone in the room would crack up laughing. It was a nonstop roasting of their boss for the entire half-hour break. Skip also had a reputation among his employees as a "penny pincher" and a "cheapskate." He was a modern-day Ebenezer Scrooge according to many of the workers at his moving and storage company.

All the workers at the warehouse would scatter like spooked turkeys the week before Thanksgiving, when *Ebenezer* would roll up in his red Fiat Spyder convertible— a small man's car if there ever was one. He would jump out of his car and speed into the main headquarters, his butt puckered so tight you could swipe a credit card down that crack.

He would walk through each department and hover over random employees, micro-managing them. If he saw something that wasn't quite up to his standard of excellence, his face would turn bright red and he would chastise the grunt right in front of other workers. In his fits of rage, I have seen him hurl a pile of papers against the wall, knock over a file cabinet, throw a hole punch through a window, bring sweet little old ladies to tears. What a jackass, I thought. He had a clipboard that he took notes on, and he had a blackboard where demerits or black marks were posted for all to see. These demerits would cost each employee two dollars to be deducted from their monthly paycheck. I am sure this was not legal, but his workers feared him and at the same time made fun of him behind his back. Since I was his son, they felt it necessary to let me know how they felt about my dad, and often.

One guy named Larry had thirty-two black marks on the blackboard, and he would whisper obscenities under his breath every time he passed it. He also had a picture of the Nazi in his locker with a mustache, beard, and devil horns drawn on with black Sharpie. "Your dad is the devil incarnate himself, the prince of fucking darkness." He one day cornered me in the bathroom and said, "If I ever see your dad alone in a dark alley in the wrong part of town, I'll take these here box cutters and render him *nutless*." He cackled as he left the men's room, without even taking the time to wash his grimy hands.

No one, and I mean *no one*, liked my dad. I was beginning to see why. Skip thought he was just a little bit better than everybody else in the room and he wasn't afraid to tell you so. When the week of my wedding arrived, he simply refused to go.

"Why would I want to go see *those* people again? *Those* people are beneath me."

I assumed he was talking about my grandparents here, and I did not appreciate his high-and-mighty attitude. I had heard that things did not end well for Skip at the end of his marriage to my mom. My grandpa had threatened to "beat the crap" out of him if he ever laid hands on her again.

Later on, in our conversation, Skip started to tear up.

He said that he was sorry for shaking me as a young boy. "It was a wakeup call for me. . . . I went to counseling for anger management after the divorce," he confessed.

At that moment, I knew that my mom's stories about the overbearing and ill-tempered Skip were all true. That sole recollection of potty training actually happened. Still, I tried one last time to convince him to come to our October wedding in Oregon.

"But Skip, my wife and I would really like you to be there, it would mean a lot to us."

Skip got curt, leaning in his face inches from mine. "Sorry. I am Christian enough of a man to forgive people who hurt me, but I'm not *crazy* enough to ever trust them again. Count me out. Don't ask me again about your *wedding thing* or I am really going to get pissed. And you never want to see your dad *pissed*. End of discussion."

(5)

The day of our wedding came and only two of my five current dads showed up for our special day.

Skip Barnes had already made it clear that he was not coming.

D.L. Kirby, my second dad, called and said, "Sorry, Pard, you've made a choice to fraternize with the enemy, that candy ass, preppy, penny loafer–wearing dickbag Skip Barnes, and I ain't a comin'. And I ain't sending no present neither." No surprises here; D.L. was a deadbeat wedding guest, just like he had been a deadbeat dad all those years when I was a kid.

Michael Melvin, Dad number three, came with his new wife all the way from Florida. If it wasn't for Melvin, I probably would be incarcerated or living on the street somewhere. He was a positive father figure in a pivotal time. I really owed my life to him. According to Mike, he had made five million dollars selling vitamin supplements and then lost all of it when he invested in the commodities market in the early eighties.

"I had a mansion, a pool and a chauffeured limousine," he said, "and then I lost everything." Melvin was always a dreamer. He was a go-big-or-go-home kind of a guy.

Daniel McCormick, Dad number five, was there and had paid for the entire $1,500 rehearsal dinner the night before. He bought rounds of drinks for my former fraternity brothers and expensive champagne for the toast to the bride and groom.

My wife, Barbara, had no idea what she was getting herself into when she married me. It was like the Brady Bunch meets the Manson Family. All of these new crazy fathers-in-law to keep track of, each with their own unique problems and issues. They were truly a cast of characters and my wife really did not trust any of them, especially when we had kids of our own.

You see, Barbara came from a large Catholic family of eight kids. They were a relatively normal family and all the brothers and sisters were there for our wedding celebration. This side of the family, my in-laws, would provide my wife and me with a great deal of stability and support in our years of marriage. My wife's mother, Melvina was a *saint*—an excellent mother and grandmother who was adored by all her family. She would always be there for Barb and me in the good times and the bad. My father-in-law Boyd was just like my grandpa Cliff: ornery, tough and lovable all at the same time. Melvina and Boyd would be married once and only once, and to each other, and for over sixty years. They would be the new adult role models in my life whom I would look up to. They would, for the first time in my adult life, provide me with a consistent, solid feeling of stability and family. I admired their relationship and aspired to have that kind of grounded, loving relationship with my wife.

After the wedding, my wife and I drove her old, dilapidated 1976 Toyota Celica down to Alhambra where I had rented a small two-bedroom apartment for the two of us. My stay in Las Angeles was short lived. We lasted only two months. My wife was pregnant, hated the hospital she was working at, and she was homesick. My dad and I were not connecting, either.

I set up a meeting to talk with my father about my situation and get some fatherly advice from him. I spilled my guts to him about my desire to gain his trust and build a deeper connection. I said that I was "stressed" being newly married with a baby on the way. I also explained that my wife was struggling with her new job and missed her family.

Skip looked at me and said, "Mark, what I've learned through my years in business is that people don't really want to hear your problems, ever. Saying you're *stressed out* or revealing to me that *your wife is homesick* is a sign of weakness. People will view you as weak, and leaders can never show weakness. Right now, I am sitting across from a weak-willed kid. Grow some balls, son! It takes *big balls* to be successful in life. You are a failure because you are *choosing* to fail. It is as simple as that."

"Hmmm . . . thanks for the advice." I got up and walked right out of his office. I was stunned by his lack of emotion, his lack of empathy. Who does he think he is?

Mr. Adolph Napoleon Hitler, telling me *I* needed *big balls*? What a joke. This single interaction with my dad would motivate me for a lifetime. I would always look to prove him wrong. His condescending words that day would mutate and harden into a giant *chip* that would reside squarely on my shoulder as I moved forward.

I left Pasadena for good. My dad wouldn't even shake my hand or look me in the eyes the day I left his office. I felt again like he did not want to have any part of the sometimes-messiness of fatherhood. He had not changed in twenty-three years. He was the same selfish person he had always been. I moved on with my life, rudderless, without a compass, carrying a solar-powered flashlight in the dark. I would never see my *real* dad again. End of discussion.

Give me a Break!

My MRI test results returned during spring break. I was called by my primary physician at the home my mom shared with Ken, Dad number eight, in Phoenix, Arizona. It was *not* good news.

My mom did not want to deal with the *crisis*, as she called it.

"Why all the drama and fuss, for God's sake, it is only a little prostate *cancer*. I know lots of men who have had prostate *cancer*. The only downside to getting prostate *cancer* is you probably will never be able to get an erection again. I have met all kinds of elderly men down here in Arizona who can't *get it up*. No biggie. It's only a teensy-weensy issue of erectile dysfunction. Quit being such a *wuss* and deal with *it* for Christ's sake."

She squeezed her pointer finger downward, giving me a visual of what my shrunken penis would soon look like. That is the only intelligent thing my mom said or did that day, and I am afraid she was right about one thing. I would have a teensy-weensy little *pocket pickle* that I would have to *dill* with sooner than later.

"There are pumps and the magic little pill that can help you out with your little problem. No worries at all here, no worries at all. Suck it up, Mark. Besides, you can please your wife in *other* ways." That last comment seemed to have crossed the healthy boundaries of a normal, mother-and-son poolside conversation.

Now my mom began to really let me have it, talking to me condescendingly like I was a naive, stupid little kid once again. The more she spewed nonsense, the angrier I got. I wanted to just ignore her, but for whatever reason she was relentless that day in her inappropriate and inconsiderate comments as we all sat by her pool and drank iced teas. Then she said something I will never forgive her for—something so bizarre and self-centered, I had no idea where it came from.

"Don't worry about me, Mark. I won't pull a Debbie Reynolds on you and die right after you go, you know, like the Carrie Fisher situation from a few months ago? I am way too strong to let stuff like *that* bother me."

"Stuff like that? You mean *stuff* like me dying?" I retorted. "What the hell, Mom. That is an awful thing to say."

My mom had absolutely no empathy for my situation. My wife and I left early from Arizona in order to run some more tests and to get away from my self-absorbed mom. And she was more than happy to see us go. We were in the way of what she was fixated on at the moment. She was consumed with shopping for a new, bigger home that Ken had always dreamed of. You see, Ken had been living in a small trailer in the suburbs of Phoenix before he met my mom.

"We are looking for a big home with a pool and a giant *man cave* for my dear Ken."

Here is what I do know about my mom after fifty-nine years of watching her operate. If you look up the word *insanity* in the dictionary, you will find her picture. You see, my mom sadly continues to make the same choices regarding the men she marries. We are talking about eight grooms here. That is a right-fielder short of a full baseball lineup. Or a bearded lady short of a full freak in circus side show! With each journey to the alter, my mom foolishly expects different results. Each of her marriages ends in a flaming crash landing, body bags galore. That, my friend, is the definition of *insanity*.

And she was never really there for me growing up. I became an intuitive child around the age of four. It took me a while to figure things out on my *own*. This intuition I had as a kid was like a sixth sense. It allowed me to foresee bad things before they happened, to visualize accidents waiting to happen and know when I was in impending danger. Believe me, I was always in *grave* danger in the Kirby household when I was young. Eventually I would make the necessary adjustments just to survive. The world to me back then was black and white. I knew the good guys from the bad guys; the characters and plotlines throughout my childhood were always easy to follow—probably because I didn't overthink things too much. That is the innocent beauty of being a kid. My mom, on the other hand, was self-absorbed, oblivious to her surroundings, and made every relationship she got involved in more complicated than it needed to be. She was utterly clueless and didn't even realize she was laying her head down next to a *monster* each night.

My journey from childhood to adulthood has seen a revolving door of incompetent, unscrupulous, and sometimes sociopathic male role models figuring as my father. I can size up a man my mom is dating in one brief encounter and tell you *good* or *no good*. I have developed a valuable skill set from surviving *it* as a child. I can detect threats instantly. I know immediately when things are unsafe for me or my kids. I am able to adapt to new situations quickly and effortlessly, can use humor to endure and survive hardships, and can learn from my mistakes on the fly. My mom never seems to learn from any of her mistakes.

If a hamburger is set down in front of me, smells like crap, looks like crap, my intuition derived from childhood tells me that burger is probably crap. I will not touch the burger, let alone take a bite of it. My mom, on the other hand, is presented with this same *shit burger*, samples it, takes several disgusting bites of it and then tries to change it, return it to the kitchen. Some cheese perhaps, lettuce, pickle and onion maybe, a sesame seed or onion bun might do the trick, or maybe some bacon might change the flavor just a bit, but sadly, it is still and always will be crap. She had ordered up another man again, this time husband number eight. I could smell the stench of poo in the air on that beautiful sunny Arizona afternoon. My mom, on the other hand, smelled desert wildflowers in bloom. She was hopelessly in love, once again.

So, I wondered that day, like I have throughout my entire life: Was I just a bother or a nuisance in my mom's pursuit of her next man or her next upward career move? I would learn once again the sad truth of it all in a time in my life when I probably needed her the most. My mom would be nowhere to be found for the nine months of tests and radiation treatments. She was too busy trying to please, bribe, and trap husband number eight. Some things in my life never seem to change.

At that very moment, I wished my grandparents were there. They had both *passed* long ago. They were always there for me as a kid and grown man. As I sat dejectedly by the pool, waiting for my Lyft driver to arrive, my feet dangling in the water, my mind began to drift off. First to a giant Tanqueray and tonic with a slice of lime. Then to that time in my young life when my mom would bring *him* into our family.

(1)

The year is 1962. She is a single mother of one living at home with her parents and working as the soda-fountain girl at the local Woolworths five-and-dime store in Tacoma, Washington. Being a single mom in the early sixties was somewhat frowned upon in society and my mom's ultra-traditional parents, Cliff and Lavina Christianson, felt that their daughter's marital failure and current situation reflected badly on their parenting. There was pressure being placed on my mom by her parents to get back in the game, find an adequate provider for her now-broken family and a good male role model for her son. The weight of this pressure was tremendous, felt every day she left her parents' house for her downtown job.

Cliff and Lavina Christianson were not high-society folks, image-seeking socialites looking for approval from a large circle of upper-class friends. No; these were salt-of-the-earth, working-class folk who had good intentions and cared for their daughter and grandson very much. My grandparents were solid, loving people, and would always be there for me as I grew up.

Grandpa Cliff was a great high school athlete, could

play all sports well. He could golf, bowl, shoot hoops, and was damn good at tennis. When I got a little older, he would teach me to play tennis while standing at the baseline, suspending a lit cigarette in his mouth the entire time. I can see him now, hitting pinpoint shots everywhere, making me chase them down with my scrawny legs and chuckling to himself, in-between puffs of smoke. He worked at the naval shipyard as a supply truck driver in nearby Bremerton and was planning on retiring early, collecting his full pension and traveling with my grandmother to exotic locations throughout the world. He would achieve all of these goals in his life.

Grandpa was not much of a talker; I can hardly ever remember him having a deep sit-down discussion with me about any subject. He had a bit of a short fuse and a temper, and if you did something that annoyed him, like misplaying a hand in pinochle, he would let you have it. He left me crying at the family card table many times growing up, but you know, I became a pretty damn good card player. He taught me to focus on two important things when playing any card game: "Always be laser-focused on the hand that you are dealt with" and "always be thinking about your next move." I would need these two skills to survive and navigate my way through trouble as a kid.

Around my grandmother, Grandpa Cliff was milk toast, a pussycat, mere putty in her hands. If my grandma scolded him, which was quite often, he would simply reply, "Yes, dear," or, even worse, "Yes, Mother." In the company of his wife, Cliff was like a docile family puppy dog; he may as well have rolled over on his back on the living room floor and let my grandmother rub his belly. He was that pathetically weak willed in her presence.

Grandma Lavina was a stay-at-home housewife who drove a school bus part time to make some extra spending money for her family. She loved to be the boss, and was indeed bossy. She enjoyed riding herd on the elementary and middle school kids she drove to Charles Wright Academy every day. Her favorite saying, even well into her late eighties: "You know kids just love me, *all* kids love me, have you ever noticed that?" She thought she was every kid's favorite grandmother. More than a tad bit narcissistic, she was always about being the *center* of attention.

Truth be told, most kids didn't love my grandma at all; they were just plain scared of her. You did not cross Lavina May Christianson. She grew up during the Great Depression and World War II, and she had to drop out of school at age fourteen to help put food on the family table. She was an accomplished piano player, never having taken a formal lesson, and began playing piano in nightclubs and bars. This is how she met Cliff, who, at the time, was nine years younger and newly enlisted in the army. They met at the bar she was playing piano at in Vancouver, British Columbia. He loved when my grandma would sit down and play the piano, and he encouraged her to play anytime family or guests were over.

My mom would learn at a very young age that the only way she could get approval from her overbearing mother was through her performance in school and extracurricular activities. And, later in life, she would continue seeking that approval through her ascending career as a college administrator. She was taught that her accomplishments and achievements would be the only way she could define herself in a male-dominated world.

When Cliff met the divorced Lavina, my mom was only three years old at the time. Little Marilyn's real dad, Kurt, had left for *another* woman, and I believe my mom never really got over this abandonment as a small girl.

One thing was for sure: Lavina wore the pants in our family and you did not mess with her. There would be hell to pay if you did. Clifford new it, their three daughters knew it, I knew it as a boy and the students of Charles Wright Academy, who rode her bus every day, knew it as well. All my mom's husbands would learn this painful lesson too, as Lavina was very protective of her three daughters, especially of her oldest and favorite daughter, Marilyn. If a man close to one of her treasured children did something not to her liking, it was the kiss of death for them. No questions asked, adios amigos!

Both of my grandparents drove for a living. My grandmother was an excellent driver; my grandpa was the worst driver ever known to man. He would drive his brand new, bright red '63 Ford Galaxy with its 427 V-8 engines and a giant steering wheel, which looked more like a ship's steering wheel than a car, like a crazy man. This car was powerful and fast, able to go from 0 to 60 in 6.9 seconds with a top end speed of 135 miles per hour. This car was a rocket ship on wheels, and my grandpa was no John Glenn. He was more like the cartoon character *Goofy*, actually. He would drive with one hand on the wheel and his head would be moving and looking in every direction except on the road itself. No one in his car ever wore seatbelts, either. He would drive, smoke, change radio stations constantly and look for his favorite *Halls* cough drops in his glove box while carrying on conversations with everyone in the car all at the same time. It was unbelievable and pretty damn scary.

"Anybody want a cough drop?"

"No! Grandpa keep your eyes on the road!" we would all reply back to him in unison.

It is the scariest *sober* exhibition of driving I have ever witnessed in my life.

(2)

My mom met Dad number two, Donald Lee Kirby, while she was working at Woolworths as a fountain girl. She worked the small soda fountain at the store each day. She was a pretty, young, single mom, trying to make some money to help feed and clothe me and help my grandparents with household expenses and incidentals. Donald was a young retail executive "on the move," according to upper-management types at the Woolworths' corporate office. He was a twenty-five-year-old retail manager of the downtown store in Tacoma, Washington— a dashing, motivated and a hardworking young gentleman. He had aspirations of climbing the corporate ladder with one of the largest retailers in the United States at the time. Everyone who worked with, or for, the well-mannered, smooth-talking and gregarious Mr. Kirby knew that he was a rising star in the company.

My mom worked for Mr. Kirby and was immediately impressed with his pleasant smile, quick wit, excellent sense of humor and keen sense of fashion. Donald was tall, dark haired, clean shaven, well built and impeccably dressed every day he went to work at his store, like many businessmen in the early sixties. He looked like a character right out of the television show *Madmen* or a model for a

Brooks Brothers catalogue. Donald wore the classic American-cut suit of the day—the gray, black and blue pinstripe with narrow lapels. He wore a white shirt and a solid-colored narrow tie, black well-shined oxford shoes, and never would be seen without a pocket square to complete his daily fashion ensemble. He was indeed "a catch" according to all the women employees in the store who would whisper and gossip about their handsome young boss as part of their daily conversations on their coffee or lunch breaks.

Only a few weeks into her new job, and my mom found her boss's visits to the fountain growing more frequent. At first, he would check in and ask how things were going and leave with a complimentary chocolate malt or fountain coke. Then it became a sit-down chat over a banana split. She showed several pictures of her young boy one day, bragging like all new moms do, and Don seemed genuinely interested in her new life in Tacoma. My mom learned lots of information about her new boss from these pleasant little chats as well.

Donald had grown up in a small town around Eugene, Oregon, played sports and left for the Korean War right out of high school. Donald loved kids and had worked as a volunteer, coaching young boys while in school. While in Korea he had grown so fond of a poor, orphaned lad that he had valiantly tried to adopt him. He now shared several pictures from his wallet of the Korean boy. This touched my mom's heart as she got to know Don, as he now asked her to refer to him as a potential husband and father. That my mom had already been married once and had a two-year-old son did not seem to faze him at all. He was inquisitive and asked my mom many pointed and polite questions in the course of the next few weeks.

"Does your boy like toy cars?" Don would coolly pull out a brand-new Matchbox police car from his suit coat, beaming with excitement. His charm and charisma, all mixed with his genuine interest in my mom, was quickly winning her over. Their small coffee and lunch break interludes at the fountain counter—my mom having a BLT sandwich with potato salad and Don a cheeseburger and fries—morphed into late-night rendezvous at the bar around the corner, where my mom would sip on a glass of wine, chatting the night away.

Don would down a few martinis or scotch-and-sodas, probing with questions about me. My mom didn't know at the time, but her new boyfriend was *grooming* her. On one of these evenings, my mom asked Don to come to my grandparent's home for dinner to meet her parents, her two younger sisters, Linda and Naomi, and of course, me. Love was in the air and it was time to meet the folks once and for all at seven o'clock on Friday night.

Donald Lee Kirby, Woolworths manager and one of Tacoma's most eligible bachelors, dressed in his finest Ralph Lauren blue pinstriped suit, bearing a bouquet of red roses for my mom, and a bottle of expensive Cabernet for my grandparents. He rang the doorbell, without an ounce of liquor on his breath for the first time in his dating life, at seven sharp. My grandparents, who loved to drink, appreciated the fine bottle of red wine. He also bore, in his other arm, a gift-wrapped present for me and an assortment of the latest 45s for my aunts. He was on a mission to win the family over, and he did. He was "suave, debonair, handsome, polite, thoughtful, and dreamy," according to all who were there that night.

Cary Grant in the best performance of his lifetime could not have done a better acting job than young Donald did that night. He was just too good to be true! And you know what they say about that. He probably was!

The *wolf* had entered my family. He walked right in the front door and my family eagerly let him in. This *wolf* had already deceived everyone, was now among the flock, and was hell-bent on fulfilling an agenda for his own twisted gain.

(3)

The Chistiansons were now dead set on their oldest daughter marrying this solid, hardworking, young and dashing gentleman Donald Kirby. My mom was a little more hesitant than her parents, however, as it had only been a few short months since her first marriage had failed so miserably. She hadn't even really dated anyone else and was in no rush to get remarried. Shouldn't she at least get to know Don a little better before pledging her life to him? She had met a young lawyer who had handled her divorce with Skip and had her eye on him as well. But the good looking, older lawyer was in the midst of his own breakup and the timing just wasn't quite right for the both of them. Maybe she just needed to date? These were all sensible, reasonable, levelheaded questions to be raised by my mom at this time in her life. Why she did not trust her first instincts, I will sadly never know. Her ultimate decision to marry Don would change *my* life forever.

With much conversation—a little yelling and screaming behind closed doors between parent and daughter, and some arm-twisting by Lavina in particular—it was to be so. My mom and Donald would be married in a quiet little wedding ceremony in my grandparent's country home with a small group of close family members in attendance and a justice of the peace presiding. Absent from the ceremony and small reception that cold and wintery December evening was all of Don's family. It would be a year before we would be introduced to the in-laws.

The first year of marriage for my mom and new dad went by swiftly, as Don spent much of his time in his new position as regional manager of Woolworths. His job required him to open up new stores in Washington, help hire and train new employees, and mentor store managers at each new location. In a year's time, he had helped open up two new stores in Bremerton and Spokane, requiring us to move and rent small apartments in each tiny town. His expectations for his wife, as he was the breadwinner of the household, were simple ones indeed and were not uncommon marital standards for the early sixties. The woman was to play the happy housewife, cooking and cleaning and taking care of the children. My mom was living the life expected of her by society, while her new husband, immersed in his career, worked long hours with frequent late nights at the office.

Three important things transpired during this first year of their life together. First, nine months into their marriage, my mom gave birth to my baby sister, Grace. This would legitimize their marriage in a proper way. Second, my new father adopted me, and my last name was changed to Kirby. Third, and soon, alarming and disturbing behaviors began to surface in him. My dad felt pressure to be a proper young gentleman with a wife and kids, and the upper management at his company expected this from their managers. But things were starting to unravel a bit already for the young retail executive.

A couple of cocktails mixed by my mom after work turned into a few drinks and several more beers throughout the evening. And then my dad started staying out and drinking after work with business colleagues. On Saturday, he began to drink early in the morning and stay well-lubricated throughout the entire duration of the weekend. Cocktails, beers and bottles of wine were being consumed by my new dad at an alarming rate and our garbage can would be filled to the brim with artifacts of Don's thirst for alcohol. My mom was becoming concerned about this continual solitary tippling by her new husband.

Don was becoming more high handed, domineering and possessive with my mom and, when drinking, he became a person my mom had not seen before. He would not allow her to get a driver's license and forbid her to drive because "your place is in the home, doing women's work!"

He also gave my mom an allowance each week of twenty-five dollars, and this dictatorial behavior drove my mom absolutely insane. Had she traded a controlling Barnes in for a more controlling Kirby? Only time would tell.

(4)

My parent's first-year anniversary came and went, and we still had not met my dad's family. The summer to follow would be the first time. I was excited to meet them that beautiful July 4th weekend in Oregon, all piled into our light-blue family station wagon, chock-full of the necessities for the long journey to our neighboring state to the south.

Little did I know that I would soon be entering a *den* of *wolves*. We drove down Interstate 5, past Eugene, Oregon, up Route 126 and along the cold and rough waters of the McKenzie River. The *wolves*, however, would be driven by their appetites. They resided in these backwoods of the upper McKenzie River, awaiting me with unquenchable thirst.

As we neared our final destination, ending the long, dreadful journey I would take many times in my youth— we drove through the little town of Vida, through the Good Pasture Bridge, proceeded slowly up a winding, mountain-logging road, until coming to a sign that read *Dead End Ahead!* Just past this sign and to the right was a long, gravel road that divided overgrown fields to the right and a wooded area to the left. At the end of this almost unnavigable road, filled with more potholes than gravel, was a tiny, pathetic hillbilly shack in the middle of nowhere. It leaned a bit to the left with a porch and roof that looked like someone had taken an axe or jackhammer to it. This was the humble abode of the James family, my new great grandparents. I was about to enter real danger for the first time in my young life here—a relentless *feeding* zone that would change my life forever.

As we drove up to the house, all of Don's family were out on the porch, sitting on lawn chairs, old rockers or the broken-down, slanted porch itself. They were all drinking a clear concoction from old mason jars and seemed in high spirits. As they excitedly got up, they had to catch themselves from falling, as either the porch was too crooked or their drink too toxic.

The first to greet me was Grandma Bonney, a real-life

modern-day Calamity Jane. She was Don's mother. She had been married to Don's father, but divorced him when Don was younger. Don's father committed suicide when Don was a teen, taking a moonlight plunge to his death in the frozen waters of the McKenzie River. No one ever talked about this subject. I only learned about it later in my life and I can't help but think this weighed heavily on my new dad's mind from time to time. It may have been *one* of the reasons he drank so much.

Bonney was a grizzled old country tomboy, born in the hills of West Virginia, who was crusty and tough and could beat you in arm wrestling or *Burn Out*, a hand-slapping game where the object was to see who could slap somebody's hand the hardest as it rests on a table. Each player took turns on that hand. Before a strike, my grandmother would lick her fingers, get a running start, and jump into the air to get more leverage, finally walloping her hand violently down onto yours. I played this game with her more than a hundred times as a kid. She always drew tears from her opponents, leaving them swollen and red. I never saw her lose a match.

You did not want to *mess* with Grandma Bonney; she had a nasty mean streak running through her veins. I watched her manhandle her husband, Ralph, a tough old codger, many times when I was a kid. But Ralph was not present the first day. Instead, he was up in Alaska searching for gold.

"That son bitch better come back with some money or gold this time or I'm a divorcin' hem!"

There were two things I absolutely loved about Grandma Bonney. One, she made the world's best corn fritters, the most delicious tasting food I have ever eaten;

and two, she always brought a giant logger's wool sock full of coined money that she would let me and my sister divide up between us. We would excitedly pour all the coins on the carpet in the living room and spend what seemed like hours dividing it up between us. The great thing about this particular day was that my grandmother had brought me my first big sock full of money and my sister was too young to care about the dividing part yet. It was all for me. I lugged that sock of coins around with me the entire weekend. It never left my sight.

After we got our luggage out of the car and settled into the tight quarters of the tiny one-bedroom shack, we made our way out to the front porch. This modest home belonged to Ankee James, Bonney's stepdad. His name was actually Frank, but young Chester, Don's seventeen-year-old brother, could not pronounce "Frank" when he was a little boy, so the name "Ankee" stuck. Ankee's wife's name was Nanno, her real name forgotten long ago by all. She was seated in the luxury-edition plastic chair in the center of the porch, like a queen presiding over her people. Her daughter, Bonney, was now seated beside her, a hillbilly princess if there ever was one.

Ankee was a retired Oregon state forestry worker and had gone back to his roots as a West Virginian Appalachian hillbilly moonshiner in his twilight years. Ankee was proud of his moonshine! All his family members waited with much anticipation and excitement at today's *low-society* function and were passing around the homemade concoction. His *still* resided a mere hundred feet from the home and a short distance from their outdoor "pottying shack," as Nanno called it. I would try to avoid this little shanty as much as possible this weekend because I had already visited there earlier after the long car ride and it stunk bad!

Ankee was seated on a log in front of the porch, doing something with a pocketknife. This stimulated my curiosity, so I meandered down to the log and immediately took up a seat close to my new great-grandfather.

"What are you doing, Mr. Ankee?" I asked.

"Well, I be whittlin' boy, whittlin'," he replied, as a broad smile flashed across his wrinkled, crackled face.

"What's whittllin'?" I asked.

Suddenly, we had a new participant in our conversation—Chester, Don's seventeen-year-old brother, chimed in: "He means *whittle*, which is a country, backward way of saying carving with wood. Have him carve you a wooden toy, kid, go on . . . ask him."

Well, welcome to the party, Chester, I thought. You are all right and I do appreciate the toy idea. At this point in my young life, the acquisition of new toys was always foremost on my mind. I paused for a moment to reflect on my new uncle, who was sunbathing with his shirt off in a lawn chair a few feet away from us—in a giant field that my great-grandparents were trying to pass off as their front lawn. What in the heck was this Chester fella doing here in the first place? Here was this muscular preppy guy in Bermuda shorts and Ray-Bans, lying on his own lounge chair he had brought from home on *hillbilly beach*. He was basted from head to toe in tanning oil, sipping an iced tea with a wedge of lemon in it, which he must have packed himself, and was casually reading a copy of *Life* magazine with Marilyn Monroe on the cover. What is up with this dude? This guy just doesn't fit in here with the rest of these country folk. But not to dwell on this strange bronzed beatnik for too long—I wanted to get back to the *toy* thing.

"Ankee, could you make me a toy, please, out of your wood there?"

"You see boy, this here wood is sycamore, and it comes from a sycamore tree, which is good for whittlin'."

"Can you make me a toy out of that seekmore wood?" I asked.

"I can make you a *whimmy-doodle*," Ankee said.

"A whimmy-doodle?

My uncle Chester now chimes in again: "He means toy! A *whimmy-doodle* is slang for 'toy or object,' ya stupid little kid."

"Yes, I would like one whimmy-doodle please."

"Comin' up, boy, one whimmy-doodle it is."

"I'll need another jar of this here moonshine to git my creative juices a flowin'!" says Ankee. "Hey, Nanno! Get me another jar full of that elixir of the Gods!" Ankee shouts for the whole county to hear.

Now with another full mason jar of moonshine in his hands, Ankee, like a master craftsman, was working his magic as he began to whittle my toy out of the hunk of wood with fury. "Oh joy," I thought, "a new toy," and I hung on his every movement as Ankee swiftly and precisely made sharp and glancing cuts with his pocketknife. He would shave and scrape, twisting and turning the "seekmore" wood over and over, wood shavings flying in every direction. I was truly watching a *master* at work. Would it be a car, a soldier or a some kind of toy weapon? The excitement was too much for me to bear.

At long last, Ankee finished and proudly held his final wood product high in the air for all the now drunken hillbillies to see.

"I present to you, young Mac, my new great-grandson, your prized whimmy-doodle!"

So, he didn't get my name quite right, and I didn't care; I was more interested in the toy. "Thanks, Ankee." I looked down at the product. "What is it?" I asked.

"Why, it's a duck whistle, boy! It's used for duck huntin'. Now blow into it, you'll see."

I was disappointed, and my excitement was immediately deflated as I now held the pathetic little whistle made from a hunk of wood in my tiny hands. Duck huntin', I thought. There are plenty of ducks at the park by my house. Why would I need a whistle? I don't need a whistle to hunt, just a bag of bread and they'll come waddlin' by the hundreds.

"Go ahead, Mac, blow the doodle. You kin do it boy, *blow* it."

"Alright," I said, putting the wooden whistle to my mouth. No sound. I blew again, this time relinquishing all the breath in my lungs. No sound again. After the fourth or fifth try, the blessed hillbilly queen, Nanno, saved the day for me.

"Ankeeee, Ankeeee!" Nanno cried out to her pack member. "How's about a goin' huntin' soes to get us some meat fuh supper tinite?"

"OK, ya old hen!" Ankee yelled, just before another big swig from the mason jar. "That's the stuff, that's the stuff," he rejoiced, a newly energized smile emerging on his wrinkly old face.

"Ankeee, take the new boy Marty with you!" Nanno could never remember my name either. "It'll give you some company."

"All right, all right, calm down you damn squink, ya old ball and chain," Ankee muttered as he grabbed me by the shoulder and began to steer me up the path to the tool shed—a shabby, old wooden structure that matched the house to a T. Ankee opened the rotted-out door, went inside and emerged once again a few minutes later, this time bearing a giant snow shovel and a burlap bag.

"Come on, boy, you take the bag and I'll carry the shovel. Let's go a huntin'."

We proceeded down the driveway and veered off into the field where Ankee's prized family truck was parked. We hopped into that rusty old red truck and proceeded down the road to the highway we had traveled on earlier that morning. After about fifteen minutes, we came to the intersection of Highway 126.

"Keep your eyes peeled boy, we're a *huntin'* now."

"What are we hunting for, Ankee? And why don't we have a gun?" This was a reasonable question, I thought.

Ankee paused for a moment and reflected. Or maybe it was just the seven mason jars of moonshine kicking in. "Boy, listen to me now, we are searching for the *elusive* possum. With possum, you don't a need a gun."

"Possum?" I say.

"Yessir . . . possum. It takes patience to hunt possum. You ever eat possum?"

"No sir."

"Well you're in for a real *treat* then."

Ankee now took a long, awkward moment of silence as an opportunity to now *touch* my little left leg with his big old wrinkly, dried up paw. Weird, I thought. Really weird, almost *creepy* in fact, as he began to rub *it* ever so *gently*, like my mom kneading bread on her kitchen cutting board. He began to touch my leg down around my knee and slowly started working his way up my thigh toward my "danger zone," as my mom called it when I started to play with myself in the tub just before bed time. It is where my *Wee Willy Winky* lives, and trust me—*Willy* was not looking to be played with by any uninvited guests on this little pleasant drive in the country. What is the old geezer doing? I thought. Why is he touching me there? If this was some bizarre version of the game Red Light, Green Light, I am calling RED LIGHT just about NOW. Ankee's hand immediately left my leg as he saw something in the road. This could not have come at a better time, as my new great-grandpa was about ready to violate me right there in his old broken-down hillbilly truck.

"Look!" Ankee yelped, as he pointed to the right lane ahead and slammed on his brakes.

There it was, the *elusive* possum. But it wasn't fast, mean or even sport, really. It was big, kind of cute, like a house cat, fuzzy and fat—lying face and feet up, its tiny pink nose sticking straight up in the air, dead as a doornail in the road. Some Good Samaritan must have shot it and left it there especially for us because they knew we were hungry. I was now *very* excited.

Ankee rolled out of the truck, stumbled and heaved as he came upon the "road keel," his "prize catch."

"Come over here, Mac, and open up yer bag."

I did as I was told. Ankee took the snow shovel, and with one swift scoop picked up the possum and plopped it in my bag. I had *bagged* my first animal on my first hunting trip. What an awesome adventure, I thought. Ankee and I had fun.

"I'll take the bag now," Ankee grinned. He tiptoed back

to the truck like he had done something sneaky or top secret. Tonight, I was to have my first fried possum belly, with my brand-new family. What a treat.

At supper, we sat outside in our musty, sundried lawn chairs and feasted on deep-fried possum belly, catheads and gravy. It took a few minutes for my grandma Bonney to talk me down off a ledge on the catheads idea, as I didn't think too kindly about eating little kitties. But she calmly told me it is a West Virginia way of saying big biscuits. I liked big biscuits, so I took two. The food was not very appetizing—bordering on disgusting—and every time I went to Nanno and Ankee's home, I always had to try something new that I had never eaten before. Bear, rabbit, quail, deer meat: all things I had tried for the first time at my great-grandparent's home with much remorse and belly discomfort. I would always try to have a peanut butter and jelly sandwich, a box of animal crackers, or a few Oreos with me for backup.

The only person who didn't partake in the meal that night was the *odd* duck of this family get-together, my uncle Chester, who had packed a sack lunch consisting of a turkey sandwich on rye, chips, a banana, an orange and Jell-O pudding. "I am training for football, don't bother me," he defended, sitting quietly on the sofa inside the house, now wearing his letterman's sweater and watching the small black-and-white television in the hillbilly home.

After dinner, Nanno broke out her guitar and sang songs. She always took requests to start off her down-home dinner show: "Duz anyone hev a song they wanna hear?"

Someone shouted, "How about playing some Johnny Cash 'Ring of Fire' or 'Puff the Magic Dragon' by Peter,

Paul and Mary?"

Nanno would quickly quip back, "I don't know any of 'em, but how's about ol' "Cripple Creek'?" She would begin playing this old Appalachian song from the 1920s that her mother had played for her as a child. This was either the only song she knew or the only song she remembered as a woman in her mid-eighties.

Gone to Cripple Creek, gone in a run
Gone to Cripple Creek, have me some fun
OH, Gone to Cripple Creek, gone in a run
Gone to Cripple Creek, having me lots a fun!

After finishing, she would excitedly ask her small audience again, "Any requests?"

Someone different this time shouted out, "How about Bobbie Vinton 'Roses Are Red My Love'?"

Nanno again, right on cue, would say, "Don't know 'em, how about some 'Cripple Creek'?"

This madness would go on for hours that night, as she and her dinner guests inebriated themselves on Ankee's homegrown moonshine, feeling no pain. As my new relatives danced by the firelight and sang out of tune to Nanno's old song, my new dad got more and more belligerently drunk, dancing the jig with a straw hat on his head.

I began to assess the situation I found myself in on this warm July night of 1963. My first thought was, what in the world was I doing here in this backwoods hillbilly estate? I also wondered why my mom, my protector, hadn't taken the time to meet my new dad's relatives before she got hitched. I thought something was real weird and my stomach grew increasingly queasy, either from the catheads I had eaten earlier or the redneck music and dancing, or both. I knew something was *rotten* in Vida that night. I couldn't figure out why my intelligent mom was not picking up on these creepy little vibes as well. She just sat there all night like a zombie, smiling, nodding her head, clapping and not saying a word.

What seemed like a relatively pleasant, albeit strange, day turned into a horrifying nightmare as the darkness of night fell upon the James' country estate. Everyone had turned in for the night. Ankee and Nanno were the first to retire to the only small bedroom in the house, the entry way closed off by· a bed sheet. My mom and dad were left to sleep in the hide-a-way bed in the living room. Bonney was sleeping outside in a tiny pup tent. Ankee had suggested that my new uncle and I should *share* a bed on the side porch, which was turned into a makeshift guest room entirely wrapped in some kind of black plastic to protect it from inclement weather. I did not feel comfortable with these sleeping arrangements; Chester had given me a *weird* feeling that afternoon. My intuition told me he was no good immediately. But no adults chimed in to produce another desirable alternative, so it was to be me on the porch bed with my new creepy uncle for the night. No further discussion.

The innocence of childhood left me that night forever, never to return again, as Chester was the first of the *wolves* to bite me, slowly chew on me and *devour* my heart, mind and soul in one ravenous meal. The terror was constant and intense, as "shhh"s turned into a hoarse and quiet, commanding "hush" from my demented and evil uncle. At some point during that horrific evening, I just gave up and submitted to *it*. I drifted off to sleep that night and for the first time of many times in my childhood I would lock *it* away in a tiny safe in the dark recesses of my mind.

I hoped as I rode back to my home that weekend that it all had been some awful, dreadful dream. If the attack had really happened, I thought, maybe my uncle was just a creep, or a weirdo, and my mom and dad would be there next time to protect me.

These were the family secrets that I discovered, hidden deep in the backwoods of the McKenzie River that fateful July weekend. My mom had unknowingly brought me into a *den* of *wolves*, and these predators would leave me with emotional scars and male trust issues that I would wrestle with for my entire life.

A SECOND Opinion

My current dilemma was far worse than anything I could have ever possibly imagined as a kid growing up. My wife wisely thought I needed a second opinion from a specialist outside of my health-care plan. I was not at all enthused about seeing another *butt* doctor that day.

On the bright side, I had learned so much in the past couple of weeks. For instance, I now knew that the prostate is a little, useless, walnut-sized organ that resides in close proximity to a man's carry-on. I was now paranoid that everyone wanted to stick something up my rear end to get a feel of my rotten walnut.

My wife and I went to a specialist in urology, Dr. Wilson, to get a second opinion. He was a kind, old, gray-haired man who spoke like Mr. Rogers. He was using an anatomic diagram made for five-year-olds to explain the prostate to us. I was already feeling uncomfortable and paranoid in his presence. Might have made me feel a tad bit better if they had asked me if I had ever been sexually abused before?

"There are three zones of the prostate: one, two, and three." Dr. Wilson smiled and pointed to each of the zones on his diagram like my wife and I were small children.

My wife asked, "Which zone would be most a cause for concern, doctor?"

"If you get cancer right here, it's not so bad. Most people get cancer here." He trembled uncontrollably, like what you might see in Parkinson's, motioning his shaky, wrinkled hand to the innermost zone of the prostate. He was using a pointer stick.

"Well that's good to know," my wife replied, now smiling at me for an instant.

"But if you get cancer in this outer zone, very bad I'm afraid. Only seven percent of patients get it *here*, and most people don't survive more than three to ten years. That's not very long, is it?"

Dr. Wilson was now smiling at me like a little old grandpa in a friendly game of checkers with his grandson, instantly giving me the creeps. Danger, Will Robinson, *danger!* I wanted to leave his office immediately.

Once he wrapped up his little Mr. Roger presentation, he instantly transformed into Mr. T from *Rocky III*.

"Well it's time for the prostate exam!" He clapped his hands three times, seemingly excited about this idea. "This might be a bit painful. You don't mind *pain,* do ya son?" He was now administering the rubber gloves to his earthquake hands. "You ever have one of these rectal exams before, boy?"

I gulped twice. "No, sir, and that sure wasn't a very smooth transition from the friendly little pictures to the rubber gloves there, Dr. Wilson."

I was now sweating and squirming in my seat. Looking at him quiver, I knew I was in for a bumpy ride here. My butt cheeks tightened instantly as an obvious defense mechanism to the impending invasion of my semi-secret stink portal.

"I remember when I first got into the military as a

young kid and they gave me one of these rectal exams. It completely changed my life forever! I knew at that very moment that I wanted to be a urologist." Dr. Wilson was now laughing to himself and applying a heavy dose of lube to his little latex feelers.

"Where do you need me?" I asked.

"Bend over the table right here. This may *hurt* just a little. I am going to gently *massage* your prostate to try and see if we can get some fluid to examine under a microscope." He laughed like a mad scientist would. This creepy little cackle scared the living shit out of me.

He had what seemed like his *whole* fist up my ass now and was holding a microscope slide under my petrified penis. He was definitely not massaging my prostate, but instead grasping and compressing it, swollen and tender, like someone does with a squeeze ball to relax. I was not relaxed at all by this violent assault on my *bunghole* and I started to have a panic attack, my throat tightening up, my lips swelling and my face turning bright red.

"I think I'm going to pee!" I was now screaming, and tears of pain were streaming down my face as I feared Dr. Wilson might *crack* my throbbing walnut.

"Peeing is a good thing! Pee, damnit, *pee!*" I was in as much pain as I have ever been in my life. Ten out of ten.

Unable to control my bladder, I urinated on his table, dribbling some thick, dark yellow liquid on his slide. It was done.

I couldn't even look at the man when I left his office, my head down in shame. I had been *violated* for the first of many times to come. Actually, I felt a little like friendly old Dr. Wilson had *molested* me that day. He certainly had taken away some of my dignity and self-esteem during that hour-long office visit. I came into his office a reasonably confident fifty-eight-year-old man and left a traumatized four-year-old boy newly born. Darkness.

(1)

Donald Lee Kirby had been lying low during the honeymoon phase of his first and only marriage. A marriage to this woman, my mom, would really only serve his purpose this one and only time, because he was not interested in the bride at all, but in her treasured, only begotten son. He had planned his work and worked his plan of attack to perfection. He had been *grooming* me every day for the past year and a half of my young childhood.

He bought me a little dog when I was a small boy. He placed a red bow on her and gave her to me right after I blew the four candles out on my chocolate-frosted birthday cake. I was ecstatic and loved my dad so much for his thoughtful little gift, a furry friend I could call my own. I named her Misty. She was a poodle mix with curly black hair, the prettiest little creature on this earth, my pride and joy—she would be my one and only true friend for six long years. My dad would make sure I never had any friends over to our house. There were way too many *secrets* inside the *Kirby* home. It was always going to be Misty and me. And my dad, of course. My dad's grooming of me was now close to complete.

He got me up every morning, dressed me and saw that my mom fed me before he left for work. In the evening, he played with me when he got home from work, bathed me after dinner and tucked me in safe and sound each night. I now trusted my new father, without knowing that this was a cold, calculated *hunt*. It was now time for Donald to move in for the kill.

I remember the night my second dad turned into a *wolf* like it was yesterday, although I have tried to block it from my memory for most of my life.

Shortly after my trip up the McKenzie River in Oregon to visit my hillbilly in-laws, Dad stealthily *snuck* into my bedroom at our new family home in Coos Bay, Oregon, a tiny coastal town to which he had just been transferred to work as manager of the new Woolworths store. Now, this was actually a demotion from his previous job. He was not happy about this downward move in the company and had turned to drinking even more intensely the past few months, soothing his fractured ego. It was Friday night, and he had been up drinking late after my mom had retired to bed a couple hours earlier. He quietly slipped into my bed and *it* happened to me again. I just could not believe *it* was true. I foolishly thought *he* was here to protect me.

Before he left that night, he said in a cold, calculated, demonic and hoarse voice, "This is our little secret, Daddy's little secret. Don't you dare tell anyone about this, especially your mom. Your mom will punish *you* for what *we* did."

He would say this to me time and time again. "Do you understand me, *Pard*?" He would now refer to me in this way, talking to me like an adult to control me even further. "Answer me, Pard, when I am talking to you!"

"Yes, sir," I would manage to squeak out, fighting back the tears.

And in the most twisted way a parent could ever manipulate their child, he told me that if I said any*thing* to *any*one ("and I mean *any*one!), that he would do *this* to *Gracie*. That he would *rape* my little sister.

"Please don't hurt my sister, please don't touch her!" I would scream.

"Quit being such a candy ass and take *it* like a man," he would say. "Pard, life's a bitch and then you die. Don't you ever say a word about this to anyone. You got me, Pard?" He yanked me by the back of the neck, shoving my face into the pillow.

I remembered nothing else that first night, my mind drifting off to happier thoughts and places. I thought of my favorite cartoons on Saturday morning television, replaying my favorite scenes of my Saturday morning cartoons in my mind.

Much of my early childhood would be stripped away by this *monster*. Gracie was only one-and-a-half at the time. She was just starting to talk. The thought of *him* touching her private parts made me sick. It would be my job as her big brother to protect her from his bite.

He would visit me time and time again over the next several years, never seeming to get enough of me. "D.L." is how I would refer to him from this day forward; Donald, the man I knew as my dad, as my protector, would die that night. D.L. had a veracious, unquenchable appetite. From that night on, he would no longer be my father but an enemy.

How did my mom let this happen to me? The signs multiplied over the first few years of their marriage—you just had to open your eyes, study the simple patterns of human motivation and interaction, and connect the dots. I now had two secrets to keep: one with my Uncle Chester and one with D.L. I was hoping and praying that someone would take the time to help me so I could just get back to being a regular kid.

(2)

It was a typically rainy, coastal morning in May of 1965 in Coos Bay, and I was now a first grader at Miller Heights Elementary School. School for me had become a sanctuary, a safe haven from *it*. Going to school each morning was a way for me to leave my family issues behind for five days a week, eight hours a day.

My mom had a driver's license now—after convincing D.L. that she needed to be part of the neighborhood carpool of women that transported their kids to school each day. This newfound freedom allowed my mom to, for the very first time in their marriage, take on two part-time sales jobs: one with the Beeline Fashion company and the other for Avon.

For me, my mom leaving our home to go to work in the evening made *it* get worse. D.L. offered to babysit me while she was away at her Beeline and Avon parties. And this, of course, was not to help *her*, but to gain more private access to *me*. When alone with me at night, *he* would offer me drinks of wine out of a big jug with a screw top, trying to drug me. Or, he would take me on long drives in secluded areas to do the same. Where was my mom when all of this was going on? Could she not smell the wine on my breath when she checked on me every night in my sleep?

(3)

I was in third-period gym class that day in May, sitting with all the other boys and girls on the floor. We were waiting for Mr. Bentley, our PE teacher, to speak.

That day, Mr. Bentley looked as he always did. He was dressed in white from head to toe. He was in his mid-forties, and he sported a military buzz cut.

Mr. Bentley was not a model of fitness. His stomach pooched way out over his belt. He slouched when he walked. He had yellow teeth and was constantly smoking cigarettes, both in and out of class.

Mr. Bentley awarded different-colored uniforms to each student according to their grade received in the previous term. "A" students received bright-red ones. "B" students received matching Kelly-green trunks and shorts, while all the average-to-under students received navy-blue ones. I had received a "C" the last term, because I could not do at least five pull-ups and climb the rope to the top of the gym ceiling, so I was sitting with my legs crisscross applesauce in my standard blue prison attire.

Mr. Bentley did not really teach PE—except for the last week of the semester when he tested all students for the Presidential Fitness Award program. He mostly rolled out the basketball, playground ball, softball or dodgeball and just let the kids play. We would choose sides for dodgeball and he would always be on the side that had the most red-uniformed "A" kids. Yup, Mr. Bentley would intentionally seek out the less athletic kids he didn't like and pelt them square in their melons just for the fun of it. The red-clad young Republican kids thought that he was vicious—a real cutthroat competitor! But most of us dressed in blue thought him to be a complete idiot and a disgrace to the teaching profession.

Bentley would yell all kinds of maniacal, meaningless mouthfuls of worthlessness as we fired away at each other.

"Battle to the death, kids! Last man standing wins!" or "Dodgeball is Social Darwinism at its finest! It's survival of the fittest, boys and girls!" He would laugh hysterically at his own immature and asinine humor, as he would *drill* a little girl in her noggin and knock her half silly just for the fun of it. I thought Mr. Bentley only a slightly better role model than my dad. He was in his own little world, on his own pernicious power trip. At least Bentley had never tried to touch me.

Today we were to play indoor whiffle ball, one of Bentley's favorite games. We chose sides first, with two of the red-uniformed kids out in front as captains, like always. Choosing sides took a grueling fifteen minutes, at least. The whole process was brutally demeaning for some of us kids, but it did allow Mr. Bentley a logical smoke break. It finally came down to me and the heavy kid in the wheelchair—and I got picked *last*, as usual. Mr. Bentley liked to play "all time pitcher," as he called it, which meant that he pitched for both sides. He would pitch with a lit cigarette in his mouth and he always threw as hard as he could. He would say, "Here comes an overhand screwball" and he would fire away. The kid at the plate would swing wildly, and Bentley would laugh and make some clever and condescending comment: "Nice swing, ya dingle berry. I got some wood at home that needs to be chopped."

In the world of teaching today, Benjamin Bentley would have probably been placed on a plan of assistance for several infractions and violations of the district teacher handbook, as well as for a general failure to employ best practices in the classroom setting. In 1965, however, "Coach B," as he was affectionately called by administrators, colleagues, parents and players on his high school baseball team, was a pillar of the community and regarded as a competent elementary PE teacher. For us students, however, he was the disconcertingly cruel Mr. Bentley.

After whiffle ball was over, Mr. Bentley gathered us in the center circle of the gym and directed us to "get down on one knee, boys and girls. Listen closely, and eyes on me." He cleared his throat.

"This, boys and girls, is a very important message from Principal Skinner..."

Miller Heights
Elementary School
Coos Bay, Oregon

Dear Parents:

The annual school carnival is just around the corner: Friday, June 5th. As always, we are looking for boys, grades 1–6, to participate in the featured event for the night, "Little Guy Rough House Boxing!" This event alone brought in over $1,200 last year, and was used to pay for two new slide projectors for the school.

All boys participating must fill out a participation slip and waiver, signed by a parent or guardian, releasing any liability to the school in case of injury during the event. We hope to see you at this year's carnival!

GO COUGARS!

Michael B. Skinner
Principal

Bentley glared out at all the big eyes looking straight back at him, hanging on his every word. "Men, I'm talking to the boys in the class right now. I have been affiliated with the Rough House Boxing event for the past fourteen years and have served as the ring-side trainer and referee for this illustrious and sacred event each and every year. As some of you know, I served in the marines during World War II and boxed while stationed in Guam. We are looking for a few proud young men to compete at the school carnival on June Fifth. Make your classmates, parents, school and the community at large proud of you by signing up today. I am now looking for four volunteers from this class—four bold and brave enough to go to *battle*. Make your fellow Cougars proud. Who from this class is man enough to volunteer?"

Three hands instantly rose as Bentley jotted each of the boy's names down on his clipboard. Mr. Bentley was now scouring the rest of us boys, head swiveling back and forth, looking for a fourth participant among us. Bentley could never remember kids' names; he had a nickname for everyone he taught. I was to his back left and he instantly spun around and suddenly stabbed his finger in my direction.

"How about you, *Hoover*?" He called me this because my last name was Kirby, like a vacuum—get it? He was glaring straight at me and smiling with his bright-yellow teeth, waiting for a reply. No answer.

"Wouldn't you like to volunteer to *box,* you little pantywaist?"

Well, that was it. I never had volunteered for anything, had no idea what boxing really was. At the time, I thought it had something to with boxes, so I was unenthused about the whole idea. My childhood intuition that day told me *boxes* were not an immediate threat to my safety and well-being. Bentley, though, was calling me out and challenging my manhood in front of my peers. I did not appreciate this.

I shot back proudly, "I volunteer. I will box at the carnival, Mr. Bentley!"

"Nice job, Hoover. That's the first time all year you haven't *sucked!*" he said, using another lame vacuum pun.

The entire classroom cracked up, laughing at Mr. Bentley's cutting wisecrack about me. All this did was inspire me even more. I will show all of you guys, I thought, including you, Mr. Bentley. I will show my parents and all the people of Coos Bay. I will be crowned the *Champion Boxer* of the first-grade class.

When I got home that night, I burst into the living room and shouted, "Mom, Mom! I am going to be part of the carnival this year as a boxer," still having no clue what I volunteered for. I thrust the information sheet and waiver form up to my mom's face and waited patiently as she slowly read it. She signed it immediately and gave me a big hug.

With a signed entrance slip and waiver turned into the office, I began to do my training for the big event. For the next couple of weeks, Mom fixed me healthier meals and rode her bike while I jogged beside her in the evening through our neighborhood. She even had developed a little fifteen-minute workout for me to do each night before bedtime. Mom had now become my *boxing* trainer. I guess I had never realized what kind of shape you had to be in to *box stuff* up. My mom knew. She had a vested interest in my success. Our family pride and honor was on the line, and if anyone had the *eye of the tiger* in May of 1965, it was certainly not me, but my mom.

The night before the match, just before bedtime, while D.L. was away on a business trip, my mom emerged from her bedroom with a large rectangular gift-wrapped box. She said, "Open this up, little champ. You deserve this for all the hard work you've been putting into training for tomorrow's bout."

As I lifted up the lid, I was surprised to find a brand-spanking-new white terry cloth robe. Now, this wasn't just any robe—it was a personalized boxing robe with the name "KIRBY" on the back. Looking back on this gift, I think it was more of a gift for my mom than it was for me.

Well, the night of the school carnival had arrived, and I spent the first hour and half of the evening playing games in the downstairs cafeteria. I threw darts at balloons, flipped ping-pong balls into little fishbowls and tossed rings onto bottles of coke. I spent the whole ten dollars that Mom had given me in an hour, and ended up walking around with fifty cents worth of trinkets and candy stuffed in my pockets.

It was about one hour before my nine o'clock match, and I stepped into the gym for the first time to see what all the fuss regarding *boxing* was about. My *bout* was with Josh Harper, a kid who lived across the street from me, and whom I had played with many times at his house the last few years. He was my best buddy. I was confident that we would have lots of fun *boxing up* stuff together.

In the middle of the gym was a large, square trampoline, I guess, with ropes around it? Seats were lined up all along the four sides, facing the trampoline about ten deep. There must have been four to five hundred people packed into this cramped, hot, sweaty, smoke-filled gym.

All the adults were smoking and shouting at the top of their lungs while the kids walked and bounced lightly toward each other on this trampoline. I sat down in an empty seat in the third row and decided to get an up-close look at the action.

Two fourth graders whom I knew from my morning bus route, Bart Wespee and Alan Mundt, were hitting each other viciously upside the head, with these big, padded *mittens* they wore on each hand. They sure were hitting each other hard, I thought. I was starting to feel ill as I watched the events unfold, now realizing that this boxing thing was a bit too violent and dangerous for my taste. I became perplexed and wondered where the boxes were. Alan was the only combatant wearing protective headgear; he had lost most of his left ear as a second grader when he was tragically run over by a street cleaner. Kids wondered, and many adults wondered as well, how in the world could someone get run over by something as slow and loud as a street cleaner?

D.L., after a few beers at a neighborhood get-together, would joke, "How in the hell do you get run over by a street cleaner? It's not like the damned thing is going to surprise you or sneak up on you suddenly." And sadly, people would laugh. I always felt sorry for poor Alan.

Tonight, as I examined the match with horror, three boys in the front row were talking trash and trying to distract Alan any way they could. Now they were all yelling in unison, "Hey, Alan, the street cleaner is coming, the street cleaner is coming!"

Alan had been glancing over at the hecklers the instant Bart struck him with a right hook to the face. Alan's knees buckled and he fell like a tree, flat on the trampoline, face first, his mouthpiece flying out of his mouth on impact. After a ten-count, referee Bentley declared Bart the winner and raised his mitted hand high in the air. Luckily, Alan wasn't knocked out or hurt badly. He had just given up and stayed down for the count. When he finally got to his feet a minute later, I was horrified to see blood gushing everywhere from Alan's bloody nose. I almost passed out, gasping, my heart leaping, a queasy, uneasy feeling coming over me. I was going to get sick.

I sped to the bathroom and tossed my cookies in the closest bathroom stall from the door. I knelt on my knees, preying to the porcelain god, and wondered, how in the world did I get myself into this awful mess? *Why* had I volunteered to box? I don't want to hit anyone and, more importantly, I don't want anyone to hit *me*. I needed to get out of this situation.

I gathered myself, wiped the few scattered remnants of spew off my shirt and rushed back down to the gym where Mrs. Bruiser was checking boxers in. I told her, wiping back the tears, "Mrs. Bruiser, I am Mark Kirby and I don't feel so good. I am not going to be able to box tonight."

She simply crossed my name off the list and said, "Thanks for letting me know, Mark! I hope you feel better soon."

Well, that was easy, I thought, but there were two people who would be really mad at me that night for wimping out. One was my opponent and friend, Josh Harper, who was now *furious* at me because I had *chickened out*. For the rest of that night and the remainder of the school year and summer, Josh would make chicken sounds under his breath whenever he saw me. If we hadn't moved that summer to the nearby town of North Bend, I am sure the chicken-clucking would have continued through the next year as well. One thing is for certain: I lost my best buddy that night because of my decision to not get into the ring with him and fight. He would be the last *human* friend that I would have until the age of eleven.

The second disappointed person was my mom. As I slipped out of the gym, I immediately spotted Mom coming down the hall, all dressed up in a light-blue flowered dress and white high-heeled shoes. She had a big smile on her face, and as she moved closer to me, extending her arms out in front of her, ready to give me a big old hug, my head dropped down. I was so embarrassed and ashamed I could not look her in the face. She instantly knew something was wrong.

"What is it?" she asked. "Why so glum?"

"I am not boxing tonight, Mom. I chickened out and got my name taken off the list."

I was hoping for some sympathy, a little under-standing and compassion, but she would not let me off the hook that easy, oh no. She grabbed me by the ear with her right pointer finger and thumb, clamping down hard, and proceeded to pull me through the hallway and out the parking lot to the car. She was *fuming*, her face beet-red as she led me around to the passenger side. "I am extremely disappointed in you, young man. And, to make matters worse, I left my Beeline fashion party early all because of *you*."

She continued to rant, shoving me in the car and slamming the car door shut. As she entered from her side, she glared at me and rebuked, "I am *removing* the family name from the back of your robe tonight and returning it to JC Penney's tomorrow morning for a full refund." It was nonstop tongue lashing, but I really didn't care. I just took it like a *man*, a six-year-old man.

You know, as I slipped into bed, not a mark on me, I pretended to be distraught by my mom's disappointment in me, but as I dozed off that night, I was glad I didn't fight. I wanted no part of it. This little *boxing* episode would be the first and last time I ever volunteered for anything in my life. I also remember this event because for the first time as a young boy, I was not thinking about *it* for several hours. School had, and would always be, a distraction from *it*.

(4)

My Grandma Lavina and Grandpa Cliff used to play cards all the time when I was growing up; bridge and pinochle were among their favorite games. Logically, if I wanted attention from these two grown-ups, whom I spent a lot of time with in my youth, I had to learn to play these games. From the time I was old enough to count, I was playing cards with my grandparents; hearts, spades, war, cribbage and pinochle were all games I learned, played regularly and eventually mastered as a boy. Through this practice and repetition, I acquired an intuitive card sense and became adept at counting cards in my head at a young age.

Poker, at its core, is about human interaction, and instinctive players always receive clues based on their opponent's physical patterns and demeanor. These clues are called *tells*. In 1968, as an eight-year-old second grader, I already possessed some of the skills necessary to be a pretty good poker player, and after months of careful observation, I had now sized up my crafty and formidable opponent, D.L. Kirby.

Mom, on the other hand, was oblivious to the hundreds of *tells* her husband was giving to her that should have warned her that he was pure evil. Sadly, she would be of no help to my safety moving forward; I would have to rely on my own instincts and abilities here.

Donald Kirby was a decent poker player. He kept his cards close to his vest. He was acutely aware that what he was doing was morally wrong and criminal. D.L. knew that being outed would cost his alter ego, Donald, everything—his career, his reputation in the community and, ultimately, his family. Drinking alcohol was just adding toxic fuel to his already demented mind.

Now that I was getting older and had been exposed to more normal male role models, Mr. Bentley excluded—it became apparent to me that D.L. was trying to use fear and intimidation to control me in almost every encounter that I had with him. He made me somehow feel responsible for what *we* had done, forcing me to keep *it* a secret. He intimidated me by making me afraid that my sister might be harmed if I told anyone.

D.L., for the entire time I knew him, enjoyed photography. He liked to take pictures and turn them into family slide shows. He would bring people over, get himself and his guests all liquored up, and perform as the Master of Ceremonies for these glorious presentations, all in splendid, living color. He even had several slides of Korea and showed pictures of himself and the young Korean boy he had so desperately and valiantly wanted to adopt. There were numerous pictures of the boy, in all kinds of settings, smiling innocently for the camera. When the melancholy D.L. would speak of this boy, he would sometimes cry. This would always touch the hearts of the people seated in his living room. No one knew it; to this day, not even my mom knows that this friendly hobby of his was one big sham. It was a cover for the pictures he really liked to take, pictures of naked boys. I know this because he showed these disgusting images to me when he was half-naked and drunk on whiskey.

As a small boy, D.L. made me want to vomit. I hated to even look at him, because all I could see behind those dark, piercing eyes was pure evil. But now I had key information at my disposal: I knew where he hid those photos, and I would use them against him when I became a much more savvy and worldly ten-year-old. He collected them deep in his closet in a black shoe box, inside a blue-and-white striped pillowcase, behind his row of shoes. No one would ever think to look behind those rows of shoes, so his little *trophies* would be safe for now.

(5)

D.L. was cruel and controlling with me in public as well, but because nobody knew what was going on behind closed doors, most people viewed his behavior as simple horseplay—tomfoolery between father and son. This public humiliation probably made me as angry, or angrier, as the mental and physical abuse that was going on inside my own home. My mom witnessed much of this mental hazing in public, and she blew it off as harmless father-and-son fun time together. Many people thought Donald as a big lovable teddy bear, while I knew him to be a wretched beast. This would always be a source of frustration for me growing up.

Fear is power in the sick mind of an abuser, and D.L. tried to possess and control me by terrorizing the living daylights out of me on a weekly basis. This mental hazing was random and without warning, which made it even more terrifying for me as a kid. I was at a heightened state of anxiety whenever I was alone with him and constantly in fear of what he might do to me next.

I had originally never been afraid of heights. D.L. would change all that. I had an intense fear of going to the carnival as a boy, a place that most kids love, because I knew at some point, D.L. would take me on the Ferris wheel and *scare* me half to death. He would always take me on the Ferris wheel alone, never with my mom or my little sister. To my mom, it was special bonding time. To me, it was a ride from hell. A short way into the ride, as the Ferris wheel began its gradual ascent into the air, D.L. would pull out a silver flask from his jacket and begin to drink. It only took a few taps of the flask for him to crank into his evil, abusive D.L. mode. As we reached the top, and away from the line of sight from my mom, who was always doing . . . the hell if I ever knew? D.L. would begin his routine of hazing me.

"Hey Pard, I think this seat seems a little bit shaky, don't ya think? Why don't we test her out a bit?"

He would begin to slowly rock his now enormous, 240-pound muscular meat sack of a body back and forth, back and forth—gaining momentum each time the seat swayed. I was now frozen, horrified, almost looking straight down at the ground below me. My hands clutched tightly to the bar, gripping like my life depended on it, as D.L. would grin wickedly and ask, "Why are holding on with two hands, Pard? Are you afraid, ya little *candy ass*?"

No—I was so petrified that I couldn't even scream. D.L. talking in my ear the entire time, taunting, *hazing*, paralyzing. I wanted to scream to my mom and sister below, "Help me, please! Save me from this evil man!" I could never muster up enough courage to do so.

When D.L. drank, the West Virginia redneck side of his personality would surface. His voice would change, even the way he put together sentences morphing into some sort of country jargon. "Hold on to your diggers, boy, we're goin' for a ride, ooh doggies, yee haw!" he would shout for everyone to hear. Observers thought him to be having a grand old time with his young son. I knew differently. Because of this torment, *by air*, on the Ferris wheel, at the hands of my dad, I am still afraid of heights. I don't like to ride in an elevator, drive over a bridge, go on a high-rise hotel patio or even climb a ladder. I have D.L. to thank.

Of course, D.L. would attack me on land as well. His favorite thing to do when he was driving alone with me was to let me *take* the wheel. I hated to ride in a car alone with him because of this psychotic game. We would cruise down the highway, and about twenty minutes into our trip, after he had taken several swigs of Wild Turkey from his silver flask, the hazing would start all over again.

He would pull me close and make me take the steering wheel as we cruised down the highway at 70 miles per hour, while of course he continued to drink. He took exceptional pleasure in messing with my little mind. "Hey Pard, watch it, don't hit that car comin' at us!" He would grab the bottom of the wheel with his right pointer finger and thumb, well below my two hands, and swerve the car ever so slightly, left and then right, scaring me to high heaven each time he did this little move. Again, his hillbilly vernacular kicked in: "Quit driving all katty-wonkered, Pard!" or "Knock that shit off, Pard! Keep your eyes on the road!" or "If you don't stop swerving, I'm a gonna havta open up a can of woopass on ya!" All howling and laughing, swigging another.

During this time of my life, I began to experience panic attacks. They were random, but occurred daily. These were strange occurrences for a kid my age, walking to school alone, walking down a crowded hallway, sitting in the cafeteria at lunchtime without a group that I could connect with, taking tests, sitting in unfamiliar groups in class, and of course any particular situation that D.L. was involved in. I had to carry around a brown paper bag with me at all times to breathe into. The other kids made fun of me. I couldn't tell them what was going on at my house. I would have really been an outcast then. At least I had Misty.

"Misty," I would say, "what's wrong with me? Why do kids hate me so much?" Misty would just stare back at me and wag her little tail or jump on my lap and comfort me. She was my best friend and could always see the goodness inside me that the other kids couldn't.

D.L.'s torture: Air and land, covered. Then one spring, my parents decided to get a family boat; now D.L. would be able torment me by sea as well. Mom had saved up her extra money from working Beeline and Avon parties, and my parents now had enough for a basic ski boat. When we got it, I did not swim very well and was a little afraid of the water. By the time D.L. got his hooks into me, my phobias spread to the water.

The Rotund Buffoon

The day after my rectal exam, I looked into the bathroom mirror to find my eyeball bright red. Dr. Wilson had squeezed my prostate so damned hard it had popped all of the blood vessels in my left eye. I looked like Arnold Schwarzenegger in one of the *Terminator* movies. I had to go to school and teach, so for the next few weeks I told my students that a "tennis ball had hit me in the eye at practice." Since I am a high school tennis coach this excuse made sense. I couldn't have told them the truth.

To survive the next two weeks, navigating my way through my high school, I used self-deprecating humor to cover up the embarrassment I felt about my grotesque-looking eye. I made fun of myself and my current predicament. I had learned this comedy technique long ago as a young boy from my mentor, the one and only *Rotund Buffoon* . . .

(1)

D.L. was up early on a Saturday morning as usual, making last-minute preparations for our trip to Loon Lake, a forty-five-minute drive from our house. He was dressed in Bermuda shorts, a tank top, flip-flops and a fedora. He always wore his signature hat to the lake, although his clothes no longer fit him well; they were too small, but he, bound and determined that they still fit like when he was younger, refused to stop wearing them. His tank top no longer covered his beer belly, and his excess flab rolled way over his shorts like an accordion. For the first time in his life, he could no longer see his own feet.

At age thirty, D.L. now looked more like the Skipper from *Gilligan's Island* than the former handsome, muscular and debonair Wolf of Woolworths! In five short years, drinking had taken its toll on D.L.'s body, and he was by his own admission now fat and out of shape. A shell of his former self, his calm, confident, friendly public persona of several years' past had morphed into that of a *Rotund Buffoon*. Self-deprecating humor playing fat for laughs.

After a few morning beers and a couple Bloody Marys, D.L. was already in rare form, giving a preview of his afternoon show to his unenthused family as they packed the station wagon and boat. As I helped lift the ice chest into the boat, D.L.'s big belly got in the way and he said, "You know, I am not fat, Pard. I'm just two feet too short." I gave him nothing in return, except for empty silence and a little scowl as he awaited my laughter like a stand-up comedian. I would not feed into his little game here.

He shot back again, this time hoping for a laugh, "You know, if someone told me to 'haul ass,' Pard, I'd probably have to make two trips," this time laughing at his own joke, his belly jiggling like Jell-O. "Here's a good one, Pard: I'm so fat, I took you two kids to the zoo, and the elephants threw peanuts at me!" He was now laughing hysterically. He suddenly realized he had no audience as I had already left to get the beach towels. What an idiot, I thought, as his laughter still reached me walking away and into the house.

The car was finally loaded, and we all piled in our 1962 baby-blue Ford Country Squire station wagon, the boat pulled behind it. D.L. would drive us up to Loon Lake. Misty jumped on my lap, and we were off. Misty loved riding in the boat.

D.L. would drive us to the lake, but my mom would be the designated driver back; at this point in the morning, he was not as completely *sauced* as he would be by late evening. Just getting warmed up for his day of drinking and debauchery.

D.L. Kirby was really a modern marvel of unhealthy habits. He was a slovenly drunken driving version of my Grandpa Cliff. He was simultaneously steering, chain-smoking Marlboros, eating beef jerky and pork rinds, while sipping on a large 40-ounce bottle of malt liquor that he would conceal in a brown paper bag. This was his way of multitasking early this Saturday morning. He would drink and tell us stupid little jokes that would get progressively more inappropriate the closer we got to the lake. Keep in mind that this was the sixties and we had no iPods or phones at our disposal to tune this idiot out. My sister and I were now trapped in the back seat of the car, forced to listen to the comedy stylings of the Rotund Buffoon.

He would always start out with something cute and kid friendly: "How does a train eat?" We never tried to guess, as we hoped at some point he would stop, but sadly he never did. "Chew, chew!" he would fire back.

"Here's another good one, kids: Where do animals go when their tails fall off?" No answer, dead silence, as his stupid jokes were now fully desensitizing my mom's brain waves. "The retail store! Get it?" We were now all hoping that he would "get it" that no one was actually listening to him.

When D.L. finally figured out that no one was paying attention to him anymore, especially my mom, his jokes would start to get dirtier. This was his way to gauge if my mom had completely tuned him out.

"What kinds of bees give milk?"

"Boo bees!" he would reply, this time smiling, laughing, reveling in his own humor.

"Why do dogs lick their balls?"

"Because they can!"

He was now in full moron mode, I thought, as I counted the minutes to the lake. Misty even gave her disapproval of D.L.'s humor by *tooting* on my lap in disgust.

"A priest, a rabbi, and a midget walk into a whore house and . . . "

"Don!" my mom was now alive again. "Quit it, there are kids in the car!"

"Anyone want some pork rinds?" Don would now pivot, trying to capture his lost audience once again.

"NOOOO!" we would all shout back in defiant unison.

This was our typical 45-minute trip to Loon Lake each weekend, which seemed more like five hours for us passengers (prisoners) in the family station wagon.

Once we got to the lake and put the boat in the water, we found a camping spot and settled in for a day of fun. Because the water was at its calmest in the morning hours, the adults would immediately take turns skiing. I would sit and watch them from the beach, marveling at their strength, coordination and balance. Some skiers started in the water behind the boat, some sat on the dock, and others started right off the beach in about a foot of water. How they started all depended on their experience and skill. I always liked the adults who started right off the beach. They were the coolest to me, because if done right, they would never even get wet at all! They would pop right up, standing in shallow water with their ski tip up, cruise around the lake and then do a beach landing, stepping right out of their ski when they hit the sand. I have seen many a crash landing of skiers trying this particular strategy as well, and my mom always carried a box of bandages in her beach bag "just in case."

All the adults were accomplished slalom skiers, meaning they skied on only one ski, except for poor old D.L. He skied like all novices did, on two skis. This was a source of much humiliation and frustration for D.L, who had hurt his left knee in high school football. He could not put all of his weight, especially now that he had gained sixty pounds in the last few years, on one leg. Feeling a little jealous and left out, and being the consummate show off, D.L. had devised some gimmicks to not only fit in but standout among the crowd of far superior skiers. Everyone at Loon Lake loved D.L.'s stunt-man sideshow antics except for me. Why, because D.L. liked to use me as a prop, like pulling a rabbit out of a hat—me being the *rabbit* of course. I will get to my role in this twisted freak show shortly.

D.L., the Rotund Buffoon, had now taken his comedy act to the water for the day. People would line up on the beach to watch his exploits, the crowds cheering and clapping, laughing, hooting and hollering, feeding into his already overinflated ego. As he struggled to squeeze into the ski belt, a floatation device that wrapped around a skier's waist, he tried to lighten the mood and distract the onlookers from his enormous belly.

"You know, I keep trying to *lose* weight, but it keeps finding me!" This crowd of morning beer drinkers found this type of humor from the "funny fat guy" absolutely hilarious.

After finally lifting his flab over the belt with two hands, a young muscular guy cinched the belt around D.L.'s waist. "This is how I roll! Let's let 'er rip, tater chip!" he shouted to the crowd as he squeezed his belly with both hands and shook it for the many onlookers gathered. Again, they found the "fat dude with the hat" to be quite entertaining.

D.L. had embraced his new funny-man persona fully. Deep down, though, he didn't like how far he had let himself slip. It's as if he knew he was losing it, so he was now making himself the giant butt of his own jokes. The comedy routine was a convenient way for him to cope with his insecurities about his appearance and weight. It was as if he was making fun of himself so no one else could beat him to the punch. I could psychoanalyze this numb nut for hours, but it was time for the first act of his show to start and I wanted to get a good seat.

D.L.'s first warm-up stunt was *long distance skiing*. He knew all the other skiers could go much faster, and cut across the wake back and forth with style and grace, so he got the crazy notion that he would be like a long-distance runner and ski for miles at a time. Wearing his favorite fedora, black sunglasses, complete with a cigarette in his mouth and 16-ounce can of beer in his claws, he would cruise around the lake, raising and toasting his beer high in the air to the many boaters, skiers, swimmers and picnickers along his aquatic parade.

After making a full circle around the lake, he would twirl his beer high in the air, signaling to the driver that he wanted to go "one more time around!" As he passed the main beach, he would shout something stupid to the entertained onlookers: "Look at me, I am faster than a one-legged man in a butt-kicking competition!" The crowd would cheer and on several occasions some other drunken fool would try to toss him a beer as he cruised by the shore. I have seen D.L. crash-land in the water trying to catch an oncoming beer.

His next bigger and better stunt would require the services of his little sidekick: me. I would wait around all day, pacing and worrying about D.L.'s next stunt, *Tandem Skiing*. This was not people riding on separate sets of skis behind one boat—oh, no, that would be far too fun and safe. This was the more terrifying and dangerously ill-conceived idea of all time: me riding on the top of D.L.'s shoulders as he cruised around the lake at 45mph with a beer in one hand. Why my mom ever signed off on this not-so-special father-and-son bonding moment, I'll never know. Where was she anyways? Anybody seen her?

When D.L. yelled, "Grab your lifejacket, Pard!" I knew it was *our* time to perform. Every time I heard that battle cry, my stomach would begin to churn; I felt like I was going to throw up. By the time, we got to our little show in the late afternoon hours, D.L. had already consumed mass quantities of liquid courage, three sheets to the wind and wobbly.

We started right in front of the main beach—the *Rotund Buffoon* always liked a large audience to perform for. We both started in the water, me clutching onto D.L.'s back as he held the rope tightly between his two skis. When the boat pulled us up and we were moving at a lower rate of speed, I gradually climbed up on his shoulders. At this point, D.L. gave me the command, "Let 'er rip, tater chip!" and that was my cue to give the boat driver a thumbs-up sign. We were going to speed.

This time, my cousin Danny was driving the boat and pushed down on the throttle all the way. Misty was seated in the passenger seat next to Danny, watching all the action, anticipating a great show once again.

Talk about being scared to death. I was holding onto D.L.'s fedora, *screaming* at the top of my lungs as we weaved in and out around other boats, downing skiers and a log or two. What always would start out at as a fun family day at the lake quickly turned into a nightmare. He again would pass by the beach and wave as I held onto him for dear life, hoping that this ride from hell would end. Luckily, we didn't take a spill that day. But on a couple of other occasions, when D.L was even more inebriated, we fell and I almost smacked my head against D.L.'s big *coconut* on the way down into the water. That would not be a good thing. How were the other adults thinking that this was somehow safe? These stunt shows seemed to be getting beyond ridiculous. Where the heck was Mom?

When we were finished, Danny pulled me into the boat, and I looked like I had just wrestled a great white shark. Inevitably, D.L. would have something clever and cutting to say to me, like "Pard, you look like you've been eaten by a bear and shat over a cliff." That is probably the most intelligent thing he had said to me all day, believe it or not, and that's pretty much how I felt at that very moment in time.

For our last stunt of the day, my drunken fool of a dad and I would be performing our grand finale trick, *Buddy Bridge Jumping*. The idea is a simple one: Find a railroad trestle or a bridge, hold the hand of your buddy and jump to your impending doom. I already explained in lengthy detail that I had become completely and utterly terrified of heights; well, this was like rubbing salt into an open wound.

I had heard a husband and wife talking as we left for the trestle say, "Look at that father and son together, isn't it neat they have so much *fun* together."

And at that moment, I wanted to scream, "Help me! This man is a monster, someone, anyone, please save me!"

I was already emotionally spent and now found myself on top of a large railroad trestle overlooking the beach and clutching my *buddy's* hand. People were cheering, and D.L. was basking in the glory of it all. Out of the corner of my eye, I saw Misty jumping up and down, barking at us. Even she knew this was a *rotten* idea. D.L. said, as he always did, "One, two, three. . . . Let 'er rip, tater chip!" and we were off, the enormous weight of my rotund buddy making the speed of our drop all the more rapid and intense. Luckily, we didn't hit rocks or find ourselves crushed at the bottom of the lake. We had dodged a bullet and I had lived to see another day. "Hallelujah, I am alive!" I said, as I touched myself all over to make sure.

We crawled onto the shore, I got to my feet, and D.L. hoisted me on his shoulders high in the air as if we had just won an Olympic gold medal. The crowd went wild and all that I could think about at that crowning moment was what a complete jerk the *Rotund Buffoon* truly was. By the way, has anyone seen my mom lately?

Later on, in my adult years, people would meet D.L. and say to me, "You know, your dad is funny. A great guy," adding something even more ridiculous like, "I bet he was a great dad when you were growing up." I would usually shake my head, just smiling and agreeing. What the heck, I didn't have several hours on my hands to tell the real story. Nobody really wants to hear *that* version anyways. It's a real *buzz kill*.

(2)

All fun and games on Loon Lake aside, D.L. Kirby had been living on death row for quite some time now. His professional life had finally hit rock bottom when he was fired from his job.

D.L. was terminated from Woolworths in the spring of 1967 because, according to upper management, "sales were down the last two quarters." But truth be told, the corporate execs had grown tired and weary of the changed Mr. Kirby of the past few years. It seemed the hard-partying *Rotund Buffoon* was not the same promising young gentleman that had graduated from their management training program in 1960. So, he was simply let go.

Looking for work, D.L. had reconnected with a former army buddy, David Rochester, who now was a pharmacist. David worked in the tiny town of Lebanon, Oregon, home of the Strawberry Festival and the World's Largest Strawberry Shortcake. David's big dream was to open up his own drug store, and he had called on his old pal to "come on over to Lebanon and run the retail side of the store for me while I run the pharmacy."

This seemed at the time to be a perfect fit for D.L. So,

our family moved *again*. This time half-way through my second-grade year to the tiny farming community of Lebanon, in the beautiful Willamette Valley, to start our new life.

On a glorious April afternoon, a reinvigorated D.L. Kirby, Retail Manager, and David James Rochester, Pharmacist, opened the doors to their brand-new business venture, R Mart. The "R" was for Rochester, of course. The grand opening had door prizes for the adults and free popcorn, soft drinks, and cotton candy for the kids. The all-new D.L. lasted about as long as a short vacation to the island of Maui, with old behaviors, patterns and habits just too hard to break. The occasional late arrival of a hungover D.L. on Monday morning was easy to dismiss as "out releasing some tension over the weekend, eh?" by young Mr. Rochester.

But, D.L. falling off a barstool and chipping a tooth, as well as showing up to work looking more *hillbilly* than store manager, was a bit more worrisome to the young pharmacist. Coming to work drunk and falling through a window display of plastic flowers in front of several customers was something entirely different indeed. Levelheaded, nondrinking partners do not appreciate drunken and disorderly ones and, in less than six months, D.L. was out of work yet again. His former army buddy had *terminated* his employment.

Two months earlier, we had purchased a rundown five-acre farmland that D.L. had vowed to restore into our family *dream* home. But after termination, our house was now in peril of being foreclosed on. To prevent this from happening, D.L. had latched on to a job as Assistant Manager of a large retail store about two hours away in the capital city of Salem.

The two-hour commute in combination with the obvious step down from his previous jobs made ol' D.L. *miserable,* and his drinking *ramped* up to an all-time high. Now he was coming home every night falling down drunk after consuming an open fifth of whiskey on the long drive home. By nine in the evening, he was either *passed out* on the couch in the living room or the bathroom floor because he had gotten sick and could not make it the bedroom. As you could well imagine, my mom was in no immediate rush to wake him from his drunken slumber. She did not want to share her bed with this disgusting, drunken fool of a husband.

(3)

One night, I decided *enough* is *enoug*h and took matters into my *own* hands. My mom had been taking night classes at a local community college. D.L. was mad at Mom for signing up for this course without his permission. He still wanted her to cook and clean and basically be his *slave.* Mom was tired and disgusted and wanted her own life. She was never in any hurry to get home. She was not eager to wait on her drunk and verbally abusive husband; I totally got it. But I was the one left alone with my sister to manage the drunken D.L.

One afternoon, like always, I was home alone after school with Gracie, now six years old. D.L. was to arrive at around five, after leaving early from work with pizza for dinner. I had set the table and my sister and I sat and waited for him to arrive. Six o'clock came, and no D.L. Seven o'clock came and went; we were starving and still no pizza. By nine, Gracie and I had eaten two Swanson TV dinners, and I had tucked Gracie into bed and read her one of her favorite books.

I had a sit-down chat with Misty in the living room.

"Misty," I said, "I am sick and tired of D.L. getting all liquored up and touching me in weird places."

Misty said nothing, her black eyes staring at me, hanging on my every word.

"Misty, be by my side tonight and give me strength. I am going to standup to D.L. once and for all and tell him to leave me alone. I want to be a kid again. We don't deserve this. I am a boy and you are my best friend and we don't deserve to be treated like this anymore."

Misty seemed like she was up to the challenge that night. She looked at me and smiled, wagged her little curly black tail and barked twice, as if to say, "I'm ready." I was also *ready* on this evening to confront my sworn enemy, the *Wolf*.

Well, D.L. arrived at nine through the back-kitchen door, trying to sneak in without anyone knowing. I could tell he had been drinking because he was having a hard time finding his key to get in the house. I could hear him fumbling, followed by an intermittent thumping sound every few seconds or so. As I peered out the window, I saw that the thumps were D.L.'s big noggin banging into the door as he stumbled to find the keyhole each time. He kept singing to himself on every unsuccessful attempt to get inside our house. Misty began to bark loudly, as she thought there was an intruder at the door.

"Oh, show meesh the way to goes home, boom, boom, boom, I tired amsh I wanna goes to bed boom, boom, boom. I had a little drinksh about an hour uh go and it went right to my head. Wheresefer I may roam, on landsh or shea or foams, shhhh . . ."

I had heard and seen enough of his idiotic act, so I opened the door and let the drunken fool in. "Thanksyooo so much, Pard, ole buddy ole pal, you are a friend indeed you are."

"*Shhh,*" he now said in a much louder voice, his finger attempting to move to his puckered lips. He would certainly not have passed the field sobriety test at this point.

"*Shhh,*" he repeated to himself, much quieter this time, hunching over and sticking his drunken mug right in my grill. "Weesh don't wanna wake yer mosher up, Pard! That would be bad, very bad," he said, now giggling to himself like a little girl. "Oh *nooo,* we wouldn't want to waksh the Mrs. up." He was talking louder now, hoping that my mom would awaken and get involved in his little one-man melodrama.

"Relax," I said. "She's not home. Now get yourself inside and have yourself a seat and I'll get you a drink of water and a cup of coffee."

I led him into the living room and sat him on the couch, while I assumed his usual man-of-the-house chair, the tan, cigarette-burn-laden Lazy Boy recliner. Misty jumped onto my lap, not knowing what to think about the drunken master of the house who slouched across from us.

D.L. tried to start a casual conversation with me, but his pickled brain and mouth were not in sync and all that came out was a garbled mess. "Ohhh shitz mish self, I've hash too mush tooo drinksh. Wooo doggiessh. Imsh ash drunksh ash a skunsh!" He was now slumped over, his head down, muttering sweet drunken nothings. "Itsh OK, itsch OK, evryshings going to be all right. You'll shee, you will shee, ol' D.L.'s gotsch it covered."

Well, I had seen enough, and quite frankly, I was just so utterly sick and tired of D.L.'s drunken act at this point, that I could have shot him and put him out of his misery right there on our living room couch.

As he sat there all slouched over, I scanned him from head to toe. For the first time in my life, I did not fear him anymore, but instead felt sorry for him, and pitied his pathetic existence on this earth. He was disheveled, his hair was all messed up, and his wrinkled blue corduroy coat and dress shirt did not match. He wore an old stained tie and high-water pants that needed to be pressed. His socks were mismatched. He was a sloppy mess, I thought— a far cry from his impeccably dressed *Madmen* days of the early sixties when his future looked so bright.

For the first time in my life, I also felt confident in what I had to do right now at this very moment in time. I spoke up assertively: "Dad, I hope you can hear me, because I have something very important that I want to say to you!"

He began to nod off, but caught himself just before fading. The assertiveness in my voice made him notice me for the first time as more than an object. He was now looking directly at me with sleepy, bloodshot eyes as I glared back, almost through him, with contempt and disgust written all over my nine-year-old face.

I spoke again. "Dad, I hope you can hear me now, because I am only going to say this once. Dad, I DO NOT want you to TOUCH me anymore. I am a grown boy now, and you are WRONG in touching me. PLEASE STOP NOW."

He now perked straight up for the first time this evening, fumbling with his coat and tie. I continued scolding the now-childlike figure before me.

"Dad, if you ever touch me again, I will call the police. Do you understand me?"

"Whatsh ya talkin about, Pard. I luvs ya. Yer my boy," he whined.

"Dad, listen to me closely, you are in *deep* trouble here. I have some of your pictures of the naked little boys you hid in that shoebox in your closet, and I am going to turn them into the police if you don't STOP NOW."

This is the most assertive I have been in my entire life. Suddenly his demeanor and tone turned from desperate to argumentative; he began to seemingly prepare a defense for court.

"Well yoush knows what, Pard, I likesh me shum womens, thatsh right, vimens!" He was now suddenly upright, demonstrative, animated in his gestures and incredibly inebriated. "Yeah that's what I likesh, vimens! I likesh the good ole biggens and, and . . . the big ole goodins!"

"What in the heck does that mean?"

"I likesh em all! Tall onesh, shortz onesh, skeeny onesh, even big fats onesh, I don't give a damn, I likes hem all I tell ya, them all." He paused for a long moment, looking down to see that he had zipped his pants, while he clumsily fumbled with his crotch area.

He continued, arguing to no one in particular, "Boysh? You want to talk about boysh, I don't likesh boysh, I like vimens, not boys . . . vimens . . . please believe me occifer, please! Pard, please don't call the cops. Those guys in jail are mean and they will kill a poor guy like me for shurz!"

He was now sobbing in alcoholic despair. He slowly put his head in his hands and wept like a little baby. "I will stop, Pard. I will stop, I will stop." He kept saying these words over and over until he finally leaned over on the armrest of the couch and passed out for the night.

"What a hopeless fool," I thought, as he lay there on the coach drooling and snoring. He and had no idea what had just hit him! I had blindsided him with a 36-inch Louisville slugger right to the head. It was actually satisfying for me to watch him break down and *lose it*, to see him struggle so. From this day forward, I would not fear him anymore. I had lost all respect for him as a human being.

Truth be told, I had taken a big chance that evening. I hadn't taken pictures from that secret shoebox. Like a good poker player, I was bluffing. I was *all in* in one of the biggest games of my life. That night I played a mind game with a deviant sexual predator to reclaim my childhood.

I *buried* D.L. that evening—not with a shovel, but with my courage to stand up to him and say no. That is by far the single bravest thing I have done in my life. I went to bed that night and slept peacefully for the first time in six long years. D.L. Kirby never did *it* to me again. For the rest of his life he would deny *it* had ever taken place. I would think about this night often growing up with much regret, however. I wish I had *finished* the job that night and told my mom, or better yet called the police.

Our little *secret* would not be shared with anyone until I was twenty years old. The longer I kept this secret inside of me, the harder it was for me growing up to share *it* with anyone. You see, as I grew older, I found out *it* was for deviants, weirdos and *worse*. I didn't want other kids to find out what I had *done*. I was terrified the other kids would make fun of me or shun me all together if they knew. Not telling any adults what I had *done* with my second dad still remains my life's regret.

(4)

D.L.'s whole life as a family man finally came *crashing* down one evening right on his very own bathroom floor.

He was lying face down on the floor, his pants pulled down around his chubby knees, his enormous, round, hairy, white bottom sticking straight up in the air. He was motionless. Was he breathing? I thought he might be dead. And I hoped so. I hoped he had perished from this earth, that his soul had left his body, which was now covered in vomit, urine and fecal matter. As I peered through the tiny keyhole once more on the old-fashioned farmhouse bathroom door, I noticed that he was now snoring and his wet and matted hair was soaked in his own regurgitations. Gross! I rapped on the door with my tiny knuckles. No movement. Then knocked three times and waited. Then knocked again.

"Move, you big pile of crap, move!" I muttered to myself.

The knocking turned to banging, as I was now frantic, agitated and stressed about the whole situation. What was I to do? I let out a blood-curdling scream and yelled . . .

"Mom, I have to *pee. Baaad!*"

"Well, why are you telling me? Just *go.*"

"I can't, he's drunk and passed out on the bathroom floor *again,* and he has locked himself in."

"Not *again,*" she sighed. "That is the third time this month for Christ's sake."

In a matter of seconds, Mom was standing right next me, pounding on the door with both fists clenched.

"Don, get up now, I am sick of this shit!"

My mom never cussed in front of me, so I knew she must be mad. No movement, no answer from inside.

Mom screamed again, this time even louder, "I am giving you to the count of three or I . . . I . . . I am going to divorce your ass!

The word "divorce" surprised me, shocked me—but to tell you the truth, it made me about as happy as I had ever been.

"One, two, three!"

"Well fine, you asked for it! I am divorcing your ass!"

She led me down the hallway, out the back kitchen, down the steps and into the large backyard that separated our house from a walnut orchard. As I looked up at my mom, I noticed that tears were streaming down her face.

She snapped, "Find a tree!"

"What?"

"Find a damn tree now and pee!"

As I skedaddled off, she left to go back inside. That was the first time my mom had ever allowed me to go the bathroom outside. I became excited and motivated, as I had a small geyser hidden in my underwear, ready to explode at any moment. I would let out this frustration on the nearest shrub. Six years of pent up anger and aggression would be taken out that morning on a poor innocent little juniper bush in my backyard. For a very short window of time in my life, I became a pretty angry kid. Prior to this occasion, Mom had always told me that "peeing outside was for *perverts*." If she really wanted to see a *pervert*, I thought, she had to look no further than our very own bathroom floor.

After relieving myself in the backyard, I skipped back

to the kitchen to find her writing a note. I peeked over her shoulder: "I am sick and tired of your drinking, I'm taking the kids with me for a week to my mom's house. Be out when I come back. Consider this a divorce!"

Divorce. There was that word again.

It was such a celebratory, liberating word, that for the first time in my young life, I was forced to hold back utter tears of joy and ecstasy. I thought to myself, hallelujah. D.L. is dead, call the hearse, pick his big fat corpse up, pop open the champagne and let's start living again!

We packed up a couple of suitcases, spent a week with my grandparents in Tacoma, and when we returned home, D.L. was gone. He had taken all his belongings and left. There were no traces of him left behind, except for the giant pyramid of empty Budweiser cans that were left on one wall of our kitchen as evidence that the *Rotund Buffoon* had completed his final act of drunkenness and had indeed left the building for good.

That evening, my mom sat Gracie and me down and said, "Your dad and I are getting a divorce, and he is moving to Alaska to work on the pipeline." I had no idea what "the pipeline" was, but I did know a little bit about Alaska and figured that Eskimos, polar bears and even wooden totem poles would be better company for old D.L. than his family in Oregon. He was an uncontrollable drunk, a disgusting human being, and I was just plain tired of him. I thought my second dad to be dead and buried for good that day, but the state of Oregon would have a much different idea.

Visitation Rights or Wrongs?

I was assigned a primary care urologist by the friendly folks at Kaiser Permanente. I was scheduled for a rectal exam by another creepy male stranger in a white lab coat. What the *fuck,* does every man in the world want to touch, examine and feel up my privates? I was more than a little paranoid at this point. As Doctor Snidely examined my sweaty *gonads* in front of my wife, I felt as ashamed as I ever have in my adult life. As I stood there, the doctor now holding my testicles in his cupped hairy right hand—I felt feeling like an anxious ten-year-old once again.

(1)
I can pinpoint the low point of my troubled childhood. I was an extremely overweight fifth grader with low self-esteem, of low socioeconomic status, from a single-parent family, on free and reduced lunch, complete with anger issues, an anxiety disorder and major league male trust issues.

To make matters worse, I lost my only real friend in the world one late August afternoon. We accidently left the backdoor open, and Misty escaped around to the front of the house and scampered out into the street. She was oblivious to her surroundings. A *screech* of car breaks and her squeals of pain drew my head to pop out the window, and I watched my poor little dog lying there motionless, blood dripping out of her mouth. I scurried to the street, screaming, picking Misty's frail, limp body up off the pavement.

The old man in the car kept saying, "I'm sorry, I'm so sorry . . . " It didn't help. He said over and over again, "I didn't see her, she just ran out in front of me!" Then his ranting and raving faded to the background as I focused my attention on my best friend.

She looked up at me one last time, whimpering softly as if to say *goodbye,* and laid her tiny head on my arm.

We buried Misty under a big old tree in our backyard on that cool summer evening, just before my bedtime. I gave a short eulogy for my beloved pet.

"Misty, you were my best friend and you were always there for me when I needed someone to talk to. You helped me get through my troubles with D.L. and I am going to miss you so very much. Rest in peace little one."

I made a cross of sticks and pounded it with a mallet into the small pile of dirt that was now her final resting place. My sister and I placed some flowers on her grave. I slumped down on my knees and wept, knowing full well that all the crying in the world wouldn't bring my Misty back.

I was really on my own now: No real friends, no one to talk to, and I was *scared* to *death* to start another school year in September.

(2)

The administrators, counselors and teachers were all on high alert as to my comings and goings when school started; I had been labeled an *at-risk* student in the friendly confines of Crawfish Elementary in Lebanon, Oregon. I was bringing a lot of baggage to school with me that fall.

My fifth-grade English teacher, Mr. Zimmer, would be my first male teacher (except for that one in gym class . . .) and a man who would leave a tremendous positive mark on my life. He was introducing our first writing assignment of the new school year: "Class, I want you to write an essay on how you spent your summer vacation. It needs to be written in ink and my expectation is that you will read this piece of writing to the *entire* class."

I was excited about the prompt because I had just spent the entire month of July and part of August in Alaska visiting D.L., Uncle Chester, Grandma Bonney and Grandpa Ralph. My mom had shipped us up to see them for six weeks (while she looked for a new man). My first thought was not to go at all, but Mom said the state of Oregon had informed her that "we had no choice!" Something about "visitation rights." I didn't get it.

Why was I being sent off to the middle of nowhere with two men who had previously molested me as a younger kid? I wished at that very moment that I had taken it one step further with D.L. and had told my mom or the police. Still, I couldn't let Gracie go alone to see my crazy relatives, so it was to be me and her as always, together through thick and thin. I would always keep my eye out for her. I would never trust the *wolves* around Gracie alone.

D.L. went to Alaska, just like my mom had told us, and got a job working as a heavy equipment operator apprentice, on the Great Alaska Pipeline in Prudhoe Bay, Alaska. He found himself an alcoholic, a *dead-beat* dad, owing money to Oregon for unpaid child support and alimony. He also found himself fitting in perfectly to his new surroundings among the other deadbeats, degenerates and dregs of society who had left the lower forty-eight for a new life in the *Last Frontier.*

Although D.L. was now "making the big bucks," according to my grandma Bonney, who had received a few letters from her oldest son—D.L. saw fit that his former family *should not* reap any of the benefits from his new job and newfound healthy income. For the first and only time in our lives, our little family of three, now living in a rundown farmhouse in Lebanon, was dirt poor. My grandma was now sending money to the state on her son's behalf to keep him in compliance with the law and out of jail.

Mom was continuing her college studies in hopes of becoming a teacher one day, working several part-time jobs to make the monthly house payment. She was extremely driven during this period of her life; she had to be just to survive, but had little time for us kids. My sister and I seldom saw her, and we often had to let ourselves in the house after school, make a giant snack tray of peanut butter and crackers, and watch hours upon hours of television alone with no supervision. The TV became my after-school baby sitter, the center of my universe.

We had little money left over for things I had always taken for granted, like food and clothing. I had one pair of jeans to my name that fit and a couple of shirts that I would rotate every other day. For the first time, kids at school teased me for the clothes I wore; they held back no punches with their cutting remarks.

Some wiseass kid with a brand-new plaid shirt, slim trousers and shiny new shoes would say to his *cool* friend right in front of me at recess, "Nice shirt, Kirby, never seen *that* one before, like two days ago."

The pain would just keep on a-comin' for the *uncool* me when a popular girl would say in front of the whole class, "Gee whiz, Mark, do you shop at the Goodwill? That looks like a shirt my brother gave away three years ago to those guys. I think it has the same stain on it, even!"

Well, with the start of a new school year and a hope for a brighter fifth-grade school experience, I sat down one afternoon and scrawled down on paper what I thought to be a dazzling piece of autobiographical writing.

I hoped to gain the approval and acceptance from my new classmates by writing a funny and interesting story that I could read aloud.

How I Spent my Summer at Kito's Cave!
By Mark Kirby
September 9, 1970

Last June, my mom told my sister Gracie and me that we would be going for a month-long summer vacation to see my dad in Petersburg Alaska. My sister and I had not seen our dad in over a year. My mom said we could not visit him because he was a "deadbeat" and a "horse's ass." She said this about him because he was not paying his monthly check to us for food and clothing and other important stuff like that. My mom wanted us out of her hair, though. She was "on the prowl for a new man," according to Grandma Bonney. So, we kids were headed to Alaska on a plane with *no* adult supervision. I felt a little bit like used and unwanted furniture. I would never let my little sister know I was scared. She needed me to be strong as always. I was the *man* of the house.

I had looked up Petersburg, Alaska's "Little Norway" in the

Encyclopedia Britannica and was excited about all of the fun wilderness adventures that we might enjoy on our trip there. I was hoping we could see La Conte Glacier, Tongass National Forest or maybe watch the humpback whales feed along the Frederick Sound on my trip to our 49th state up north. Well, unfortunately we didn't spend much time outside on our vacation to Alaska at all. We spent most of our time in a trailer park, or in other exotic places like Harbor Bar, Kito's Cave and the Petersburg Municipal Garbage Dump.

Gracie and I boarded an Alaska Airlines flight from Portland on an early Sunday morning in June. We were both a little nervous. It was the first time we had ever flown without our parents. The stewardesses were all very nice to us, and after a four-hour flight, we bounced, rattled, shook and swayed our way into the tiny Petersburg Airport, situated on the north end of Mitkof island in the southeastern part of Alaska.

I was told by an old man behind me, "Son, if the plane bounces only three times when landing in Alaska, consider it a good one!" I guess it was good, then, even though I had to hold on to the armrests for dear life as we screeched to a stop on the narrow, rain-slicked runway! I received a *Jr. Pilot Wings* pin for my bravery from the co-pilot as we left the plane. Mission accomplished.

We were picked up at the Petersburg Airport by my dad in a beat-up old car that looked like the latest loser in a demolition derby. I called my dad "D.L." now, because he did a bunch of creepy and weird stuff to me a while ago, and I don't really like him that much anymore. I basically tolerate him, like all of my family does. My mom says that "D.L." stands for "Daily Loaded" because she says my dad "drinks from sunup to sundown, seven days a week."

D.L. thinks he is funny and clever and most of us think otherwise. He was really no different from the last time that I saw him, other than the types of jokes he now liked to tell had changed. He used to like to tell *fat* jokes, but now I noticed that his humor revolved around two basic topics: his anger toward "stupid Oregonians," and his resentment for "lower 48ers" in general. D.L. was a big fat *sour grape*, I had concluded, because his work and his family had basically kicked him out of the state of Oregon for good.

As my sister and I were riding in the back seat of the car from the airport and my Uncle Chester was "riding shotgun," as he called it, my dad began to work his newfound comedy magic on us.

"Do you know why Jesus couldn't have been born in one of the lower 48 states?" D.L. asked.

"No," I reluctantly replied.

"Because they couldn't find three wise men and a virgin down there!"

"Get it?" he belched, pounding his fist on the steering wheel and laughing hysterically. We kids said nothing and my uncle gave him a quick pity glance.

"What is the difference between a bucket of shit and an Oregonian?"

No answer, dead silence from the three trapped passengers.

"The bucket," he spat out, barely able to hold his humor in. "That is so true, it is *hilarious*."

My sister and I, both Oregonians, did not find this funny at all.

My uncle slowly turned his head to the driver-now-turned-comic and said, real proper and *prissy* like, "Don, we have all had about enough of your nonsense here, you illiterate *country bumpkin*, just shut your *pie hole* and drive for goodness sake."

One thing I had noticed about my Uncle Chester on this trip was that he indeed had changed a whole bunch. For one thing, he let us kids know right off the bat that he wanted to be called "Chet." He said, "Chester is a damned redneck name." My new Uncle Chet was much more flamboyant than my old Uncle Chester. It seemed strange how he had changed so much, all of sudden refined. He now pronounced his words perfectly and precisely when talking, almost lisping like my buddy Wally did back at home. When he walked now, it was as if he was walking daintily on lily pads across a big old pond. I thought my Uncle Chet might make a great dance instructor or tightrope walker, floating in his shiny new penny loafers to and from the car. It all reminded me of my Uncle Bill, my grandma Lavina's brother. He and my dad must have had a talk, because neither of them touched me anymore. D.L. had indeed paid attention to my threat a year ago.

We finally arrived at the trailer park, the third mobile home on the right with the killer whale mailbox. This was the residence of my grandparents, Bonney and Ralph Bedford.

As we walked into the trailer, we were caught off guard by the sight of my grandpa Ralph seated in the dead center of the trailer's small living room in a kitchen chair, wearing only his *wife beater* T-shirt, tighty-whitey undies, and thick wool logging socks, with a lit cigarette sticking out of his mouth. My grandpa preferred *hands-free* smoking, talking and puffing, while never removing the cigarette from his mouth. It was really an amazing trick.

Chester went to put the suitcases away in the bedrooms, and the rest of us sat in the living room to observe Grandma Bedford's *frontier courtroom* proceedings for the *accused* Ralph G. Bedford, my grandad.

"Ralph G. Bedford, you son bitch," my grandma started with her opening remarks to the court, its members now seated in fur-covered furniture. "You old, tired, mangy son bitch, I told ya to never come home with liquor on yer breath, and here you sit, drunk as David's saw and pissed as a newt."

I later learned that my Grandpa Ralph had stopped by the bar for one drink after going to the grocery store. Well, Ralph was not to ever even have one tiny drink because he was an alcoholic, sober for seven years now. One drink with the boys turned into a few, and a few turned into a lot. Ralph was staggering drunk when he arrived at the Bonney estate.

Sober, my grandpa is one of the most amazing men you will ever meet. He is a direct descendent of William Bonney, alias Billy The Kid, the famous wild west outlaw and gunman. My grandpa had some of that same tough guy blood running through his veins as well, as he had panned for gold on the Klondike River in his younger years. He liked to do things in front of us grandkids to show off his *manly* strength. His first feat of strength was usually fifty one-armed pushups adorned by a lit cigarette in his mouth. I am convinced he slept and showered with a smoke as well.

He'd say something ridiculous like, "Twenty bucks to each person in the room if I burn a hole in my old lady's carpet." My grandma would have "tanned his hide, but good" if one fiber of her carpet were charred. I was always impressed with this display of strength, but wished just once he would have burned my grandma's carpet. I would have been twenty bucks richer, and would have enjoyed seeing my grandma kick his butt but good.

He also liked to stand on his head, and he could do this for hours if he had to. The first five minutes "neat," the next five "impressive," after fifteen minutes or so we would be shouting, "Come on grandpa, enough is enough! You are blocking my favorite program on television, get down."

My grandpa found himself in a real pickle this evening, however, as my grandma was hell-bent this evening on teaching her drunken old husband a lesson. "OK, Ralph Bedford, you old worthless tit. If you want to drink, then drinks so be it!" She was feeding him straight shots of whiskey every few minutes or so and he was downing them like a real pro. What started out as a fun "drinking game" for the wily old codger turned into agony and alcoholic despair, as my grandma would not let up on her relentless speed-bartending tactics.

His periodic belches turned into him begging, as the *wasted* old man now fervently wanted no more to drink: "NO MORE, BUD," his pet name for my grandma, "NO MORE!"

"You wanted to get drunk with the boys, so I am a fixin' to get you drunk, Ralph Bedford!"

"For God's sakes, Bud, ol 'Budderoo, you miserable ol 'fushin bitch. Stop! Imma gonna get sicksh." My grandpa was a sloppy, pickled mess. Finally, he had enough of this "nonsensh," as he called it. He staggered to his feet, rumbled to the kitchen like a "runaway freight train," opened up a kitchen drawer, pulled out a large, sharpened cutting knife and headed directly for my grandma in the tiny trailer living room. He wielded the knife high above his head and shouted out a savage war cry, "Die, you devil woman, die!"

Out of nowhere *leaped* my Uncle Chet from one of the adjoining bedrooms. He had been taking a little *catnap* and had been aroused by his parents feuding. He tackled my grandpa to the ground in a matter of seconds and now was wielding the knife above his father's own head.

"You want to introduce a knife into a fight, old man, do ya? Then you better be prepared to have it used against you, you dumb, ignorant bastard! Do you understand me, you crazy motherfucker?! Look who is tough now, little man. I am the motherfucker NOW, holding *your* knife, and you're about to become *my* little bitch, you drunk old fuck!"

Well, to say the least, we were all sitting there in horror as the friendly frontier courtroom of Judge Bonney Bedford, complete with life lessons for her drunken husband, had quickly turned into a rollicking and violet barroom brawl.

After moments of dead silence in the room, Ralph replied in a defeated and deflated whimper, "No, boy, I don't want to fight no more or driksh. I just want to go to bed and sleep this off. Now he was starting to cry, "I am a drunk, a miserable old drunk." His blubbering turned into cries of despair. "Help me lord, please help me and forgive me. I won't drink no more, I promise," as he looked right through his son and up to the heavens. Chet helped his dad up, his arms now practically carrying the old man, and assisted him to the master bedroom and tucked him in for the night.

My grandma—not missing a beat, acting as if nothing had ever happened—chuckled and said, "OK, kids, now who's in for a game of burnout with your old grandma Bonney?"

That was my first night in Petersburg, Alaska. It would only get more exciting in the next few weeks.

Every morning when I got up, my grandma would make me a big "hearty, man-sized breakfast," as she liked to call it. Back home I would usually just pour a bowl of cereal and that would be my simple, boring breakfast before school. My mom usually did not let me eat a lot of the real good sugary cereals like Froot Loops or Lucky Charms. She said they weren't healthy, and for me that pretty much sucked. My grandma Bonney, on the other hand, was the complete opposite of my mom, and it was great! The first day we were in Petersburg, my grandma took me shopping and we loaded up on Captain Crunch with Crunch Berries, Sugar Smacks, Sugar Puffs, Super Sugar Crisp, and Fruity Pebbles. I would usually start off my morning with a bowl or two of sugar yumminess, while my grandma was cooking up the hot portion of my meal. She would make me my favorite corn fritters every morning, followed by eggs and bacon, sausage or ham. Some mornings she would make me biscuits from scratch, covered with sausage gravy. I was in heaven and eating like a king. My grandma saw to that.

D.L. would sometimes peek in the kitchen while I was eating and make some wisecrack about me being too skinny. "You're so damn skinny, Pard, you could hula hoop with a Cheerio," or the one that really got me scared and confused, "You're so skinny, your nipples touch." That would really creep me out and after he left, I would immediately lift my shirt and check my nipples out.

We spent most of the day with my dad while my grandma slaved away at the only dry-cleaning business in Petersburg. We would check in with her every day, and I have never seen anyone work as hard as she did in my entire life. While she was "busting her hump," Chet went to work for Alaska Airlines as a baggage handler, and D.L. who was off for a month from his Prudhoe Bay job, tended a bar. Now, keep in mind that D.L. did not work as a bartender. Instead, he tended to loiter all day at the two main bars that this tiny little commercial fishing town had to offer.

In the morning, we frequented Harbor Bar and usually stayed there through lunch. The bartender Steve would greet us and usually have something clever to say to us about Petersburg or Alaska in general.

"Kids, there are two seasons in Petersburg: fishing season and waiting for fishing season," or "The four major food groups in Alaska are fish, moose, beer, and whiskey." He would flash a broad smile and ask us what we wanted to drink, just like he did to the grown-ups. This made us both feel pretty special and important. We liked Steve and wished we could hang out with him all day instead of D.L.

Gracie and I had our usual drinks for the day, a Roy Rogers with two cherries for me and a Shirley Temple for my sister with just one cherry and an orange wedge. My sister and I must have drunk about a thousand of those delicious drinks between us in the month we stayed there. By the time we left Alaska, we were what the locals here call "bar flies" —people who frequent bars all the time. I had a drawer full of Japanese paper umbrellas in my nightstand as evidence of my *bar hopping* prowess. My sister and I were really not very proud of this moniker at all, as we were merely just *tagalongs* with the *Lord of the Bar Flies* himself, D.L. Kirby.

D.L. was a self-proclaimed "master bullshitter," and he would work his magic at the bar with anyone who would bend his or her ear and listen to him. D.L. would usually bribe them by buying a round of drinks, and the *victim* would have to listen to him for at least as long as it took them to swizzle down a cool concoction of alcohol. Gracie and I would watch the ships come and go and play twenty questions, hang man, or any old card game to pass the time away. I would always have one ear open, however, listening intently to whatever worthless BS was spewing from the mouth of our adult chaperone, the *Big Gasbag*. D.L. was going *fishing* this morning, and he was looking for a *sucker*fish. I had seen this act a thousand times over.

"Hey, Pard," he was now conversing with some poor, innocent shmuck, dumb enough to take the bait and listen to him. "I used to live in Oregon, and I hate that place. Got nothing good to say about it at all. Left my job and my old lady down there because I couldn't take it any longer. Hey, I got a good one for ya: You know the difference between an Oregonian and a Halibut?"

"No?" the innocent fish replies. D.L. had caught his first *live* one of the morning hook, line and sinker.

"Well, one is a bottom-feeding scum-sucker and the other is a fish. Get it?"

He would slap the sorry sap on the back, dislodging the *hook* from his mouth, and now the *poor fish* was trapped, being forced to listen to D. L's mindless, pointless nonsense for the better part of the morning.

"Why don't girls play hide-and-seek in Oregon?" D.L was now finding his groove.

"I don't know?" said the helpless, flopping little *fish*.

"Tell us. Come on man, *tell* us." Now one fish had become a whole *school* of 'em, haplessly swimming around the old blowhard's barstool.

"No one would look for them!" They were all actually laughing at this point.

"Hey guys, here's a good one: Why do Oregonians smell bad?"

"I don't know, D.L. *Tell* us," some noodle fritz in a blue cap filled with fishing hooks replies.

"So, blind people can hate 'em too!" Laughter now bellows from the entire group of morons.

This kind of insane, asinine adolescent behavior would go on for hours each morning, as my sister and I were left to either listen, shoot a game of pool, or play a game of darts. By the end of the summer we became pretty darn good at both.

I was always anxious for lunchtime to come. They had pretty good chow at Harbor, and D.L. always splurged to keep us busy for another hour while he drank. I would always order a "Hair of the Dog" special, which was a giant kielbasa sausage dog smothered in chili, cheese, onions, and sauerkraut and a giant helping of potato salad on the side. I also ordered a giant plate of fries as well, because I knew I was going to be here for a while and I needed something to do.

At around one o'clock in the afternoon, we would take a short and very dangerous drive to the other *hot*spot of Petersburg, Kito's Cave, as D.L. was now very well lubricated. It was a sleazy bar in the sleaziest part of a sleazy little town. What a great place to take your two kids for a little *bonding* time. You should truly be *proud* of yourself, D.L., you insensitive, sleazy, slimy, slippery, worthless son of Satan!

Regardless of its total inappropriateness as a place for kids to dwell, Kito's Cave was by far my favorite summertime destination. Cave had it all—a surly bartender, pool, and foosball tables, dart boards, air hockey, a juke box in the corner and twenty-two drunken commercial fishermen for every one woman in this place. Today in the bar there were exactly twenty-three customers, twenty-two degenerate *deadbeat* dads, former wife beaters, sex offenders and criminals running from the law from all parts of the lower forty-eight. There would also be one female, my little sister—innocent, sweet, pigtails and all of seven years old. Little *Gracie*. I wondered what she was thinking at this very moment.

I am sure it was *not* "Oh thank you, Daddy, Kito's Cave, isn't it *just* beautiful. It's the place I always *dreamed* of. Maybe you can bring me back here when I am twenty-one!" I always felt sorry for Gracie, but I knew I could never leave her alone, never let her out of my sight.

D.L. switched from Bloody Marys and Crown Royal whiskeys in the morning to Olympia Beer in the afternoon to "mellow his buzz." He would explain this to me each day on the drive over—as if that is actually something a ten-year-old would really need to know.

"Give me an 'Oly,'" he would shout, as he arrived at his favorite afternoon watering hole.

"Hey, Pard, come here," he motioned me to the bar. He now summoned me into his dark domain at the dimly lit dive bar, leaving my petrified little sister sitting alone at a tiny roundtable with a red candle lit in the center—unattended among the unscrupulous and mangy mob of *cave dwellers*. I had one eye on her *all* of the time.

"Pard, looky here," he was now whispering and peeling the label off the brown "Oly" beer bottle. "Looky here, you see it?" He pulled me close, and this is probably as excited as I have ever seen old D.L. in his entire life. He was acting as if he had just uncovered one of Willy Wonka's *golden tickets*. "It's a Four Dotter, Pard, a *four dotter*!"

"So, what?" I replied.

"Shih, keep it down, Pard, turn your volume down, we don't want anyone to know."

"Know what?" I say.

"About the *secret*."

"The secret?" I asked, as I was now about six inches away from the label, staring down at the four printed dots on the back like someone inspecting a valuable stamp or coin.

"Yes, the secret of this mysterious, wondrous Oly!" he said, as he now was holding his beer up in the air like an Olympic torch.

"Go on," I say, still fixated on the four dots.

"This is a rare and priceless collectible from the Olympia Brewing Company in Tumwater, Washington. The Oly beer guys employ little *artisan* fellas at their brewery to carry *artisan* water to their brewery every day by the bucketful from there *magic* well," he gloated.

"I had no idea, go on."

"Well, this here *four dotter* signifies that this here beer is of the finest quality. Beers are ranked by the Oly guys from one to four dots, depending on how many artisan fellas had stirred the beer before it was bottled. This here bottle was mixed with the magical power of four little artisan *rascals*."

"*Amazing*," I feigned, as I thought this would sound a lot like Willy Wonka.

"One in every hundred bottles of Olympia beer is a *four dotter*. You, my boy, is a proud owner of one of them," he now handed me the humid label.

"Gee, thanks!" I retorted, slipping the label into my front jeans pocket.

"One last thing, Pard, and this is very important: Come a little closer cuz I need to whisper this too you cuz it's so *top secret* that the Oly beer undercover cops could storm on in here and sweep us both up for sharing this valuable information to others."

"OK, I'm all ears," I said, as I bent my ear slowly over to his now cupped hand.

"If you get a young lady to *sign* the back of your four-dotter label, she has to, has to . . . "

"Yes, go on."

"She has to show you her, her . . . "

"Out with it man, out with it," I said.

"Her, her . . . *boobies*."

"Her BOOBIES, holy beer bottles Batman, drink some more of those Olys, D.L., so I can get me some more of them four dotters!"

At about five o'clock each evening, we would take the even scarier ride home to the trailer each night, with our now completely intoxicated bar guide at the wheel. How my sister and I did not die on one of these many *white-knuckles* rides home, I will never know. I have seen better driving by kids in bumper cars than by D.L. on these hair-raising hellish rides. This would be our routine for the duration of our vacation, as D.L. did not deviate from this schedule.

Occasionally I or my sister would ask, "Can we go to the movies, Daddy?" or "How about the museum today?"

D.L. would always reply in the same sarcastic way: "Why would we waste our time on seeing some artsy-fartsy crap anyways, that stuff will just pollute your young minds."

I had come to the conclusion that D.L. was a big, fat, unrefined idiot and preferred *polluting* our minds in his own irresponsible and delinquent way.

When we would arrive at home, my grandma Bonney, the hardest-working woman on the planet, would be fixing us a home-cooked meal. Her idea of *home* cooked revolved completely around her *giant* deep fryer that she always kept in plain sight right beside the can opener and toaster on her kitchen counter. It was the centerpiece of her cooking world. She would load the deep fryer up with mounds of Crisco oil and make us grandkids many delectable and delicious deep-fried foods each night for dinner. One night it would be beer battered halibut or cod fish and chips. I would have six to eight pieces of fish and a large mountain of greasy fries, habitually returning for seconds. The next night, it would be crispy shrimp and fries, and the following meal we might have deep-fried chicken and JoJo potatoes.

I would gorge myself. It almost became a little contest each night to see how much the "little fella" could eat. D.L. would encourage my consumption of mass quantities of food by piling more food on my plate, dismissing my unhealthy eating habits with comments on my weight. "Pard, we need to fatten you up! You're so skinny, when you turn sideways, we can't see you at all!" Everyone would think these little jokes were funny, their laughter trembling the tiny kitchen table.

My grandma would take me and Gracie to the garbage

dump almost every night for entertainment, while my dad frequented the local Petersburg bars until all hours of the night. We would bring our lawn chairs and I would have a giant grocery bag full of hot-buttered popcorn that I had popped back at the trailer.

Before my dad would leave for the Cave each night, he would make some comment about my weight as I was popping the corn: "Make two batches, Pard! You're so skinny, I could grate cheese on those ribs!" I was happy to oblige him and usually poured an extra cup of real butter on the freshly popped corn for good measure.

When we got to the dump, we would take out the chairs, get a good seat and watch the black bears come out to eat. My grandma called them *garbage* bears, and for hours they basically just rummaged around for food within the many piles of disposed human waste. We would sit and watch the bears like it was great theater, eat popcorn and drink root beer for hours.

The one thing that excited me on our many evening trips to the dump was how animated Gracie got when the bears came out. For the entire day, she was disengaged and bored, as D.L. rarely talked to her. She was basically carry-on luggage to D.L.'s many trips to the bars, an inanimate object he just had to *deal* with. But when the bears would come out every night, it was as if she came to life. "Look, Grandma Bonney! It's a momma bear and her babies, isn't that cute!" I was content to know that my sister was finally having some fun.

During the first week of our trip, when I was out walking around at the dump just waiting for the *bear show* to begin, I found a giant bald eagle feather on the ground. It was about a foot-and-a-half long. My grandma told me to keep it for good luck, so that night I put it in my nightstand drawer with my drink umbrellas and four-dotter collection for safekeeping.

One morning, I tried to fit into my pants and just couldn't make them fit. No matter how hard I tugged or squeezed or tried to suck in my gut, I couldn't button up my britches. My shirts didn't fit either, as I found myself not being able to pull them all the way down over my inflated belly. My shirts and pants used to fit me real loose at the end of the last school year. Now I looked in the mirror and noticed the bulge. "Grandma Bonney," I screamed, "come! I think I'm *pregnated!*"

"Hold your horsies there, little one, hold your horsies, let me have look," she soothed as she made her way to the bedroom.

"Look, Grandma! My clothes don't fit anymore!" I said.

"Well I'll be, you're a hittin' your growth spurt," she said. "This is a perfect opportunity to go a shoppin' for some new Alaskan *duds.*"

I was thinking that was a nice way of saying *I was getting fat*, but I was game for some new clothes just the same, so we hopped into her old pickup truck and headed downtown. We went to the only clothing store in town, and just like with the cereal before, she let me pick out a variety of new stuff to wear. I picked out six new *Alaska* shirts with different wild animal designs—a grizzly bear, a polar bear, an eagle, a killer whale, a moose and a king salmon. I chose three pairs of camouflage pants, all with elastic waistbands to accommodate my *growth spurt*, and a brand-new pair of army-style black boots.

As I was ready to leave the store, a bag in each hand, my grandma said, "Hold on there, boy, you need yourself a new Alaskan hat." She proceeded to plop one on my head and I found the closest mirror and took a look. It was perfect. A camouflage Australian Bush hat, with a snap-up side and a drawstring to cinch around my neck.

I said, "Thanks, Grandma Bonney, you're the best. This hat will go perfect with my new camo pants and boots."

When I got to the trailer, I stuck that giant old eagle feather in my hat, and in one afternoon I had completely reinvented myself with a new wardrobe and a new rough-and-rugged *Alaskan* image. I was all set to make an impression on my new classmates for my fifth-grade school year.

I left Alaska, thirty pounds heavier and ten years wiser in the ways of the world, an eagle feather in my hat and a pristine collection of thirty-eight *four dotter* Olympia Beer bottle labels. I was rejuvenated, excited and motivated and I was fixing to see plenty of *boobies* on my return trip to the lower forty-eight.

THE END

(3)

When I came up that ramp and into the Portland International airport—sporting my new eagle-feathered hat, my cheeks all puffed out with the additional thirty pounds added to my tiny ten-year-old frame—my mom about nearly *died*. For the first time in my life, I had grown me a fine pair of *man boobs*. It would *not* be the *last* time. My mother was in tears as she led me through the airport and down to the baggage claim. I had only had this feeling of humiliation once before as she hurried me down to get my luggage—the night of that damned boxing match when I was a first grader. I was again an embarrassment to her.

"The first thing that's going to happen when we get home young man is that I am putting you on a diet!" And my mom kept her word on that, trust me. Little boys with *man boobs* were simply not acceptable in the Kirby household, no way, no how!

I turned in my twelve-paged, typed, double-spaced paper to Mr. Zimmer. It took me an entire week after school to type that thing, one peck at a time. It is the only time I can recall not watching the television for an entire week growing up. I was that motivated to tell my story to the other kids. I now had to wait anxiously for an "A," some positive feedback on my written work, and a date and time slot for my read-aloud to the class.

A few short days later, I found myself sitting in the counselor's office in a large black leather chair across the desk facing Mrs. Grimm, head counselor for Crawfish Elementary School. She was a very large woman, sitting with horned-rim glasses on her face, reading my essay silently to herself. She read for a while, looked up at me, shook her head slowly back and forth, gave me an unpleasant frown, and turned to reading again.

She slowly read and flipped the pages one by one, her "tsk, tsk, tsk"s turning to "OH my goodness" and to "you've got be KIDDING me." Later, she squeaked screams and cries of disbelief. "BOOBIES?!" she yelped. "Eeally, *really*, BOOBIES?" She was now glaring at me, shaking her head in slow motion, back and forth, back and forth.

I couldn't take this silent treatment too much longer; there was a giant elephant looming in the room, and I'm not talking about Mrs. Grimm here. I finally blurted it out, "Well . . . did you like it?"

"Like it? Well, to tell you the truth young man, that may be the most inappropriate story that I have EVER read, and I'm not just talking about in school, but EVER." She even took the time to spell it out for me real slow: "E-V-E-R, EVER."

"Well, I guess that means I'm probably not going to be able to read my story out loud to the rest of the class?" I asked, all sheepish.

"Young man, I am turning this over to the principal, Mr. Todman. We'll see what he has to say about your little *story*."

The next day, I was called to Mr. Todman's office and led by the secretary to the adjoining conference room, where all of the *Supreme Court* members of Crawfish

Elementary were seated around a long table. The secretary placed me in the chair next to my mom, who had been subpoenaed earlier this morning by this *kangaroo* court and had been briefed minutes ago about the contents of my "inappropriate story." She had hastily left work, and had decided to join the key *stakeholders* in the education of young Mr. Kirby for my "risk assessment" meeting. Seated around the table were the principal, the vice-principal, the dean of students, the two school counselors, the school psychologist, Mr. Zimmer, and my fourth-grade teacher from last year, Mrs. Maddox.

The vice principal glared at me for a while, sizing me up real good, and was the first to speak. He turned to the principal and said, "You know it's times like these, when you got a real problem on your hands, a little troublemaker who needs to be taught a lesson, you got to just nip the problem in the bud! That's right, nip it! Nip it right in the bud."

Holy moly, he just stole Barney Fife's favorite catch phrase from one of my all-time most favorite television sitcoms, I said to myself, almost blurting it out loud in front of all the adults at the table. What a *moron*. At that very moment, I felt as though I had *crash*-landed in an episode of *The Andy Griffith Show*.

Here I was, Little Opie in a Mayberry courthouse, sitting around the table were Sherriff Andy Taylor, Deputy Barney Fife, Goober, his brother Gomer, Floyd the barber and my guardian, good ol' Aunt Bee. I knew this wasn't going to turn out well for me, and it certainly would not have a happy ending like the TV show always did.

Here is a quick rundown of the court proceedings that day.

Vice Principal Fife read aloud the parts of my paper that he had highlighted and deemed "school inappropriate." You know the boozing it up at the bars with D.L. parts, the knife fight and the paragraphs that had the word *booby* in it. After much discussion and deliberation by the panel, it was decided that "I was not a threat to myself or others in the school." It was also decided that I would serve two weeks of lunch detention and write a more appropriate story to be submitted at the end of my prison sentence to Mr. Zimmer. Case *closed*.

Nice, very nice, you bunch of incompetent numskulls, I thought to myself. I was now twiddling my sweaty fingers under the long table while the adults thought somehow that they had solved this very troubling situation for the safety and welfare of *all* the students in their sacred school, except for me. You guys are education professionals, sworn to some damn oath of double-die sworn secrecy that you are empowered and obligated to be *mandatory reporters* of suspected child abuse. I knew this because, in third grade, I had written something that was "school inappropriate" about my dad *touching* me, and my teacher called the state detective guys, who later called my mom.

"No problems at home!" Mom yelled into the phone at the top of her lungs. You are living under a rock, I thought to myself. She hung up in disgust.

The teacher later apologized to me, saying, "Sorry, Mark, but I am a *mandatory* reporter." That is where I picked up on this top-secret, underground educational term.

Why aren't you guys making a call to the state on my behalf and reporting this potential abuse? Could you not see the cries for help in my paper, which was now residing in the middle of the long boardroom table, facedown in shame, never to be read by anyone ever again? I tried to include little *clues* about my abusive Dad subtly (or not so subtly) in my writing. I thought I made it clear that D.L. was not the best of dads. *Help* me guys. You didn't even have to read in between the lines here. My *abusive* home life was staring you right in the face.

I did *not* want to be in his custody ever again. Not for one minute, and certainly not for a summer vacation from hell. It's like, through my writing I was hoping, praying desperately for someone here at school to throw a lifeline and save me.

I also put another blatant clue in my story: "He and my dad must have had a talk, because neither of them *touched* me anymore." I was *screaming* for help, but no one cared to take the time to rescue me that day. Barney and the rest of the Mayberry clan were only interested in the shock value of a kid writing the word *boobies,* I guess.

And the panel didn't even bother asking me *why* I had written that "inappropriate" paper. I would have simply told them I was just telling the truth! I could have also presented evidence that day from my month-long adventure with D.L. in Alaska.

Exhibit A: an Australian Bush hat, with a real Bald Eagle feather in it.

Exhibit B: 120 paper drink umbrellas, evidence of the many Roy Rogers I guzzled that past summer while bar hopping with D.L. and my sister.

Exhibit C: thirty-eight "four dotter" Oly Beer bottle labels (all unsigned, as of today).

Exhibit D: a before-and-after picture of me, proving

that I had indeed put on thirty pounds of fat in thirty days, eating bar food, grocery bags of popcorn and my grandma's tasty fried-food delicacies. I was *railroaded* that day, and all of my concrete physical evidence of a summer gone *bad* was *not* admissible in this shabbily run court of law.

Only one person came to my defense that day, and it wasn't my mom. No, good old Aunt Bee just sat there and nodded, apologizing for my *shameful* behavior. Instead, it was good old Mr. Zimmer. Goober and Gomer said nothing. Floyd the Barber doodled on his note pad. When Principal Taylor and Vice Principal Fife were meting out their punishment, Mr. Zimmer chose this moment as an opportunity to *help* me—reach out to me and not *punish* me like the rest of the adults in the room. He decided to ask me a few pointed questions and pick my brain.

"Mark, do you like sports?" he asked.

"I don't know, I have never really played much?"

"Who are you *mad* at, Mark?" he asked, pursuing his perceptive hunch. "It seems like you got a huge *chip* on your shoulder, young man, and I think I can help."

"I am mad at my dad, you know, that D.L. in the story? He is *mean* and he is . . . *no good.*"

"I see. Have you ever played on a team before?"

"No, why?" I asked, because for the first time today, an adult in this room was trying to make a personal connection with me.

"Mark, here's the deal. I am the fifth-/sixth-grade football coach and I want you to come play for me this fall. It will do you some good, get you outdoors with boys your own age. You'll get yourself in shape, and the game of football can teach you some positive life lessons you can take with you everywhere. Football is a great way for you to channel some of that anger you are feeling in a positive way. What do you say, son?"

"I'm game, I *guess*."

And that is has how little *miracles* happen. A connection was made on that day that would transform a small boy's life for the better. And that small boy was *me,* a *lost* kid who needed a strong adult male role model in his life. Zimmer was the first teacher I ever had that took in interest in me outside of teaching me *just* content.

Mr. Zimmer went on to coach me in football that fifth-grade year. It would be the first of my thirty years playing and coaching the game. That year, he gave me the job of center on the team because "I was smart" and he could "trust me to do this very important job for the team." Team sports would always provide me a strong sense of family and feeling of self-worth. Coach Zimmer used the team endeavor to teach me the character traits of self-discipline, hard work, perseverance and teamwork. He encouraged me to get in shape. I lost that thirty pounds and was a healthy, happy kid again.

I would always remember Mr. Zimmer. He would leave a lasting, positive impression on my life. He would inspire me to become an educator when I got older. *He* was indeed that *hero* I needed as a ten-year-old boy.

THIRD Times a Charm?

When it rains, it pours. That is the reality of my situation. The hits just keep on a coming. Body blows to my midsection, blows to the head. I'm taking punches from all directions. It was time for another damn test. I was none too happy about this idea, because the only way to get to your prostate is to enter through the top-secret backdoor entrance of your body. It was no *secret* to anyone now; my *backdoor* had already seen enough combat action the last couple of weeks to last a lifetime.

The biopsy was the most invasive test that I have ever had to endure. Before going to the doctor that day, my wife had to give me an enema to "flush my system out," as she put it. I wept on the bathroom floor as she administered the fluid into my lubed-up anus. At that very moment, I thought that *this* was the lowest point in my adult life. But, just when you think you've hit rock bottom, *it* will deliver you another low blow to your dignity and self-worth right smack dab in your *nut sack*.

I thought of my third dad, Michael Melvin, for the first time in a long time. He was the most influential man in my life in my teenage years. As I lay there on the floor, my bloated bowels filled to the brim with water, my mind full of self-pity, I remembered the words of my Uncle Tim,

Melvin's younger brother. Uncle Tim had told me long ago that when times got *bad* to stop being such a big v-a-g-i-n-a, *vagina*.

(1)

In the spring of 1971, as I was finishing up my fifth-grade school year, I was for the first time becoming more aware of the world outside of the little Oregon town in which I lived. I was starting to question things for the first time in my life, and I thought I had mastered a new language—the top-secret, underground, locker-room talk of *swearing*.

I had become interested in current events, as we had taken the time to read the *Weekly Reader* last year in class. Change was happening globally, as the birth of *Greenpeace* signaled a need for all of mankind to question how we managed our natural resources. In the United States, the 26th amendment to the Constitution was ratified, lowering the voting age to eighteen. Walt Disney opened up his bigger, better theme park, Disneyworld. And as an eleven-year-old poor kid, I really didn't give a damn, as I had never even been to Disneyland yet, no mind *Disneyworld*. What the *hell*, those Disney guys are really rubbing their new theme park right in my face here.

A lot of changes were taking place in the Kirby family as well. I had survived the teasing from my peers for being the "fat kid"; my two most difficult school years were behind me. I had miraculously dumped thirty pounds of *excess baggage* accumulated thanks to that summer in Alaska. It had been almost two years now since an adult male had *violated* me in any way. I did not *trust* men, however, and would never fully trust males growing up, especially those in positions of power. I would always believe they had *ulterior* motives.

I was beginning to feel like a regular kid for the first time in my life though, and I was experiencing a refreshing feeling of freedom in and out of school. I was noticing taking notice of girls, and they were taking an interest in me. Kids were not picking on me or bullying me anymore, and I was finally going to have a human friend for the first time in my life.

Gracie did not miss her dad at all. D.L. hardly had ever paid attention to her, anyways. She *never* had any clue that any abuse was going on in our house. Why? D.L. preferred young boys. *She* wasn't *his* type. Gracie was growing like a weed. It was *amazing*. She would always be the tallest girl in her class, always gangly growing up. And she did have her crushes, like most girls her age. She had replaced the bedroom-wall posters of Davey Jones to those of *The Monkees* and her new heartthrob, Donny Osmond. Her Etch A Sketch had now been replaced by her new evening pastime, Lite-Brite.

Our mom had also changed and *reinvented* herself, as she was finishing up her last year of college at Oregon State University in nearby Corvallis. She had gotten two part-time jobs and planted a giant garden of cucumbers, selling them on a roadside stand to help pay for her education. This would become her *cucumber story* that she would spin at job interviews, educational seminars and as a highly paid motivational speaker later on in her life. It was her rags-to-riches tale—the account of an abandoned single mom with no money, alone with her two kids on a rundown farm, improving her situation through the *power* of education.

She was anxious to get started on her new career as a Home Economics teacher. She had always liked to cook and sew, and these skills that she had honed for years as a stay-at-home housewife and mother would now be taught to enthusiastic high school students—hopefully in the fall. For a graduation present, her proud parents, Cliff and Lavina, had purchased her a brand-new, navy-blue Ford Mustang. She was on a mission to make her parents proud of her once again. She had been a failure in her first two marriages, but she could now control her own destiny through her career as an educator. Maybe she should stay single and not get married, she silently surmised? But soon I would learn: my insecure mom would always need a man in her life—good, bad or otherwise. It didn't matter, really. She just needed a warm, smelly, hairy body to snuggle up to at night. It was sad and kinda gross.

My mom and I shared *one* passion during this time. Something we would *share* for *entire* lives. Our *love* of film. On occasion, she would treat me to a picture at the Saturday matinee in the local downtown theater. Just the *two* of us. No *men* allowed. We both loved popcorn. With *lots* of butter. It was something we both looked forward to. It also provided us with a common topic to talk about in our home. For two hours, we could escape our mundane reality, living on that run-down country farm, and enter a world full of color, music and magic. I think this experience gave us both hope for a better *future* moving forward. At least, that is what I certainly *longed* for. We were consumed by the wondrous imagery that only Hollywood can provide.

"Mark, do you think I'll ever find love like *they* do in the movies. Ya know, *happily* ever *after*?"

"Sure. Just quit trying so hard to *make* it *happen*, Mom. Have some patience. Stop settling for *second* best. You deserve *better* than that."

"I do?"

"Yes. You *do*. Trust me on that idea."

Grandma Bonney and Grandpa Ralph purchased a two-acre parcel of land next to our farm home in Lebanon and planned to put a double-wide trailer on the property when they retired and moved down from Alaska; they wanted to be close to their grandkids. I was excited about this proposition. Corn fritters in the morning and fried delicacies at night. My mouth was already watering.

(2)

Spring had sprung and love was in the air, as the top movie at the box office for that year was *Love Story* with Ryan O'Neal and Ali McGraw. Coincidentally, or not, *love* came knocking at the Kirby household in the form of Michael Melvin, my soon-to-be third Dad.

My first impression of Melvin, chatting with him in our living room as Mom got ready for their first blind date? I bet this dude likes to smoke weed. He had all the classic signs of someone who is *high*, I thought. He was emotionally sensitive; he had commented on our "beautiful flower bed" right as he walked through the door. He would laugh inappropriately, awkwardly right in the middle of a sentence. He also talked in a drowsy, dreamy, low and monotone voice. It sounded as though he was *stoned* out of his mind.

"This is a *groovy* place you got here, Mark, ha, ha . . . ha, ha, ha," he giggled. "Do you like living in the country?"

"I guess it is . . . *groovy*," I replied, "but I would rather live closer to town so I could walk to the movie theater."

"Do you like movies?"

"Yes, sir."

"No need to call me sir, ha, ha . . . you can call me Mike." He chuckled again. "What movies have you seen lately?"

"Well, *The Love Bug* and *The Planet of the Apes*."

"Cool man, very *cool*. Smart cars and talking apes, *very* cool."

"Do you like movies, Mr. Melvin? My mom sure does. She wants to live happily ever after."

"Groovy. I *dig* movies."

His laid-back demeanor and lazy, hazy, goofy-ass smile smelled to me like a big, fat, *lit doobie*. I bet he is one of those dope-smoking, reformed-hippie commune fellas, maybe even a former *Moonie*, now trying to blend in with society and take advantage of my innocent, sweet mom. I began to grill Melvin with some probing questions about his intentions regarding my mom for that evening.

"What time do you plan on bringing my mom home, Mr. Melvin?" I asked.

"We're just going to take it at as she goes man, let the evening *flow*, ya dig?" he replied, calling up the Shaggy character from *Scooby Doo*.

I dig, you . . . you . . . big, goofy-ass *stoner*, I thought to myself, as I began to probe the demented dope fiend even deeper, my hands now clinched in fisted rage under our bamboo-and-glass coffee table.

"Do you s*moke*?" I asked, as I now inched an ashtray to the center of the coffee table.

"No thanks, little man."

"How about some *Cheetos*?" I asked, thinking Melvin

might be getting the *munchies* after *firing up* the old bong before his first date.

"No thanks, man. I only snack on healthy foods like *trail mix*. Do you have any of that?"

"No," I said, still convinced even more now that he was some *granola*-munching hippie.

"Is your favorite song 'Puff the Magic Dragon?'"

"Wait a minute, kid, are you asking me if I . . . smoke *grass?*"

"Well, kind of. In a roundabout way, I guess?"

"Look, kid, I believe in an alcohol- and drug-free, organic, whole-food lifestyle, sprinkled with wisdom, spirituality, yoga, meditation and *love* for all living creatures, *ya dig?*"

Nice answer, I thought to myself, as I continued my aggressive line of questioning.

"Do you need to make a collect call to your . . . your friend . . . *Mary Jane?*"

"Woah now, hold on there, little buddy . . . I like you kid, you're *funny* and you got a vivid imagination, and I like the way you're looking out for your mom's interest here," he answered, as a broad smile flashed across his face. In that moment, as he was now animated and full of infectious enthusiasm, I knew this guy wasn't *high* on drugs at all—he was *high* on life and I thought that was cool, *very* cool.

"Let me ask you this question, young man," he smiled, drawing a little closer to me with his left hand now cupping the side of his mouth. "You're not dabbling in the *cannabis*, little buddy, are you? You seem a bit . . . paranoid."

What a crazy question, I thought.

"Why, heavens *no*. If you want to talk to some crazy, meat-eating, inbred, *cannibuses*, you need to go up to the McKenzie River and meet my former in-laws, Nanno, Ankee and Uncle Chester."

Melvin flashed a disconcerted look, knowing full well I was confused with his question and the meaning of the word *cannabis*. Just then, Mom came from the bathroom to meet her young suitor.

"I'm ready," Mom said, as the couple now exchanged casual pleasantries.

As she stood there chatting with Mike, I thought that she looked beautiful tonight, all prettied-up in a V-neck, granny-print dress, and ready to have some fun on the town. Good for her, she deserves it!

I said goodbye to my mom and Mike as I walked them to the door, sending them off on their very first date. Melvin was an interesting guy, I thought. Much more real and down to earth, self-aware and smarter than D.L. He had a vulnerability about him that I would always appreciate. He could laugh at himself, and I would always admire this particular quality in him. As they drove off, I felt almost like a dad, watching my treasured loved one be driven away by a complete stranger. I hoped she would be safe in the company of young Mr. Melvin. I already *liked* him. Right off. He thought movies were *groovy*.

(3)

Michael Melvin was actually the perfect suitor. He was the twenty-eight-year-old, successful, well-respected Parks and Recreation director for the neighboring town of Albany, Oregon. His leadership and vision had helped open new city parks and improve existing parks in the area. He was a leader in his community and someone who would soon swoop my mom right off her feet and to the alter for her third attempt at marriage. In the back of my mind, I knew this meant that we were about to move again.

In the short eleven years of my life, I had lived in three states, eight different cities, and gone to four different schools. I would complete sixth grade in my fifth school in seven years, as my mom was about to get married *again*. I would mask my insecurities during this time period with teenage toilet humor, a box of Tic Tacs at my ready, and heavy doses of Old Spice doused all over my body. I would find out, through trial and error, that the two best ways for me to fit in as a new student would be to play team sports and be the *funny* kid, the *class clown*. This would be my identity, my persona, all throughout my secondary years of schooling. It was my way of surviving at school in a sometimes-hostile adolescent world. My mentor during this time would be my Uncle Tim, Melvin's younger brother. He would be the first *human* friend I would ever have. I idolized this *dude* in my early teenage years. He was absolutely hilarious.

As an incoming sixth grader, my life was to dramatically change again, only this time for the better. Mike and my mom dated for only a few months, enjoying dinners and movies together, skiing adventures in the mountains and weekend trips to the beach. The wedding was set for Saturday June 5th and was to be a backyard, garden-variety wedding, complete with the soundtrack music from the film *Love Story*.

(4)

It was a beautiful garden wedding in the backyard of Mike Melvin's simple ranch home—two acres of property on the outskirts of town. Melvin had purchased this home a few years ago, and when his father passed away, his mom, Mel, short for Melinda, and younger brother Tim came to live with him. This would be our new family home, as my Grandma Mel and Uncle Tim had now moved into a new apartment complex a few blocks away. We would move into our new home after my parents got back from their honeymoon.

The ceremony itself was complete with sundresses, ugly brown-and-burgundy seventies' men's suits, flowers everywhere, handwritten vows by the bride and groom, a justice of the peace presiding, and all immediate family members playing roles: I was to give my mom away under a flowered wedding arch, Gracie was the maid of honor, and my Uncle Tim served as the best man for this blended family affair. Mom, a beautiful, young bride of thirty-two years, wore a yellow crocheted wedding dress. My new dad of twenty-eight wore a brown bell-bottom suit and a wide yellow tie to match.

I escorted her up the lawn, through the lined chairs on both sides of the narrow walkway, proud to be able to do something responsible and adult like that for her. Looking back, I have never regretted that walk by my mom's side; it just seemed right. Both Mom and Mike shed a tear as they exchanged their thoughtful, heartfelt messages to one another. The crowd cheered as the justice of the peace declared, "I now pronounce you man and wife, you may *kiss* the bride." This journey with Dad number three was to begin.

All of the main players of my family were there that

day. Many members of my mom's family had made the long trip from Canada to be there. My mom was born in Canada and became an American citizen at age eighteen. All my Canadian relatives drank a lot of beer and talked funny, ending every phrase with "eh."

Grandma Lavina and Grandpa Cliff had too much champagne as always and danced the afternoon away like they had been sent back in a time machine to the end of World War II. When my grandma got tipsy, she would always try to do two things: play the piano and sing. She could play the piano all right, actually very well, but when it came to singing, she sounded a bit like a squeaky and nervous kindergarten girl. As soon as she started to sing, Uncle Bill, my grandma's protective little brother, intercepted this potential train wreck and whisked her away to the dance floor for some swinging to Benny Goodman's orchestra.

Uncle Bill, who had come down form Vancouver, was there that day with his good old pal Stan. They were both wearing matching, white, zip-up jumpsuits with white-buckled shoes and gold peace-symbol medallions around their necks. Each wore giant black sunglasses, strolling around together and admiring the many wedding flowers on display. I stood there in fascination as they began to comment on the floral centerpiece at the long gift table.

"Look at these lovely flowers, Bill," said the shorter, squatty Stan, who looked a lot like Liberace, the famous piano player.

"The purple irises, blue hyacinth, and pussy willows make for a nice arrangement," replied Bill, who resembled Elvis—not the "cool" fifties' Elvis, but the heftier *Vegas* version of the *King* of rock and roll.

"I don't like *pussy* willows very much," Stan replied in a squeaky little voice.

"I *know* you don't like *pussy* willows," smiled Bill as he puffed on a Tipperillo cigar and shared a quick wink.

My new Uncle Tim was totally different than Uncle Bill—and Uncle Chet, who was obviously not there that day. Uncle Tim and I instantly connected when we met at a small family picnic at Timber Linn Memorial Park. Tim was cool and had a sense of humor that I could relate to. He was not perverted like Chet, who had turned into a hairy, creepy old aunt.

My Uncle Bill and Stan, on the other hand, were just . . . different. I could not quite put my finger on it, but I was starting to think that they might be "homos."

It's important to note here that this word comes from my sixth-grade world, where its mere mention in front of the guys would have led to an ass-kicking on the playground. I made a vow to myself to never touch this sensitive subject—until it came up in a casual conversation at the reception with the much worldlier Uncle Tim.

He and I were sitting on two plastic chairs, eating our second piece of wedding cake and watching the dance floor. Uncle Bill and Stan were dancing together, and it quickly caught my eye; I had never seen two guys dance with each other before.

I started the conversation. "Do you think my uncle and his buddy over there in the matching white outfits are uh . . . uh . . . "

"Come on, out with it, man."

"You know . . . 'homos'?"

"You mean Homo . . . *sapiens*," he quipped, knowing full well what I was talking about.

"No, I mean, you know . . . " I was now cupping my hand and whispering to him. *"Light in the loafers,* you know . . . *twinkie toes?"*

"OH, you mean *homosexuals?"* Tim exclaimed, and two elderly women glared at him, shaking their heads in disgust.

"Shhh, quiet down, man. Do you want us to get our asses kicked?"

"Oh, *they* won't beat me up, cuz I'm much smaller than you are," he joked. "They'll kick your *bigger* ass first!"

Sadly, Tim was right; he was a half a head shorter than me. A tiny, pathetic little shrimp of a dude. His favorite actor in the world was Mickey Rooney. He had been around military bases all his life and picked up a lot of *colorful* language from the GIs.

"Let me put it this way, Mark. I bet your uncle Bill and Stan's favorite ride at Disneyland is the *Butt Pirates* of the Caribbean!"

"I don't get it?"

"Let me put it another way: if Bill and Stan went to a carnival food booth, they would choose *wieners* over *tacos."*

"Oh, I get *it."* But I actually had no clue as to what my clever, crude uncle was saying.

Our conversation had sparked Tim's mood for a comedy interlude—he decided this would be the perfect opportunity to share some of the jokes he learned as an army brat.

"What's the difference between snowmen and snowwomen?" he asked.

"I got no idea?"

"Snowballs! Get it?" he chuckled. "Now why don't you

try one. Come on, make it a good one now, make it a good one!"

"OK, here goes," I said. "Why did Tigger look in the toilet? He was looking for Poo! Pretty good huh?"

"Now that is the lamest *shit* I have ever heard!" Tim scorned.

"What do you mean?"

"I mean, who did you *steal* that joke from, a *fucking* first grader on the school bus? Here is a really good joke, you big *butt weasel*," Tim fired away. "Why isn't there a pregnant Barbie doll?"

"I don't know, Tim, why?"

"Because Ken *comes* in another box!" Tim was now laughing out loud at his own lame-ass joke. "Get it?"

"Sure," I say, the joke going completely over my head like a *whizzing* bullet.

While everyone danced, my new uncle and I engaged in our own special brand of highly sophisticated entertainment. We first decided to *cannonball* root beer until it came out our noses. We then tried to see how much cake we could jam into our mouths all at one time. We made fart noises with our armpits and laughed hysterically. To top it all off, Tim completed our mature and highly refined uncle-and-nephew bonding session by lighting his farts on fire. The bewildered elderly women nearby *gasped* in disbelief. Man, now that guy has got *real* talent, I thought. What fun we were having at the reception, and we were only just getting started.

We now moved to the front of the house where the bride and groom's getaway car, Mom's new Mustang, was parked in the driveway. We had a *blast* spraying the car with shaving cream and Silly String. After sufficient dousing, it was now time to put on the finishing touches with messages on all the windows. Being a pretty creative writer, I was the first one to take a stab with a bar of soap in hand: "Just Married!"

Tim said in disgust after reading my simple, thoughtful message, "Let me see that soap, you BIG pussy!"

He snatched the soap from my hand and began to scrawl. "Behold!" he said, as he now stepped aside from the car so he could read his message loudly and proudly to his crowd of one.

It read, "Honk if you're horny!"

"I don't think my mom and your brother are going to like that, Tim," sounding a little bit like the Boo-Boo to his Yogi Bear.

Tim scoffed, "You are the world's *biggest* vagina." His eyes suddenly lighting up, "Hey, that gives me an idea." He began to scribble again, this time in even bigger block letters: "My wife has a hairy bush, would you like to see it?"

"Tim, what in the hell are you thinking?" I yelled. "Are you out of your mind? That's my mom you're talking about."

"Vagina, vagina, vagina. Next time you turn in an assignment at school, don't forget to put your name on it . . . first name *Hairy* last name V-a-g-i-n-a, *Vagina*."

Uncle Tim was out of control now; the mountain of root beers consumed had gone directly to the rational side of his brain, saturating and polluting his already-twisted and warped mind. "They won't even see these messages, because it will be *dark* when they leave," Tim cackled, waving his hands in the air as if to scratch God. He continued on, with his one-way ticket to hell in hand, covering the car with crude messages written in baby blue Dove soap.

Most of the time, I thought Uncle Tim to be hilarious— but this time, he had *crossed* the line and I knew there would be hell to pay once the bride and groom sobered up in the morning and saw the bar soap graffiti. What was I going to do, as I knew this would guarantee us both some severe punishment from my parents. Against my better judgment, I left the car decorated as it was, and returned to the backyard for the rest of the wedding reception.

Well, the wedding reception lasted into the late hours of the night, as Tiki torches were lit and people danced to "Joy to the World" by Three Dog Night and "Tie a Yellow Ribbon Around the Old Oak Tree" by Tony Orlando and Dawn and other undanceable tunes of the early seventies. Lots of fun was to be had by everyone that night.

In the end, we all lined up in front of the house and threw streams of rice on the bride and groom as they made their way into the now profane and desecrated getaway car. As they drove off on their two-hour trip up Interstate 5 to Portland for their honeymoon night, I now wished I had *not* conspired with Uncle Tim earlier that afternoon in the decoration of the once-friendly, innocent Ford Mustang. My parents were now unknowingly strapped into the recently modified *Pootang Mobile,* a navy-blue billboard of blasphemy.

It was a big mistake to have gotten involved with my disturbed new uncle. What could have I possibly been thinking? I already knew that Timmy Melvin was bad news, a *problem child.* I just knew that this had been a *bad* idea from the very beginning.

(5)

Uncle Tim, alias Timmy Melvin, was a *mistake* from the very beginning. He was the exceptionally annoying, hyperactive, offspring of Mel and the late Master Sergeant Max Melvin Senior. He was the youngest child of three boys, seventeen years younger than Mike. Uncle Timmy was actually three months younger than me, yet I probably had three years of emotional maturity on him.

His enabling mom, my Grandma Mel, claimed that her "poor little boy" suffered from a rare condition called "jargon aphasia" anytime he would get himself in trouble, which was always. According to her, it is a *disease* that causes people to blurt out random, crude and sometimes inappropriate words. But Uncle Timmy really required no medical diagnosis; he was a mischievous, deviant little shit, unstable and bordering on mentally ill. I had concluded this in a short matter of time and had no advanced degrees or medical expertise to speak of. But I would hang out with good old Uncle Timmy during my middle school years, and he was the first real friend I ever had, for *better* or for *worse*.

Gracie and I spent my parent's wedding night with our new Grandma Mel at her apartment, and would stay there until our parents got home from their honeymoon in Reno.

But early in the morning, I was awakened by Grandma Mel to see that Tim was already sitting on the coach, crying his eyes out. Apparently, my new dad had already called his mother earlier that morning, disconcerted by what had transpired the previous evening on his ride to the Portland area. Apparently, several drivers on I-5, the most heavily traveled highway in Oregon, had harassed my mom and new dad after they had left from the wedding that night. People were honking, sticking their heads out of their windows, hooting, hollering and pointing at the Mustang's newly decorated car windows.

"Nice fucking message," one belligerent guy yelled, wielding a can of Budweiser while hanging out the passenger window in the left-hand lane.

A redneck driver passed by my parents and shouted out of his moving Chevy farm truck, "Ima honkin', Ima honkin'!" as he wailed on the truck horn, "and Ima horneeeeey! Yee haw!"

When one car of college girls pressed their large bare breasts up to the side window and another car's passenger gave my parents a BA, Mike Melvin had seen enough, and decided to pull the wedding getaway car over onto the side of the road. As he inspected his car with a flash light, with his loving, protective arm around his new wife, he was shocked and horrified to find out that someone had *rat fucked* his car. He surveyed the entire car, reading all of the lewd comments, and paused for a moment to reflect on the sequence of events during and following the wedding reception. One and one make two, and Mike had now pinpointed in his mind the two responsible parties of this dastardly and disturbing deed. Tim and I had been caught red-handed in Melvin's mind, on a lonely highway somewhere between Woodburn and Wilsonville, the Dove soap residue coating our grimy little guilty fingers back at home in Albany.

That morning, as I sat on Grandma Mel's brown-and-yellow flowered couch next to Uncle Timmy, I knew I was in deep shit! One thing about Mel Melvin: you knew she wasn't going to "pussy foot" around the situation here. She had been a military wife for thirty-five years, Master Sergeant Melvin's commanding officer at home. I would today for the first time learn that she was indeed a straight shooter, and I began to hope, from this day forward, that I would not again land in her bad graces moving forward.

"Timmy, what the hell were you boys thinking, writing all that filthy garbage on the car windows?" asked Mel, more inquisitive than accusing.

At this moment, I knew my brand-new uncle was about to throw me under the bus. I could just feel it, deep down inside my gut, knowing he was really a bigger pussy than I was. And *he did*. No clarifying questions asked, no look my way, he took me by my narrow shoulders and heaved me under a moving bus, and I was squashed like a helpless June bug on the pavement! He said in a now boisterous and animated way, "I tried to stop him, but he was out of control! He was a maniac with the soap and I couldn't *stop* him, Mommy, no matter how hard I tried." Tim was pointing at me, and I sadly now realized that the whole crime was being dumped on my lap like a big steamy shit sandwich by my sneaky little shit of an uncle.

I was tongue-tied for a brief moment as Officer Mel glared at me, as if she had now captured a Viet Cong prisoner of war behind enemy lines. I tried to rise to my own defense, but I couldn't seem to find any logical words to express my disappointment, anger, and frustration toward the pathetic little shit, sitting all innocent like. I wanted to cry and scream, but just sat there silently, dumbfounded, looking guilty as charged.

"Well. What do you have to say for yourself, Mark?"

"Well I, I tried, I mean I told him to, I was going to . . .

ah . . . ah . . . Gee whiz, Grandma Mel, I'm, I'm . . . " I was at complete loss for words here and said nothing more . . . except for "I am sorry," bowing my head before her in reverence of her authority, and in total shame for my actions of yesterday afternoon. I began to cry before my commanding officer.

"Well, I appreciate your honesty and taking responsibility for your actions," reasoned Mel. "Do you have anything else you would like to say before I punish you?"

"I'm sorry," I said. Those were the only two words I could come up with in my rattled little head.

"Mark, those are the two biggest words in the dictionary, and I am glad you owned up to your mistake."

"Thank you, ma'am."

"Because you were so forthright about your behavior, Mark, I am only grounding you a week. Your new father recommended that I ground the both of you for two weeks. And Timmy, because you were a mischievous little follower here, it is two nights without television for you, young man. Now who wants some breakfast?" Grandma Mel left for the kitchen and started to prepare the morning meal.

As the smell of bacon drifted into the living room, Tim looked directly at me for the very first time and whispered, "Nice job, ya big pussy. Way to take it for the both of us like a real champ, I mean chump." He now was giving me two thumbs-up and beaming at me with his silly-ass little smile.

"Fuck off."

"Hey, no hard feelings, man. Give me five," he reached his palm in the air, and I reluctantly requited. "Operation

Pootang" was now a done deal.

I had taken it like a man, but for the first of many situations I would find myself in with Uncle Timmy, I simply *pussed* out and took the heat for the both of us. Maybe the little shit was right; my first name was *Hairy* and my last name was *Vagina.*

V-a-g-i-n-a.

I actually enjoyed my many adventures with Tim and was sort of sad to see him go when he and his mom left for Hawaii after my eighth-grade year. We had had some fun together—although I *did* take the fall for our many misguided and immature adventures. It was a love–hate relationship with my uncle, Timmy Melvin; his antics and our fun together made me seldom think of my previous life with D.L. I was thankful for his friendship during this important transition in my life.

Over a period of two years, I had learned that laughter was indeed the best medicine for any problem. I wanted to be funny just like him. I was now enjoying my middle school years and making other kids laugh. Laughter and comedy would serve as a protective barrier from others during these awkward years. No one would be able to break this impenetrable force field I had put up as a teenager and get to know the *real* me.

(6)

Our first several years with Mike Melvin were awesome. It was a time of *firsts* for the Kirby kids, as we were now afforded opportunities we had never had before. We had gone from living on government cheese and food stamps, without clothes, and in a rundown farmhouse, to living like normal, regular middle-class families do. Both of our parents had good jobs and, judging from the things we had and the places we went to, I could see that we had money for the first time, probably the first time in my entire life.

Melvin was known, respected and networked in our small community. He received the distinguished honor of Junior First Citizen, which is the highest award given to a citizen of the city under the age of thirty. Jesse Owens, the famous African American Olympic sprinter, had presented him with the award at a special dinner in his honor, and I got my picture taken with him and my new dad. Our family was very proud of his accomplishments and the work that he was doing in the city. Mike was able to get me a job when young, keeping score at City League slow-pitch softball games. Now, I had my own spending money. I loved watching movies and would spend some of my earnings going to the local theater every Saturday.

My mom was a Home Economics teacher at the brand-new high school in town, and she could walk to work. She was enjoying her new profession, impacting kids in a positive way, and I had never seen her so happy and relaxed in the company of a man before. This is as *well rounded* as I had ever seen my mom's life. She would never fully attain this balance again.

Melvin would see to it that I got swim lessons at the downtown pool he oversaw, and, for the first time ever, I was not afraid of the water. With this small gift of swim lessons, he paid huge dividends to the construction of my self-esteem. Occasionally he would take me to the local go-cart track outside of town, and we would drive our own cars and race each other. I now had no fear of being behind the wheel of a vehicle; little by little, Melvin was unwittingly helping to erase the harmful effects of my abuse as a small boy. I was beginning to trust a man for the first time in my life and was eager to please him. He would help me with my homework at night and got me involved in football and basketball through the local Boy's Club. For the first time as a kid, I felt *safe*. I felt like I belonged. I had a real family and I was a normal kid.

It was decided in a family meeting one evening at the dinner table that my sister and I would call Mike "Dad" instead of his first name. I liked that, because I wanted to be *his* son. I always respected him as a father, role model and man. He was a *good* one. Looking back now, he was someone that I would *revere* and look up to my entire life. I would *aspire* to be a dad like him. He embodied the attributes of an excellent father.

In December, during our Christmas break from school in my seventh-grade year, our family got to know Disneyland. I took back all those evil things I said about those Disney guys, watching fireworks with my family on a warm evening in Anaheim, the happiest kid in the *"happiest place on earth."* My life had changed for the better—perfect at age thirteen.

Schmelvin

I found myself again lying down, only a flimsy patient gown on, trembling in fear. My bare ass fully exposed for all the world to see.

This biopsy would prove once and for all how much *It* had spread and at what stage *It* was at. My urologist had me lie on my side. My prostate was numbed up by a giant needle attached to a solid metal *roto rooter* attachment and twelve pieces of my rotten walnut were *removed* by what felt like a pair of small metal hedge clippers. I cringed with each *snip*.

I wish *Schmelvin* was here with me right now. He would know what to say. He would give me a great big hug sporting that seventies' 'fro, and say something *dorky* like "I *love* you, man."

The excruciating became the unbearable; I needed an escape from the pressure and horror of *It* all. So, I just closed my eyes, took a deep breath, let the pain meds kick in and my mind drift off to the happiest time of my childhood . . .

(1)
Not to get nitpicky here, but my new dad was not without faults.

Good old Michael Melvin was a bit of a *Schmelvin,* as I would sometimes refer to him as a smart-ass teenager growing up. With Melvin, it was like getting two dads for the price of one. *Schmelvin* was like the alter ego of my calm, cool, rational, level-headed dad Michael Melvin. *He* was a bit of an uncoordinated and awkward klutz, who got himself into some pretty funny predicaments over the years. He was a great source of humorous entertainment for me on a consistent basis, while I was growing up.

Besides watching movies at the local theater, I had learned much about life through watching, in my humble opinion, the greatest invention in the world: color television. As a latch-key kid in my earlier years as my mom was going to school and working, I would come home and watch the "idiot box," as Grandpa Cliff referred to it, for hours on end. I was a walking encyclopedia of worthless information. I could tell you everything there was to know about *Gilligan's Island,* because I had seen every episode twice. *The Flintstones, Batman, I Dream of Jeannie, Gomer Pyle, The Munsters,* and *The Partridge Family* were all my favorite shows growing up.

From 1969 to 1975, my favorite television show on earth was *The Brady Bunch.* I would make up a giant yellow Tupperware bowl of hot buttered popcorn, all set to munch on every Friday night at eight o'clock sharp. Sometimes our whole family would sit in our den and watch this show. Mike Melvin was actually a lot like the dad Mike Brady. They were both intelligent, loving, caring fathers who could help solve any problem that would come a kid's way. They both wore their hair straight and neatly parted on the side and dressed in business attire to go to work. That all changed in 1972, the fourth season of *The*

Brady Bunch, and year two of my mom's marriage to Michael Melvin.

Season four of *The Brady Bunch* debuted with much anticipation in the Melvin/Kirby household. The Bradys were going to Hawaii, and it was to be a two-part episode shot on location at the Sheraton Hotel in Waikiki Beach. The actor Robert Reed, who played Mr. Brady, had let his hair grow naturally curly during the taping, and Melvin had the first of his many not-so-bright *Aha!* moments of the seventies!

As we were watching episode one, part one, in the den, Melvin suddenly came alive: "Man, I like that new hairstyle that Mr. Brady has! What do you think, Mark?"

"I don't know, Dad. He looks a little *strange*."

"Hey, honey, come here for a minute," my dad yells, as Mom suddenly appears from the kitchen with my huge bowl of popcorn in her hand.

"What do you think of Mr. Brady's new hairstyle?" he inquires.

"Ooh! I like it a lot," she says, handing me the bowl.

"Do you think you could get my hair to look like that, honey?" Mike always let his wife cut his hair at home to save money.

"Absolutely! We'll need a perm kit, though, and some curlers," she remarked, her face lighting up. "I'll go to Safeway this week and get you what you need."

"Then it's a date," he smiled. "Next week, during *part two* of the show, your good old dad's going to get a . . . a . . . *man perm!* Just like Mr. Brady has!"

We all clapped in a real weird, creepy, *Brady Bunch* kind of way for our dad and shouted, "Yippee," "Groovy," and "It's going to be so cool!" Sitting there and watching

Dad clap like a middle school cheerleader reminded me of the *fruity* little shenanigans my Uncle Chester used to pull back in the day. I was definitely not enthused about any of this silliness moving forward.

The following Friday evening we were all seated in our den for part two of the *Brady Bunch Hawaiian Adventure*. I was seated with my popcorn as usual, my sister on the couch as always. But the whole scene got a whole lot weirder as Mike Melvin now sat in the middle of the room with a plastic smock draped over him, his hair now fully wrapped in several of my Grandma Mel's pink plastic curlers.

"It's time to apply the perm solution, kids!" Mom beamed.

After the show, she took out the curlers and rinsed off Melvin's hair in the sink. He reentered the room several minutes later, after combing and primping his new hairdo in the bathroom. His proud, goofy-ass smile led me to believe that he was expecting applause or loud compliments thrown his way from the small family audience assembled in the den. What he got was *gut-busting* laughter from his two new step kids and my mom. We just couldn't contain ourselves.

I can pinpoint exactly the start of Mike Melvin's slow, gradual, but inevitable, demise and fall from my mom's good graces, and it was the night he got that hideous *man perm*. It was as if the perm solution went directly from his scalp to his brain and he instantly became *Schmelvin*.

Now let's make one thing perfectly clear: Mike Melvin was never the most coordinated individual in the first place. He was probably, as a kid growing up, *that* child who got picked last for every team at recess. He was tall, skinny and lanky, arms hanging down past his knees with clown feet that he tripped over when he walked. He had grown a large pimp mustache on his face, and this made him look even more ridiculous. True, his new stupid-ass Afro had added six more inches to his height, but this goofy white man could not play basketball to save his life. And when he got that new Afro, he also developed a newfound sense of *over*confidence, believing in his own confused and poisoned mind that he was the second coming of *Dr. J*, Julius Erving.

Michael oversaw the Albany City League Basketball Association as the Parks and Recreation Director, and the Parks Department had their very own basketball team. Because he was the boss, and because he now had a cool Afro, he thought that he now had *mad* basketball skills. He appointed himself Player/Coach of the PRD team. As the coach, he also conveniently named himself the starting shooting guard—to everyone's disappointment and disgust. *Schmelvin* would show up before game time with his super-tight, long-distance runner short-shorts on, hiked up to his belly button, stretched-up white knee socks, black high-top tennis shoes, a red tie-dyed tank top and a white cotton headband, thinking that he was a real *badass baller*!

His teammates hated playing for him and with him. They were in a bit of a *pickle*. However, as their boss, there was not much they could really do but quietly bitch among themselves. On one occasion during a time out, when Schmelvin was in the bathroom, the players began to loudly voice their anger and frustrations. I watched and listened from the stands.

"That guy is the biggest piece of *shit* basketball player

I have ever seen."

"He totally sucks, man."

"I wish his stupid-ass tight little shorts would cut off his blood flow to his ball sack and he would pass out and die!"

"Melvin is the fucking *black hole*, man."

"Totally, dude, totally."

His teammates called him the "black hole," because if you were stupid enough to pass him the ball, he would *always* shoot, no matter where he was on the court. You could tell he had never played on an organized team; he had no *court sense*, whatsoever. I was playing basketball on my middle school teams and had become a pretty good player for my age, so I knew *Schmelvin* had no idea what he was doing out there.

He would *chuck it* from anywhere on the floor off one foot, shooting from the hip and looking like some *dipshit* from the 1940s playing basketball with peach baskets for hoops. Thirty feet, *shoot*. Forty-five feet, "Oh no, he's *shooting* it again!" Half-court, two running steps, "Are you kidding me?" "He shoots off one foot from sixty feet, *air ball!*"

"What a goofy assed *dildo*," one teammate commented from the bench as *Schmelvin* launched up another ridiculous shot from *no man's land*.

The guy would end up with eight points in the game, and he would be the leading scorer on his team, but keep in mind that he made four out of thirty-four shots for the night and *pissed* off all of his teammates in the process. His team lost EVERY game that *Schmelvin* played in and only won two games all season—the two games that *Schmelvin* missed. His teammates despised him so much, they would give him the wrong directions to the gym or purposely give him the wrong game time; anything to "keep the big, curly-haired *dipshit* from showing up."

I was growing a little concerned about my new dad's lack of intuition in regard to what others were thinking about him behind his back. I knew it was that new crazy hairdo; I wished he would cut it off and relieve some of the strain it was putting on the rationale side of his brain.

Mike Melvin's behaviors began to become crazier and more reckless as time wore on. In January, Schmelvin was driving us in the snow and, thinking he was Mario Andretti at the Indy 500, yanked a hairpin turn on the mountain pass road, plowing us into a snowbank at 60 miles per hour. This totaled my mom's beautiful Mustang. Luckily none of us were injured, although as my dazed dad left the vehicle, about a hundred pounds of snow plummeted from a large fir tree above the wrecked car, *crashing* down on Schmelvin's giant noggin and paralyzing him on the icy ground for several minutes.

"Are you alright, Dad?" I asked, as he lay there motionless, an Afro covered in snow.

"I'm OK. Whew, that was a close one! Lucky I had this head of hair as *protection* or I might've died!"

"Let me help you up," I said, as I got him to his feet. He looked like a giant snow cone in the middle of the road. He was truly pathetic, and I couldn't help but just laugh; he was hysterical.

As I looked at the mustang, its front end completely destroyed, I knew that my once-beloved *Poontang Mobile* was now *dead* and needed to be put to rest in a junkyard somewhere. It would be the last nice car we would ever own as a family. For the first time, I saw my mom visibly pissed at my dad for going "way too fast" for such hazardous road conditions.

"I told you to *slow down* for miles, and you just wouldn't listen to me."

"You're right, you're right," he admitted, shaking the loose shavings of ice from his snow-cone head.

"What a *Schmelvin*," I said, as I watched the tow truck driver drive away with my mom's once shiny and new mustang. "Get a haircut, you big pudwhacker," I mumbled to myself. I was also beginning to think that my first instincts from long ago might have been right. *Schmelvin* may very well be smoking dope; his behavior had shaken itself of sense.

Michael Melvin was now writing checks with his *ugly-ass* perm hairdo that his gangly, uncoordinated body could not cash. In February, my mom warned him that the roof was "WAY too slick," and to not go up on the roof to adjust the television antenna.

"I can handle it," my dad said, beaming. "I was an *expert* rock climber in college."

"Don't go, Mike. You'll be sorry." Mom warned.

Five minutes later, we would hear the thud of good intentions, of metal joining human skull, followed by a blood-curdling, "Oh no, no . . . Holy crap, Jesus Christ . . . I'M GONNA DIE!" A loud WHOOOSH sound as 180 pounds of human flesh flew down into the prickly backyard hedge below. Michael would appear in the kitchen five minutes later, dejected, picking various twigs, stickers and leaves out of his enormous Afro.

"I told you not to go up on that roof, Mike," Mom scolded him as she would me.

"You were right, you were right," he conceded, picking

foliage from his tattered and torn *schmo-fro* as he left for the bathroom to tend to the cuts on his battered body. I knew now that either Michael Melvin had gone insane, or he was secretly snorting cocaine in his study. I knew that marijuana was going to be a gateway drug to something worse, and my deepest fears had now been realized. *Die you evil* perm, die, I thought, finishing the boloney sandwich I had made for lunch.

A month later, in March, Melvin decided to fix our toilet in the main bathroom—against my mom's fervent wishes.

"Please *don't* fix it yourself, Michael," Mom said, now remembering her husband's failed attempt at fixing the family dishwasher. After my dad "attended" to it, water leaked everywhere and the kitchen flooded, leaving two inches of standing water in three rooms of the house.

"I can do it, you got to believe me. I've been reading a book on plumbing and I can fix it!"

"Don't do it, you'll be sorry."

"All's I need to do is disassemble the main down pipe under the toilet with a monkey wrench, crawl under the basement, and I will have it fixed in a jiffy," he flexed.

"Michael Melvin, this is not going to end well.

"Honey, just make sure no one, and I mean no one, uses the main bathroom. I am going to be working directly under the toilet and . . . well, you get the idea. No restroom, no *flushing.*"

Well Grandma Mel had stopped by for lunch, and my mom was busy on the phone with a plumber "just in case," when Mel suddenly felt an urgency to use the john. The chili dog that she ate for lunch had not mixed well with the Denver omelet she had for breakfast and a *three-alarm fire* was burning in her bowels. My mom had turned her back on Mel, peering out the window to watch the mail being delivered, and Mel was off in a flash to relieve the war raging in her stomach. Mel went in, filled the toilet to the brim, and *flushed*.

Mom dropped the phone on the floor, screaming bloody murder as the flush ricocheted through the pipes. Another scream was heard from the basement, this one from her husband—the plumber's apprentice.

"Nooo. Oh *crap*, nooo. *Holy* Moses, who flushed the freakin' toilet? Oh, God no . . . I am covered in CRAP!"

Five minutes later, Michael Melvin appeared in the kitchen, holding a messy monkey wrench in his hand. We kids were finishing up our chili dogs with Grandma Mel, and this would be the first time I ever heard my dad cuss. "Who in the FUCK flushed the toilet?" he said. "I told you guys not to flush the FUCKING toilet, didn't I?"

My mom appeared now from around the corner and said, "Your mom flushed it, blame it on your mother. I was on the phone and she went to the bathroom and flushed it. Sorry, dear."

Michael Melvin was standing before us soaked in disgusting, vile-smelling *Mel poo*. I about threw up on my chili dog, it stunk so bad.

"I told you not to fix it. I told you to get a plumber, but *oh no,* you had to do it yourself, *you* standing there all covered in . . . in . . . *poo.*" She began to laugh.

My dad now scanned down his soiled body and began to laugh, too. We looked at our dad standing there, covered from head to toe in human waste, pieces of toilet paper dangling off his chocolate brown *schmo-fro*. Suddenly the whole kitchen was laughing at the whole *crappy* situation.

Michael Melvin, you indeed, sir, are a big time *Schmelvin*. But I dig your style man, I *dig* it.

(2)

Before my eighth-grade school year, my family moved once again. This time, my parents had purchased a large, five-bedroom home, just across town, with an extensive basement and four bathrooms. "Operation: Shitty Perm," as Grandma Mel referred to it—whenever she got loaded on whiskey sours, which was often—may have prompted my mom and dad to look for a house with more toilets in it. This new home was definitely a trade-up, as we had moved to a better part of town, in a nice neighborhood with excellent schools.

Gracie and I made new friends. The closest friends I have ever made in my life were in this two-year period. It was pivotal in my young life, looking back on it; I was gaining tremendous confidence and feeling good about my surroundings and myself. I felt safe. We were as close as we had ever been or would ever be as a family. I loved my mom and dad very much and appreciated all that they were providing for me.

I played school sports: football, basketball, baseball and track. My mom was a teacher in the school district, and I was connected with teachers and coaches because of her. This made my life at school a whole lot easier. I was the president of my ninth-grade class and an honor roll student. My heart was set on graduating with my buddies at West Albany High School.

In the summer, I would visit my grandparents in Tacoma, Washington. My sister and I would stay there for a couple of weeks each summer break. Grandpa Cliff and

I would play tennis every day for hours on end. He was so confident in his abilities, or so addicted to nicotine, he smoked the entire time he played. It was unfathomable to me that he could move and hit, hit and move, while smoking a cigarette the entire time. He loved to win *every* point and *every* game when I was younger. He never conceded anything to me, and I respected him for that. I always knew where I stood in relation to his tennis prowess and it was easy for me to measure my improvement every summer.

I remember the fourth summer, when I was eleven, I won my first game off my grandpa, elated. He got mad and threw down his racquet and cigarette in disgust at the same time, making the win *that* much *sweeter* for me. I began to learn each summer as I began to get stronger and quicker, that if I ran my grandpa all around the court, back and forth, up and back, he would eventually make a mistake and either hit the ball out or into the net. I became a rabbit—a quick, *human backboard*, returning everything the old man hit my way. I learned through trial and error that I just had to be *patient* and keep the ball *in* play. It was as *simple* as that. The more points *he* would lose, the *angrier he* got. Once *he* got angry, I knew *he* would *beat* himself. The next summer I could win at least four games each match we would play. The next summer we frequently split sets, but I would ultimately lose. By the time, I was a ninth grader, I was beating my grandpa on a regular basis and he wasn't as excited to play me anymore.

"Why don't we go fishing today instead?" he would ask, just to avoid playing me.

Again, my grandpa wasn't a big talker. He never said, "You know, Mark, you've gotten to be a pretty good tennis player," or "Nice win today." *That* generation of men wasn't like that. They were not *wired* that way. But I knew I had garnered his respect and I respected him as a man who was always there for me in my life. My many dads would come and go, but my grandpa was *always* there for me. He was like a *rock*. A *rock*, that would rather *smoke* than *talk*.

I would sometimes visit Grandma Bonney and Grandpa Ralph on the weekend and eat corn fritters, devour fried food plate after plate, and watch professional football games all day on Sunday with Grandpa Ralph. We would shoot billiards for big bucks after the games were over for hours on end. I became quite the little pool shark and convinced my parents to invest in a pool table at our house.

During one of my weekend stays with my grandparents, I was introduced to my first true love—a passion of mine that would stand the test of time and bring me pleasure every fall and winter season for the rest of my life. That *love* was the Pittsburgh Steelers.

One Sunday morning, I sat and watched the AFC playoff game between the Pittsburgh Steelers and Oakland Raiders at Three Rivers Stadium in Pittsburgh, Pennsylvania. With the Steelers trailing in the last thirty seconds of the game, their quarterback, Terry Bradshaw, threw a pass attempt to a guy named John "Frenchy" Fuqua. The ball bounced off the hands of the Raiders' safety, Jack Tatum, and or Fuqua and, as it fell toward the ground, Franco caught the ball right of his shoe tops and ran in for a game-winning touchdown. This play became the "Immaculate Reception," one of the most famous plays in NFL history and one of the defining moments in my young life. From that moment on, the Steelers became *my* team, and I would visit my grandpa on game days to watch. I was lucky; I had two awesome grandpas to look up to and spend quality time with.

Then, without warning, *he* and *it* would come back into my life once *again,* turning my whole world *upside* down.

(3)

D.L. would occasionally visit Gracie and me in Oregon at our new home. He was a *deadbeat* dad now, owing tens of thousands of dollars to the state of Oregon. His wages were now being garnished. He *hated* my mom and Michel Melvin for this. They had taken him to court. He was a pissed-off old drunk. We would no longer visit him as children in Alaska. D.L. would drop by, out of the blue, and visit us at our family home, giving none of us any warning. My mom and dad would always let D.L. visit us, even though Grace and I begged them not to let him in the front door.

On one such occasion in the summer, D.L. brought a cute, innocent, dark-haired boy—about six or seven years old—with him to our home in Albany. He was Shawn, a "family friend's kid," whom D.L had graciously offered to take on an "exciting trip down the Alcan highway" in his new motorhome. I knew what was up the minute I laid my eyes on the poor, helpless little guy. D.L., that fucking, disgusting monster, was molesting him. How in the hell did Shawn's parents think that D.L. Kirby would be an appropriate and responsible chaperone to their young boy for a month-long trip to Oregon and back? I imagined all the sickening things he probably did with that little boy, eyeballing that nasty motorhome in our family driveway. I about threw up on the sidewalk.

For the first time, I felt guilty for not turning D.L. into the cops when I was ten years old. D.L. had apparently continued to *molest* other little boys after he stopped touching me, and I now felt responsible for Shawn's abuse as well. This was a heavy burden for any teenage kid to bear; this guilt would never go away, haunting me at night when I became a father myself. The entire time Shawn visited us that long weekend, I could barely look at him.

D.L. would not let Shawn out of his sight, or allow him to talk to me alone the whole weekend. He knew that I knew what he was up to, smiling at me the whole time, almost taunting me. Evil.

We all sat sharing a backyard barbecue the night before our two guests were to return to Alaska. D.L. was already sloppy drunk and had his arm around the young boy.

"This here boy is my little Pard, 'Shawner.' Yes, sir, aren't ya little man?" "Yes, sir," Shawn replied, barely audible to the rest of us. He began to cry to himself, whimpering like an infant. We all stared at Shawn, not knowing what to do or say next.

"My little Shawner here has an earache and needs to go to bed." D.L. *whisked* the boy up over his shoulder and carried him off to the motorhome like a load of dirty laundry. "Good night, everyone!" he shouted in his usual drunken and boisterous way. He slammed the door behind him, trapping the two inside that disgusting RV for the rest of the evening. As I looked at that shiny new motorhome, it reminded me of Nanno and Ankee's rundown hillbilly shack. It brought me back to that *first* night up the

McKenzie River, when I had been molested by my uncle Chester as a four-year-old boy.

Before the light went off in the trailer, Shawn's tiny head appeared from behind the cream-colored curtains. He seemed to stare straight at me, eyes wide and shaking. He mouthed a cry for *HELP!*

I wanted to scream, but I just couldn't. Suddenly *he* was gone. D.L. had pulled him away from the window, putting his bloated hand over the boy's mouth. No one else saw this cry for help from the little guy. I, on the other hand, was rendered temporarily paralyzed, *mortified* by what I had just seen. Not a word or sound would be heard after that night, leaving early the next morning without a goodbye. It felt like a perverse midnight getaway: the predator, D.L., leaving in haste with his young prey helplessly strapped to the passenger seat beside him.

No one seemed to make anything of it. No one seemed to care. I, of course, said nothing because I was too *weak willed* to stand up for someone smaller and weaker than me. That little *secret* that I had carried with me from my childhood weighed even heavier on my narrow teenage shoulders now. I went to bed early that night, indignant with myself. I locked my bedroom door and cried myself to sleep. I hoped and prayed that D.L. Kirby would never come and visit us again. Yet he was to continue *coming*, popping in unannounced and uninvited, looking for a place to park his filthy trailer for days on end. My second dad, the devil incarnate.

(4)

The next two years held my best memories as a kid growing up. We would be at the pinnacle of our happiness together as a blended family. Melvin was a *Schmelvin*, but he was cool. He was the kind of intuitive dad that I aspired to be one day, when I had kids of my own.

I had been bothering my mom to buy me a new dog for months. I had always loved dogs and although I thought of Misty from time to time, I was ready to move on and have a new little furry friend to call my own. My dad must have overheard my constant pleading; lo and behold, he gifted me a pup for my fourteenth birthday. I was overjoyed and appreciative my dad's kindness, sensitivity and generosity. It was the best birthday of my young life, with my new little dog—black and curly, resembling Misty when she was a puppy. She waddled when she walked, so I named her Waddles. She would be my best friend all through high school—lying at the end of my bed each night, keeping me company. Waddles was definitely my dog. She would always be loyal and comfort me when times got bad. And when Mom was involved, times tended to go bad.

In late December of 1973, after just turning fourteen earlier that month, I wanted to see the new movie *The Exorcist*. I had read a film review in my middle school library—instead of working on my assigned history research paper—and I became mesmerized, fixated on watching this scary, gory flick. I also read that people were leaving the theater in haste in the middle because it was just so damn scary. People were passing out and vomiting in the aisles; I had to see it. For whatever goofy reason, it became my obsession. I wasn't going to be truly satisfied until I bopped in to the downtown theater. But there was a problem: This movie was rated "R," which meant that I had to be eighteen or accompanied by an adult to purchase a ticket.

One night, I approached my dad to go with me. He conferred with my mom to get her approval, and we were off on a Friday night to the theater. If course, I was petrified for just about the entire film, but it was a *fun* scared—not anywhere near the terror I experienced hanging out with D.L. I did have nightmares for weeks, but what was so amazing to me was that I had formed this strong bond with my dad. I would be loyal to him from that night forward. We would go and see all kinds of adult movies together. *The Longest Yard*, a football movie starring Burt Reynolds, was one of my favorites. I also enjoyed all of Richard Pryor's films, and my dad would take me to see every one of them, knowing that much of this material was not recommended for kids my age. Melvin was now treating me like a young adult, and that had a tremendous impact on my life as a teenager. He trusted me and I trusted him. I would make good choices to *please* him. I studied, got good grades, and made the honor roll.

My mom's loyalty to my dad, on the other hand, began to *fade* after four measly years. Mom could never find total happiness with any man. Melvin always loved my mom to death, but he had other *issues* that started to surface. *Little* things sometimes become big things, and my dad had one *little* annoying habit that used to drive my mom *absolutely* crazy.

(5)

My favorite word in the eighth grade was *shit*— probably because I had seen so many Richard Pryor movies, had snuck in so many of his comedy albums to listen to in my bedroom. It was my Swiss army knife of words: I could use it as a noun, pronoun, adjective, verb, or adverb. I could have used it one hundred times here to describe my dad's little problem. But, for the sake of storytelling, I'll try to tone it down just a little bit.

Dad was a collector of *shit,* and what started out as a "cute little habit" turned into something larger and more burdensome for everyone in our family. You see, deep down, Melvin was a dreamer; he wanted more from his life, always. These thoughts, I believe, haunted him in his sleep; it is the only plausible explanation for his unexplained irrational behavior—except for drug use, of course. He was never satisfied with what he had. And more worrisome in the short term, he was always looking for a *good deal.* From the moment he met my mom, he had always had this little hobby. It just grew and grew and **grew** until it completely got *out of control.*

Let's start with the simple little *shitty* things that my dad liked to collect first: He was big into antiques, and he liked going to estate sales, garage sales and auctions, trying always to find a good deal. We had to live in and among this worthless *shit* from dawn until dusk.

In my bedroom, for example, I had an antique dresser with missing knobs and a cracked mirror. I had nightmares about that enormous fifty-pound broken mirror falling on my head, breaking into a million pieces and me dying a bloody death right there on my bedroom carpet. He collected hundreds of other castoff items that nobody wanted, but that he perceived to have potential value. *Rare* and *collectible* items in his perm-covered mind. They really were worthless pieces of *shit* nobody else wanted.

In our living and family rooms alone, we had a shabby grandfather clock with a broken pendulum, a coffee table with three legs, a jukebox that didn't work or light up, old crates of outdated records, antique framed pictures with other people's family members in them, a crappy-looking phone from early 1900s, a broken radio from the 1930s with a cracked face, and the list goes on and on and *on*. Our house was full of these old heirlooms from *other* people's family trees. To tell you the truth, some rooms in our house looked like someone living among us had a *hoarding* addiction.

Then he moved to bigger, shittier, clunkier things to collect—vehicles, campers, boats. After he wrecked my mom's Mustang, he was hell-bent on acquiring every misfit heap of scrap metal known to man. Let's keep in mind that Grandpa Cliff and Grandma Lavina, who were retired and on a fixed income, did not think too highly of Mike after he wrecked their four-wheeled graduation gift to Mom; in fact, they would hold it against him forever. I thought Melvin to be a Schmelvin, but my grandparents thought Michael Melvin to be a deranged lunatic from the local insane asylum, and at times they believed he was indeed the *anti-Christ* himself. Lucky for Melvin, they had moved to Hawaii and would be gone when his little *habit* of collecting became a full-fledged *addiction*. But my grandparents would return to the *crime scene* much later in the game and it would not be pretty for the sadistic shopaholic when they would come knocking at his farmhouse door.

Michael Melvin was always shopping for *shitty* rides, and the *shittier* the better, he imagined. As a fifteen-year-old boy, getting ready to drive for the first time, I thought our family vehicles to be the worst *fleet* of cars in town. Absolutely embarrassing. I even had pet names and acronyms for the many worthless four-wheeled items that my dad would bring home from auctions.

One week my dad would drive up in a broken-down, rusty Ford pickup truck with bald tires. It was a BPOS, a big piece of . . . shit. This hunk of junk would be bestowed upon me when I turned sixteen, and it would be my main *ride* in high school. I affectionately called *him* The Beast. Every time I would let up on the gas pedal, *The Beast* would backfire and scare every little kid, dog and elderly person in the area. *He* was a real gem.

As soon as our dad adopted The Beast into our family, he decided it was time to adopt a little friend for it to *play* with. This friend came in the form of a ski boat.

"It's high time we get ourselves a *new* ski boat," he announced to all of us at the dinner table one night. "I used to be an accomplished skier back in the day, so let's *do* this thing. Some fun in the great outdoors, a little family bonding time, some exercise—what could possibly be better than that?" as he waved a fork full of mashed potatoes at us like a wizard waving a magic wand.

I was not keen on this idea at all; D.L. had tormented me on family ski trips as a young boy, and I did not want to replicate this kind of unhealthy family "bonding" experience anytime soon. This time around, I wasn't scared for my own personal safety, but more for Schmelvin's. He was definitely a klutz on land, and I knew he would be much worse behind the wheel of a high-powered ski boat.

My dad came driving up one late spring day in The Beast, pulling his *new* ski boat. "Honey, kids!" he shouted.

"I want you all to see our new ski boat! Isn't it freakin' amazing?!"

Obviously, my dad had a different definition of *new*. This was the ugliest, oxidized, barnacle-laden baby-blue boat I had ever seen. It looked more like an *old* tugboat than a *new* ski boat. My dad was indeed full of shit if he thought *this* sad, sorry hunk of junk was something worth being seen out on the lake in.

"How did you get the money to buy it?" was the first logical question my mom had for her husband.

"You know that cookie jar you keep up on top of the refrigerator, the one with all the extra cash you keep for a rainy day?"

"Uh-huh . . . ?"

"Well, it's *raining!*" *Schmelvin,* reappearing suddenly again, raised his hands high in the air like he had just hit a jackpot. "I couldn't pass up a *deal* like this one, honey."

"Michael, you know I was saving that five hundred to go toward a brand-new Singer sewing machine that I've always wanted."

"I know, dear, but this boat was just *too* good of a deal to pass up." He reached into his pocket, pulled a crinkly twenty-dollar bill and plopped it onto my mom's open hand.

"What's this, Michael?"

"It's the change of course. The asking price was five hundred and I talked the man *all* the way down to four eighty. Here is a twenty to start your *rainy-day* fund again. I will pay you back, honey, I promise."

Mom looked at Old Blue, as I would fondly call our family boat from that day forward, threw the twenty-dollar bill into my dad's face, and began to cry. She ran into the house, *wailing* out loud, the door slamming shut behind her.

Schmelvin instantly knew my mom was angry, but tried to *pivot* back to his excitement for his new aquatic toy. "What do you think, Mark?" I shrugged my shoulders and said nothing, not really knowing what to say or how to say it.

Schmelvin pivoted again, making the fatal mistake of asking Gracie, who never minced words, what she thought.

"Dad, I think that baby-blue eyesore over there really sucks, and I mean big time. I think you should back that ugly piece of crap off a cliff, into the ocean, and give it a proper burial at sea." Gracie threw her hands up into the air, cried to the heavens and said, "What will all my friends say when they see in me that, in that *thing* at the lake." She ran inside crying and slammed the door behind her.

Schmelvin looked at me, sheepishly shrugging his shoulders. I looked at him and did the same, yet he was not finished that beautiful spring afternoon, seemingly unfazed by the negative emotions of the entire female population of our household. This was one of the greatest days of his life—like for most boaters, the day he bought his wondrous boat. And Schmelvin's second greatest day as a boater would be the day he sold it. We will get to that later.

Schmelvin once again looked at me, still gleaming with pride, walked over to his new boat, and said, "Listen to me, Mark. We can fix her up, make her look brand new. A little paint here, some paint there, a little elbow grease, new upholstery, a refurbished engine, new sparkplugs, some spit shine, some polish . . . and this little gem, she will sparkle just like new!"

I knew our new boat was an accident just waiting to happen, but I just couldn't hurt my dad's feelings. My childhood intuition kicked in and I sensed for the first time that my dad might be losing it, and *that* scared the *shit* out me. I patted my dad on the back, knowing fully that this was not going to end well, and said, "Let's hop up and take a look at *her*, Dad."

We spent at least two hours sitting in that mangy, musty old boat, my dad the whole time telling me over and over again just "how good we were going to make her look" and "how much fun we were going to have in our *new* boat." Schmelvin's little annoying habit of buying other people's shit wouldn't stop with *Old Blue*.

My dad sadly could never stop shopping, and things would get much worse for all of us as we were moving *again*. This is a bunch of shit, I thought. We were leaving the home, the town, and the school that I loved. I would especially miss all the friends I had made in Albany.

This time we would be moving fifty miles away to the country, near the town of Stayton, Oregon, home of Flavor Pack frozen vegetables. Michael Melvin had gotten the hair-brained idea in his fluffy noggin that *farm living is the life for me*. So . . . green acres, here we come!

Green Acres Is the Place to Be?

I got the results from my biopsy promptly; it was too late to do surgery, so the options for my treatment were limited. *It* had spread to my lymph nodes and my seminal vesicle. I was in stage-four crisis mode, at this point frightened for my future. I bet this is how *Schmelvin* must have felt when he was brainwashed and beat down by a badgering bunch of new-age life coaches at the Ramada Inn in Eugene, Oregon long ago. After laying down two hundred and fifty bucks for a two-week "sensitivity training" seminar called "Lifespring," Michael Melvin returned home a blithering basket case. I knew he never should have joined that self-help, mind-controlling, money-grubbing cult. They did not care one bit about helping my dad; they just wanted the cash. It was painful to watch a grown man *lose it* like that. I was on the verge of losing it myself. We should never have moved to that damned farm in the country . . .

(1)

The farmhouse in Aumsville, Oregon was definitely a trade *down* for the Kirby/Melvin family. This humble and not-so-happy home would be the final resting place for poor Michael Melvin. The five-bedroom home out in the middle of nowhere, on ten acres of God-forsaken property, would be Melvin's final and greatest accomplishment in junk acquisition, and he would reach the pinnacle of *Schmelviness* with this one real estate deal. Melvin thought this renovation project to be "a great deal, a real steal."

Gracie and I thought otherwise. We felt our dad had completely *lost* his mind.

My sister in confidence said to me one day, "I can't believe we traded all of our friends in Albany in for *this* place. It's a complete shithole!"

For the first time, I was seeing a side I had never seen in Gracie before—one of pent-up frustration and contempt for her life and for the many moves we had made as kids growing up.

Our new home was not *new* at all. It was very rundown and needed lots of work, like a new roof, new gutters, new paint, new tile, new carpet, new wood floors—and the list goes on and on. But in my dad's cloudy mind, he could see his dream home with three to five years of hard work. He was *all in* and invested in such an undertaking; my mom, on the other hand, was not. From the very start.

I would spend my sophomore and junior years in the farmhouse. Time would go by quickly for me, because I was exceptionally active in school, involved in sports and lots of extracurriculars. I played football, basketball and tennis, all the while enjoying the drama club as well. I always had to work *extra* hard to be good at sports, sitting on the bench in basketball for long periods of time just to be part of the team.

Acting, on the other hand, came naturally to me. It was my little *gift* from God, allowing me to escape my reality and become someone else. My childhood survival skill of play-acting—as a way to temporarily escape my abuse—probably had prepared me well for a life on stage. I was a *natural* born actor, and this skill would serve me well throughout my entire life, especially when I became a teacher.

My dad was *not* a farmer. He did not have the time to put into farming or the knowledge to pull off his new avocation successfully. He believed in his heart of hearts that he could teach himself to farm by reading books. He and my mom both had full-time jobs. They were commuting to the capital city of Salem for work, about a twenty-minute drive each day. My mom was working for the State Department of Education and my dad was now working for Chemekata Community College.

My mom's new job would be a step up for her in her educational career in terms of title, responsibility, and salary—and my dad's, a step down. He was working in a program to help inmates at the state prison in Salem obtain their GED, and he didn't enjoy this work as much as his past job as Director of Parks and Recreation. My mom got the new, *bigger, better* job with a huge raise. He latched onto any job he could find—a job just for a paycheck, until something better came his way. This was not the ideal situation for his career, but he believed in his own convoluted head that he was going to be a subsistence farmer, living off the land and growing enough food for his family. This would be his source of self-esteem and sense of accomplishment, his *life's* work, he thought. Not his eight-to-five routine job.

Farming did not start off well for my dad. The first week that we got settled in our new home in the month of June, he came rolling into our gravel driveway with his new tractor. The tractor was not really *new*, however, as he had gotten a "great deal" at a local auction and purchased this "little beauty" for two hundred bucks. He pulled this once-fine piece of farming equipment from the year 1952 into our driveway from a John Deer graveyard somewhere in Oregon. It was chained down to an old trailer, my dad pulling it with our old truck. It had no tires and no steering wheel. Even The Beast knew this tractor was no good as he backfired in disgust, pulling up next to the dilapidated barn. The tractor sat there for two years— never fixed, never driven. My dad found the feeble farm vehicle two new *friends*. These two tractors were in even worse shape. The three just sat there, tired, helpless with nothing to do. All the cats in the neighborhood liked to climb and play on these old relics, so at least these old-timers served some purpose in life. *They* were *blots* on the landscape and my mom hated them in every way possible.

"Get rid of those damn tractors, Mike. We look like a bunch of hillbillies, for God's sake."

Melvin would defend. "I can't get rid of those tractors, honey. They were all great deals and I can fix them, you'll see."

As I walked to catch the bus one morning, I swore I saw the ghosts of Nanno and Ankee bouncing on those tractors, dueling banjos, and singing to good old "Cripple Creek." It scared the hell out of me for a moment; I began to worry about my dad, as I was way past the point of making sport of his silly little antics. I was becoming concerned for his mental and emotional well-being. I didn't even think of him as Schmelvin anymore, as I believed he was about to hit rock bottom.

Things would only get worse when he began to bring

animals to the farm—he brought dozens of little chicks to a small hen house he had restored. They all died. My dad had turned up the incubator too high and he had fried them to death. His shenanigans used to be funny and we all would just laugh. Now, for the first time, other living creatures were left dying in his wake. He bought three calves our first spring there, and by the following fall, they had all died as well. I rarely ever saw him cry growing up, but he was visibly distraught and shaken when the third little guy passed away in October. For the first time, I felt sorry for him. My mom believed his antics as a sign of weakness and began to ride him mercilessly.

He decided to buy three one-year-old steers in the summer. "They are healthy and strong," he beamed, "and in a year, we will have plenty of beef to go around for our family and all of our relatives!" He was leading them through the gate with the help of the experienced farmer he had purchased them from. In this time, it might have been wise for my dad to inspect his fence before purchasing these three large beasts.

"This is Farmer Johnson, down the road!" the neighbor, Farmer Johnson, would holler through the phone. "Your cows are in our corn again, you horse's ass!"

Gracie and I had to chase these big dopes all over the countryside; we weren't too happy about it. We not so affectionately referred to them as the "Three Stooges," Larry, Curly and Mo.

The final straw for my mom came when the *stooges* had escaped one afternoon, and *she* was called away from work to help chase down her husband's little "shit burgers!" We were all not very fond of Farmer Melvin's four-legged bovine buddies, and we were now secretly drawing straws to see which one us would put them out of their misery for good.

"Fetch them critters of yours NOW, before I shoot 'em right between their butt cheeks!" screamed Farmer Johnson on the phone.

"I'll be there shortly," my mom curtly replied, now fuming.

Well, we chased those stupid creatures all over the creation and beyond, until we finally had them cornered and corralled at the top of Bull Head Mountain with a five-foot-high rock wall on three sides of the tired and weary animals. Their tongues were hanging out, all thirsty, famished and exhausted. Here is where *Schmelvin* reappeared for one last, shining magic moment—an encore, a curtain call, if you will. I hoped this would be the last time I would see my dad's alter ego.

"I've got an *idea*," Schmelvin remarked.

"Oh *no*, I know what happens when you get your not-so-bright *ideas*." My mom was in no mood for his little games here, as the heat, her high heels and the time spent away from her work was grating on her nerves. "OK, Señor Smarty Pants, out with it then, *what* is your brilliant *plan* here?"

"Well, I've got this roll of chicken wire right her, ya see," he said, motioning to the large roll of thin metal wire.

"Oh, you've got to be *kidding* me," my mom now chuckled out loud at her delusional husband.

"No, now listen here," he said, his voice lowering as if he had a top-secret plan and didn't want the little *shit burgers* to listen in on it. "I'm going to pull this wire out, like this. Everyone's going to hold on tight and we're going to create a *wall* with this wire, see."

He was now getting fired up, thinking that he had created a *giant* wall that would somehow stop the tired and angry steers from stampeding us. As I shut my eyes, mightily clutching on to the thin metal chicken wire and praying to the Lord above, I knew that this was a ludicrous idea. Suddenly and without warning, the steers charged at our pathetic little fence.

My mom screamed, "Holy shit, we're all gonna die!"

Schmelvin screamed STOP! At the top of his lungs, hoping the three agitated steers would listen to the scrawny Afro-haired matador betting on his chicken wire cape.

The three stooges broke through our *last stand* on Bull Head Mountain and set off again to—who the hell knows where. And you know, I did not even care if I ever saw those ignorant beasts again, and neither did my mom. Mom chewed my dad a *new one* right in front of us kids, and I needed a translator to make sense of the garbled, nonsensical swear words she was spewing at her husband, the now-dejected amateur cattle rancher.

My dad slouched as he made his way over to *The Beast*, carrying a roll of chicken wire. I was following close behind. He heaved the chicken wire in the bed of the truck, obviously angered and frustrated by the day's events. My mom and sister drove home in the other car, not talking or even looking at my dad on the way to their vehicle. Dad said nothing the entire way back to the farmhouse, but I could see tears *trickling* down his face. He tried to wipe them, so I wouldn't see them. I knew he was a *broken* man that day.

One week later, my desperate dad sold those three steers to Farmer Johnson for half their market value. My dad sadly realized he was *never* going to be a farmer, but he never stopped trying, until it was *way* too late.

(2)

Melvin was looking for something—*anything*—that could bring him out of this incredible funk he found himself in. He knew he was in a slump, so he had to find something in his life that would bring him joy and happiness once again. He turned to Old Blue.

Our last summer together, my dad thought it would be a great idea to take Blue out and show her off to everyone at the lake. For the last three years, my dad and I had been fixing *her* up, little by little. New paint, brand new upholstery, a refurbished engine. We took the time this past spring to really polish her up, and she sparkled like new. It became a father-son project for us, Blue shimmering under the sun in our family driveway. She was a source of tremendous pride for him.

"Look at that beautiful boat. I told you, son, didn't I? I just knew that we could and *would* fix her up and make her look brand new."

"You were right, Dad, she looks awesome."

Even my sister couldn't deny our efforts. "That boat actually looks good, guys. I can't believe it."

My dad was really itching to show her off, so he organized a weekend camping trip to Detroit Lake. Each of us kids could bring a friend, and we were excited about this idea. I invited my best friend Riley, while my sister invited her good friend Cindy. We all expected a great weekend of camping, picnicking and boating, and I was confident Old Blue would be up to the challenge; my dad and I had put a lot of blood, sweat and tears into fixing her up, and my sister and I no longer viewed Blue as a source of family shame.

But looks can be deceiving. Unbeknownst to me, Schmelvin had cut a few corners on getting Blue's engine refurbished, commissioning a cousin of a coworker to fix her motor. The novice mechanic was currently out on parole and looking for work. This tidbit of information didn't seem to faze my dad in the slightest.

The mechanic assured my dad on the phone, "Hell, this will be a *piece of cake*, Mike. I don't know much about boat engines, but I got lots of experience fixin' up lawn mower motors, motorcycles, concrete mixers, scooters, and go-carts. That's why folks around these here parts call me 'Fix-It-All Paul' Conklin." Besides, I'll give yous a good deal since you a friend of kin."

That's all my dad needed to hear, and "Fix-It-All Paul" would be his go-to guy in the summer of 1977. This decision would come back to bite him square in his ass and pocketbook.

On Saturday, we were all loaded up in The Beast, the four of us kids riding in the bed of the pickup with Waddles by my side. In the late seventies, this was seen as *safe* as long as you sat up next to the back window of the cab. This idea seems frightening to me now—a thirty-minute drive up Highway 22 East, past the little town of Mill City and Detroit Reservoir. We would put our boat in the water, set up camp, have lunch and begin our fun-filled day of skiing. During the past three summers, my sister and I had learned to ski behind Blue. By the second summer, I could ski on one ski; no more riding on D.L.'s shoulders around the lake for me. Those days were long gone.

I had gained confidence on the water during these

years, and I have Schmelvin to thank for that. He wasn't exaggerating; he was actually an accomplished skier. He took the time to teach me how to ski. Those days on Detroit Lake, learning to ski, spending time with my family—these would be some of my fondest memories growing up. I would try to emulate these experiences for my own kids—minus Melvin's many malfunctions and mishaps.

Our early afternoon ski session on the lake went without a hitch, everyone skiing behind Blue. The problem came when we went out for a second time, around four o'clock, just before dinner.

Before we all left, my mom, who was staying behind at the camp, said, "You guys have fun! Dinner will be ready by six."

My dad yelled back, "No worries, we'll be back on time, honey." He gave her two big thumbs-up, flashing that gigantic goofy smile.

Not more than five minutes toward the calmer part of the lake, I started noticing that Blue's engine was smoking a bit.

"Dad, what's going on with the engine? It seems to be smoking some."

"No worries, no worries at all. We're probably just burning a little oil, that's all."

Then I began noticing these rattling, knocking noises from the engine. Blue was sputtering, and it sounded like she had a bad case of the hiccups. Then it sounded like someone had dropped a bucket of marbles into her engine. I know very little about boat engines, but I knew something wasn't quite right here.

"Dad, what's going on with Blue?"

"We probably just need to clean out her gas line, let me

fix it. Everyone stand near the front of the boat while I throttle her up." My dad commanded us like a self-assured, veteran sea captain.

We all moved to the bow of the boat, clinging on for dear life to the sides, rails, seats—anything we could latch onto. My dad pushed the throttle down all the way, not having warmed the boat up gradually. "Here we go!" he screamed, and the two girls fell backwards on their rear ends, and then *it* just happened.

Blue's propeller *flew* off the engine; she erupted in black smoke and we suddenly came to a complete stop. My dad, for whatever reason, knew immediately what had happened and cried, "*Holy Criminy*, I'm going to rescue that propeller. I used to be a *champion* diver back in high school!"

Schmelvin was back. Holy shit, I thought to myself, here we go again.

Schmelvin dove into the water wearing his brand-new pair of sunglasses. "*Bonsai!*" he cried, with a loud *ka-wump*!

We all gave a loud "Ouch!" in unison as the permed cliff diver belly-flopped into the lake, causing many water fowl to scatter.

After a minute or two, Schmelvin came to the surface, some slimy, green lake sludge in his enormous Afro. I noticed his glasses were gone.

"Dad, you lost your sunglasses!" I shouted.

"*Holy moly*, I'm goin' back down to try and save them!" He submerged again, his giant sandaled feet sticking straight in the air. This time he was down for almost *three* minutes. *Schmelvin* came back up gasping for air sporting that goofy-ass smile of his. "I got 'em, I got my sunglasses!"

"What about the propeller?" Riley asked, rather calmly and casually.

"*Golly gosh*, I knew I forgot something!" He dove down again, a duck ducking around for food.

Schmelvin spent the next half an hour diving down again and again, trying desperately to find Blue's propeller. He finally climbed aboard, having lost all hope, soaking wet and shivering from head to toe. Once again, he suddenly became distraught and started to hastily pat down all the pockets of his cargo shorts.

He stared at me as if *he* was the child and *I* was his father, looking at me, like he had made a big mistake and he knew *he* was going to get in big trouble. "Dammit, Mark! I lost my wallet! I can't believe it. It has all my cash and credit cards."

He dove back in the water, not saying anything to us. He gave a loud battle cry once again, "*Geronimo*," belly-flopping off the side of the boat with a loud *ka-wump,* and he was back in the water again.

Riley felt a need to comment on the situation. "Your dad seems a little *crazy* to me?"

"He has his days, he has his days, I'm afraid."

We both started to laugh. The girls started to laugh. The *Schmelvin Aquatic Sideshow* had begun, and the more the gangly *merman* dove back down into the water, the more we couldn't stop laughing.

Each time he would come up for air, he would say something silly like "*Oh, diddly squat!*" or "*Oh, fiddly foo!*" as each dive *came up empty* for the permed Jacques Cousteau. He would relentlessly dive down into that water for another hour, looking for his cherished wallet.

As you could imagine, this reconnaissance mission took quite some time here. Darkness fell over the lake. I knew my mom would be worried sick back at camp. I'm sure she had dinner waiting for us. We four kids rowed Old Blue into shore near our camp with four water skis, each of us paddling like crazy for about two hours, our arms feeling like they were going to fall off at any moment. *Schmelvin* stood at the bow of the boat, hopelessly looking for his lost propeller and wallet with a small flashlight.

The skiing part of the weekend was over. My mom let *Schmelvin* really *have it* that night in front of our friends at the campfire for being *late*. After finding out from her husband that he had gotten the boat engine refurbished by ex-con Fix-It-All Paul, she went on a *tirade* in front of all of us.

"What in the hell were you thinking, Mike? A guy on parole for God's sake? A novice mechanic, who works on scooters and go-carts? I am really getting tired of this shit, you and your crazy ideas, half-baked schemes, always trying to get a *good deal*!"

My mom went to bed in the tent alone, the rest of us roasting marshmallows and telling scary stories into the early hours of the morning. My dad slept upright, fully clothed, sunglasses on, in a lawn chair with a blanket over him, passing out after downing several Bacardi and Diet Cokes. I rarely saw my dad drink more than a couple of beers. I knew today's events rattled him greatly, and now I was preoccupied for *him* and for the preservation of *our* family. I also knew that my mom has always had little patience in matters of matrimony. I loved my dad and didn't want to *lose* him.

When we got home, my dad and I took Blue to the local

marina. We found out from a certified boat mechanic that Blue's engine was indeed *fried* and her transmission was tragically *toast*. A new engine would cost several thousand dollars. My dad's head dropped when he heard this news. We could not afford to fix *her*. We would lose a family member that fateful summer—a boat that gave me so much joy as a teenager.

Two weeks later, *Schmelvin* sold the engineless Blue for four hundred dollars, one hundred less than he had originally paid for her three years ago. With the selling of his *treasured* boat, some of Schmelvin's carefree, fun-loving personality and spirit would be lost as well.

(3)

Michael Melvin now found himself depressed for the first time in his life, suffering from what I believed to be a major-league, and a little bit early, mid-life crisis at age thirty-five. The farming idea was not working out; he was in a job that he hated, and the house had become, according to my mom, a *money pit* requiring much more work than they had planned. I also believe that for the first time in their marriage, my parents were arguing about finances.

Grandpa Cliff and Grandma Lavina had recently moved from Hawaii to a small town thirty minutes away from us, and this really made matters worse for my dad. They were over at our house quite often, quite unpleased with what they were seeing. In the wintertime, our two new calves that my dad recently bought at an auction were wallowing around in mud up to their knees, and the barn was not a safe place to escape the inclement weather. On one visit to our place, my grandparents had seen enough of their crazy son-in-law's act and let him have it.

"Mike, you don't know diddly about taking care of animals," lectured my grandma, puffing on her cigarette in disgust.

"This is a bunch of *bull crap,* Mike!" my grandpa egged on, not clever enough to be making a *pun* here.

"If you don't get your act together, young man, we are going to turn you into the Humane Society!" Lavina declared.

"I know, I know," he said, as he stumbled away to feed his two precious little calves. I knew that he did not appreciate the butt-chewing he got from my grandparents, but he took it like a man, never arguing with his elders. I respected this character quality in him. He was obviously a lost and broken man who needed a break.

My dad needed something, *anything,* to kick-start his life back into gear. He was a desperate man looking for a new direction and a new career path. However, the final *nail* in his own *coffin* came when he enrolled in the "human potential training program," Lifespring. He would do this against my mom's wishes, because she had *warned* him one week earlier:

"Mike, you either get professional help, OR ELSE . . . " I had seen Mom this angry before and I knew that the "or else" in that tone meant *divorce.* I did not want her to get a divorce from my dad. I loved him and still believed him to be a loving and caring father, despite his obvious shortcomings.

Well, my dad charged two hundred and fifty on his Visa credit card, the cost of five days' "Basic Sensitivity Training" at the Ramada Inn in Eugene, Oregon.

Lifespring was one of the many self-help encounter groups of the late seventies, and Mike Melvin was anxious to get started. Melvin was enthusiastic for the first time in months, as Lifespring's brochure claimed that, through a series of lectures and role-play, participants might learn alternative ways of dealing with life's situations and struggles. I believed him to be struggling mightily at this point in his life, and I was hoping and praying for the best.

Mom gave him . . . not much hope. "He's a *wacko*," she resigned.

My grandma was even less sympathetic. "That crazy bastard has joined a *cult*."

"It's a bunch of nonsense. He may as well have taken up *voodoo* or *witchcraft*, the dumb son of a bitch," my grandpa theorized.

Well, as you can imagine, Melvin ate this New Age shit up, and not hesitating to go back for seconds. He "drank the Kool-Aid" by the gallon-full and believed himself to be a "changed man!" When he arrived at our farmhouse door after five days of intense therapy at the Ramada Inn, he was bright-eyed, animated, and that goofy-ass smile of long ago had returned to his face.

Michael C. Melvin declared, "Lifespring is my game-changer, a life-changer!"

My mom claimed it to be, "A homewrecker and a marriage-breaker!"

As we sat in the living room as a family, we listened intently to Dad's experiences.

"You know, I used to be afraid of taking risks, guys," he beamed. "I was living my life in a rut. I used to be stiff and rigid, and now I am more sensitive, more in touch with my feminine side. I have learned to reach out and *hug* people."

One by one, *Schmelvin* reached his long, gangly arms out and hugged each one of us, crying like a baby and bearing his soul for all of us to see. It was eerily transparent and raw. For the next few weeks, *Schmelvin* would randomly come up and give me a "drive-by hug" with an "I love you, man!" It just plain scared the *living shit* out of me every time. He was like a giant mummy with an Afro, wanting to *hug* everyone, *all* the time.

Schmelvin would shed a few tears and say something weird like, "I have learned the art of positive presumption and I want to spread the glory of godly goodness to all of you." I was getting *creeped* out by all the hugging and touching. Keep in mind that I had been abused as a child, all the while appreciating Melvin's *hands-off* approach to parenting before Lifespring.

"You know, Mark, the *climax* changed me forever!"

"What is the *climax,* Dad?"

"Sorry, son, I am sworn to secrecy. Something terrible will happen to me if I ever share these dark and mysterious *secrets* of the *inner sanctum* with you—*mums* the word." He placed two fingers to his mouth as if he was locking his lips.

What a deranged *doofus*, I thought, as he "locked the safe and threw away the key." Secrets, eh? I've been in the *secrets* game before with other strange and creepy dudes from my past, and I was none too fond of playing *that* game again. I believed my dad to be a bit of a lost soul at this point in his life, and I just wished for now that he would *chill* out and *quit* being so damned hard on himself.

(4)

My mom was not that patient. "Mike, I'm filing for *divorce.*"

Curses, foiled again, I thought. Three strikes and you're *out* at the old ballgame.

My senior year, we moved once more—this time only ten minutes away from my high school. My sister and I could take a short, pleasant walk to school each day or, if I really wanted to scare the *shit* out of the people in the neighborhood, I would drive to school in The Beast and let it *backfire* at every intersection along the way.

My mom went to a national School Administrator's Conference in Anchorage, Alaska, around the time of her breakup with Melvin. She was back, dating someone immediately. This time, a handsome high school counselor from Olympia, Washington, who, according to her, was "absolutely dreamy."

The timing of *this* new romance seemed a bit *odd* to me at the time. Reflecting on this as an adult, more than forty years later, I wonder how committed my mom was in *saving* her marriage to Melvin. Maybe she had fallen in love with this dude while my dad was going through his Lifespring *thing*? Mom never had much patience with men—or maybe she had *too* much? It seemed to me, as a younger man, that she oftentimes spent *too* long with the wrong man and *not* enough time with the right ones. I could never seem to figure this conundrum out; it would only get more befuddling to me as I got older.

Michael Melvin would move to the city of Salem, and I would sadly see him only a few more times after they divorced. He did call me many times over the summer before I went to college. Each time I saw him or he called, he would try to sell me on some new *get rich quick* sales scheme he was *big into* at the moment. You see, Schmelvin finally stopped buying *shit*. There was no money in that, only pain and heartache. He got into the business of selling *shit* to people instead. Maybe he had finally learned his lesson?

My dad quit his well-paying job with the community college on the following logic: "Mark, my job just wasn't giving me the emotional satisfaction I needed and the healthy income I desire now in my life." He would call me and say in true *Schmelvin* fashion, "Hey Mark, I got this *great* part-time job opportunity for *you* while you're going to college; it's called *Amway*. You *got* to see the potential earnings here! Besides, you can make money and get all the household products you need at a huge discount."

No thanks, Dad. I'll just stick to working at the Flavor Pack cannery for minimum wage this summer. It's a safer bet.

"You'll be sorry, son. You're missing out on a great opportunity here. Next time you see your old dad, I will be cruising up to your house in a brand-new, red, turbo-charged Porsche 911 sports car. That's the dream man, that's *my* dream." Michael Melvin, the once-promising young Parks and Recreation director, had vacated his former body and was *gone*, nowhere to be found. All that remained was Schmelvin, 24/7. All day, all the time. It was *Invasion of the Body Snatchers* playing out before me.

"Drop by and see me when you get that Porsche, Dad. I would love to go for a ride in it." I would get off the phone and chuckle to myself. Porsche 911? The guy is delusional.

The next time I saw him, he picked me up in his *new* white 1972 Cadillac Eldorado with leopard-cloth interior and whitewall tires. He was going to take me to lunch just before my high school graduation.

"Where's your Porsche, Dad?" I asked, sliding into the passenger side of *Shaft's* former luxury automobile.

"I'm working on it."

"Where did you get this little beauty?"

"I bought it at a police auction the other day," he informed me, glowing with excitement. It was as happy as I had seen the man in years.

"Hmmm, looks like this car could have belonged to a drug dealer or a pimp," I half-joked.

"Possibly. No matter, I got a great deal on it, and it's got a *huge* trunk to haul all of my merchandise in."

"Merchandise?" I hoped Schmelvin hadn't turned to selling illegal narcotics, or making pornographic films in his new apartment at night. I tried to wipe that image from my mind. "How is the, ah . . . Amway business going?"

"Amway, shamway. I'm into something *much* better now. It's a line of gold-and-silver-plated jewelry. It's made here locally by a company called *Dis CO*. Get it, Dis *CO*?"

Mack Daddy Schmelvin gave me one of his new business cards with his name on it: "Michael C. Melvin, Account Executive." The card had a logo of a diamond-engraved disco ball in the upper-right corner. I looked at it and said, "Yeah, I get it. Very impressive."

Schmelvin was wearing about fifty pounds of jewelry that day: necklaces, chains, bracelets. A giant, fake gold Rolex watch and a ring on every finger. He was still sporting that man perm, but now it was *ginormous*, almost touching the ceiling of the car. He was wearing a white leather disco jumpsuit, black platform shoes, and rose-tinted glasses. I started to laugh out loud as I eyed him from head to toe, holding my breath for what seemed like five minutes. Schmelvin looked just like some skeevy pimp cruising on the town that day. I was kind of embarrassed to go to lunch with him in our small rural town. I feared he might get *shot* by some rednecks that day.

Schmelvin was beaming, that goofy-ass smile of yesteryear. He had both of his hands clenching tight on to the white-furred steering wheel, and we were driving down the road listening to KC and the Sunshine Band's "Get Down Tonight." Schmelvin and I were singing along with the radio and having a grand old time that sunny June afternoon.

Suddenly, Schmelvin looked my way, turned down the radio and lowered his voice like he was revealing some top-secret information. "Do you want in on a piece of the *action* with my new sales venture, Mark?"

"No, thanks. I am going to college at Oregon State in a couple of months and that should keep me plenty busy."

"You'll be sorry. This is the opportunity of a lifetime."

I knew he would be off to something *new* by next week. He was like a giant, goofy, teenage kid with a bad case of ADHD; the guy had the attention span of a gnat, moving from one *dream* to the next.

We had only two places to go out to eat in our small town of Stayton: A&W and Dairy Queen. I chose Dairy Queen, figuring I wouldn't see many people I knew there that day.

Once we pulled into the parking lot, everyone inside and outside of the building was staring at us. I don't know who people thought we were or what we were doing at friendly ol' DQ, but we did not look like we were father and son, there for dinner and a couple of Dilly Bars, no—

we looked more like a pimp and his apprentice scouting around for some new *hoes* to add to *our* stable of women. Everyone stared at us the entire time we were there. I was worried a couple of the rougher-looking dudes with the blue-jean overalls and work boots in the corner booth might launch burlap bags over our heads, throw us in back of their hay wagon and hang us from a tree in the countryside. We ate quickly that day, took two Dilly Bars *to go* and got the hell out of there.

Schmelvin would call me from time to time that summer before college. It was always something *new* and *exciting* he was selling every time I talked to the man.

"Mark, I'm working for a company called Cutco Knives. I'm recruiting people to work under me. These knives practically sell themselves. You can cut through a pop can with one of these babies."

"I think I'm going to have pass on that one, Dad."

"Mark, are you feeling rundown? Not enough energy to do the things you need to do every day? Well, then try *VitaPlus,* the natural, healthy vitamin supplement that can replace fifty assorted fruits and vegetables ALL in one tablet."

"No thanks, Dad. The FDA is probably going to *kill* that one for sure. Sounds too good to be true, and probably is."

"Mark, this is it!" Schmelvin screamed one night into the receiver. "Do you know how much money there is in the emerging sex toy industry!?"

"Dad, no and NO!"

Schmelvin just stopped calling. The last words out of his mouth to me were "sex toy industry." It would be the last time I would talk to my third father until I would see him at my wedding in 1986. I'd miss him—the joy, the laughter, the heartache, the falling, the accidents, the craziness. I would never miss that heinous 1970's man perm, though; it always seemed to me a source of bad luck. Looking back now, Melvin was like a tall, gangly, goofy version of Inspector Clouseau from the *Pink Panther* movies I had loved growing up. And I loved Melvin. He was a one-man circus, always full of surprises. I would always miss my time spent with him, the father I desperately needed in those critical teenage years of my life.

I would be angry with my mom for divorcing Mike Melvin, and for a very long time. I would take this anger, now a *giant chip* on my shoulder, to Oregon State University in the fall. I would have five more fathers down the road, but Melvin would be the last man that I would ever call "Dad."

Good FOUR Nothing!

My wife, two kids and I had an appointment with Dr. Johnson, my radiology oncologist. "Dr. Johnson, isn't that ironic," I tittered to my wife as we drove to the clinic. "*Johnson*, a slang name for a man's *wiener schnitzel*, the perfect name for a guy who is about to do some alien probing up my *Planet Uranus*. The guy's name may as well have been *Dover*, Dr. *Ben Dover*, for goodness sake."

My wife did not think this dark humor was at all funny. Although she is my age, she has always seemed twenty years more mature than me in any *adult* scenario. Especially now, as I felt like she was the only person holding it together in this particular situation. She squeezed my hand and smiled confidently, giving me a small dose of courage as we entered the clinic's main door and checked in.

We spent two long hours at the clinic. And after all was said and done, it was decided by my family that I would undergo two years of hormone therapy in the form of Lupron injections, along with eight weeks of radiation treatments. The rationale for the hormone treatment is to cut off your testosterone, which *it* feeds off of. I had no idea about the testosterone thing, but I got this strategy immediately. The first rule in the art of warfare is to "starve the enemy." Once the enemy is weak, you *radiate* the living daylights out of it. It was one of the hardest decisions I ever made, because one of the many side effects of these female hormone treatments is that they can have a long-term effect on a man's ability to ever get an erection again.

"Cutting off your testosterone is essentially like going through male menopause," Dr. Johnson said in an eerily simplified way, waving the waiver in front of me. "You will *hate* this treatment. Most men can't take the side effects for more than a year. You will have hot flashes, you will gain weight, you will lose muscle mass . . . short-term effects can be depression and long-term effects can be bone loss, osteoporosis, and *worse*."

Worse? Holy crap, this all sounds bad enough, but I just couldn't get past the damn penis *thing*. "And what about the erectile dysfunction issue, Dr. Johnson?" I inquired, trying to sound calm as I felt my own *little Johnson* quivering and shaking in my jeans, as my voice squeaked like a pubescent teenage boy.

"Your penis becomes *lifeless*, unable to become *erect* anymore, because there is no blood flow to your organ," Dr. Johnson said.

I know what you're thinking here, because I was hoping for some *silver* lining in this very troubling health predicament.

"Viagra, pumps, you name it, they won't help either," he added. "Basically, *ding-dong, your dick is dead*."

I was now bordering on petrified as the waiver form was thrust into my face by the good doctor once again.

"Well, it sounds like my wife and I are going to live out

our lives as a couple of old lesbians," I said.

Dr. Johnson thought this remark to be funny. Of course, he did, I thought. This twisted, old Dr. Frankenstein made a living sticking his grimy fingers up *dudes'* rectums. Why wouldn't he find my pathetic attempt at dark humor delightful at this very morbid moment?

"Your time is running out. The pulmonary embolism should have been a *major* warning sign to you here." The good doctor was scolding me like a child. "It should have."

So, in my own troubled mind, my short-term decision became, a *stiffy* or *life*? Seems kind of superficial, immature and silly really, but like most men, I had grown quite fond of my ability to get a *hard-on*. And like most men, my maturity level has always been just below that of a teenage boy.

I got the hormone shot that day before I left the hospital, knowing full well that by next year at this same exact time I will probably have lost all of my muscle mass, my body hair and will have grown me a nice pair of *man boobs* for the *second* time in my life. I needed to focus on the bigger problem at hand, however, instead of thinking about where I was going to purchase my first adult training bra. Suck it up, man, *suck* it up.

I was looking for answers here, reasonable, rational explanations for *why* I got *it* in the first place. What a complete screw-up I had been. I knew I should have had my prostate checked way earlier, probably in my late forties or early fifties. Maybe God was *punishing* me, shutting my entire system down, my indoor and outdoor plumbing, because I had been such an incredible *dick* to women in my twenties? At this particular juncture in my life, this seemed to be the most plausible explanation for my predicament. Is this how it was going to end for me?

This thought process made me think about my fourth dad. Why you ask? His name just happened to be *Dick*. If my fourth dad was here with me today at the clinic, he couldn't have cared less about consoling me. He'd most likely be screwing one of the cute, young nurses in a broom closet or mounting the pretty blonde receptionist on a waiting room leather couch just for the sport of it. He was no *dad* to me, nothing more than a skirt-chasing womanizer. Dick, you should be ashamed of yourself for what you did to my mom and to women everywhere.

As Dr. Johnson gave me one last rectal exam for old time's sake, I closed my eyes and thought about my reckless womanizing youth, realizing how much my fourth dad and I were *so* much alike back in the good old days of the early eighties when I was a boorish and preppy college kid . . .

(1)

Grandma Bonney died my senior year. She came to watch my last varsity football game when I was a senior and died of a heart attack two weeks later. I just knew it had to have been all of those damned corn fritters she had eaten her entire life. She would be missed.

Almost immediately after my grandma was laid to rest, Grandpa Ralph began corresponding with a woman in Korea. He had purchased a "mail-order bride," according to my mom. I just did not get it at all, the whole *buying* a wife idea. But Gloria would be my step-grandma until Ralph passed away ten years later. She couldn't make corn fritters, but she could make the best Korean barbecue ever.

After Ralph remarried, things changed between us,

and I seldom visited him. He had a new Korean wife and a new batch of Korean kids that Gloria had shipped over one at a time from her country. It was strange, really—I felt like an outsider when I visited my grandpa now. We just drifted apart.

College. For the first time in my life, I would be separated from my mom. Isolated from all of my family. I felt all alone, with no one to turn to. I was a little scared, but anxious to get away from the drama of my home life. My mom and my sister would stay in Stayton while my sister finished high school. My mom and I would lead parallel lives for the next six years, committing acts of inhumane proportions—not on other people, but on ourselves.

Two parallel behavioral patterns emerged for my mom and me during this time: we both chose people and situations that led to much disappointment, failure and mistreatment in our lives. We knew better, but we still did it anyway. And two, we completely ignored and/or rejected the attempt of other family members to help us break out of our continuous cycles of self-inflicted pain.

In the fall of 1978, I left for college at Oregon State University, nestled right in the heart of the beautiful Willamette Valley in Corvallis, Oregon. Why did I go there? My best friend from Stayton High School, Riley, was on his way to school there to study pre-veterinary medicine. He had a purpose, a plan, laser-like focus, a goal and a clear direction on how he wanted to achieve his mental objective. I did not have a goal, a plan, or anything else that resembled a rational, logical thought process. I did like Riley, however, and I thought it might be fun to go to school with a friend. I decided to major in business because it sounded levelheaded; I had absolutely no idea what I wanted to do with my life at eighteen.

My first two terms in the dorms were dismal; I was just scraping by with a 2.50 grade point average, homesick and lost. But I was studying some, and, for the first time, had an occasional beer at an off-campus party—that I would pay to get into. I did not like the taste of beer or understand all the fuss.

Why was I struggling so mightily here at college? In high school, I played sports, involved myself in drama and clubs. Much of my identity and self-esteem was derived from these extracurricular activities. At Oregon State, I was bored and disconnected, a little depressed.

I was now feeling some empathy for what Michel Melvin had gone through the past few years at the farmhouse. Like Schmelvin, I was searching for something outside of my current life to make me happy. He found inner peace and harmony at a five-day *Lifespring* seminar. In the Ramada Inn. I would find my happiness at the corner of 25th and Harrison Streets in a giant *frat castle* with seventy-four brainwashed *douchebags* practicing acts of *douchebaggery* on a daily basis for three long years.

I had been noticing these guys around campus walking in groups, laughing, joking and apparently having great fun together with what I thought at the time to be matching *Egyptian hieroglyphics* imprinted on their shirts and sweatshirts. In the coming weeks, I would later learn at a party that those fun-loving groups of guys littering our campus were *frat guys*. I made a connection immediately to the world of Hollywood—one of the top movies of 1978 was *Animal House* with John Belushi, and I had seen it twice the summer before college. Because this film was hilarious, fraternity life seemed like loads of fun to me.

(2)

So, joining a frat became my fateful Aha! moment for the year 1979. I went through informal rush, visited many *frats* on campus. By spring term, I had pledged the *Kappa* house. I moved out of the dorm and now found myself living among seventy-four hand-selected secret members of our organization: my new fraternity brothers.

My first term in the house, I was a *dick bag* in training. I was a mere pledge, or "puke," as my elderly mentors liked to say when they would summon me to do various menial tasks around the house. I would scrub toilets with a toothbrush, wash the showers with a squirt gun, and serve the elder members of the house in a white dinner jacket and boxer shorts.

The worst job I ever had as a pledge was my time spent as "Rook Wake." The job description was a simple one: try to wake up all of the older members of the house in the morning at individual set times without getting the crap beat out of you. We had two sleeping porches in our house. The Fire Marshall wouldn't let us sleep in our rooms, so thirty-six guys slept on each porch, twelve bunk beds stacked three high. Guys snored, walked and talked in their sleep. Occasionally, after a long night of partying, some would either pee or vomit in your bed. It was a dark, cold danger zone, and I hated the sleeping porch with a passion. The beds were all numbered and there was a corresponding pegboard in the hallway that had tags next to each wake-up time from 6:00 to 8:00 a.m. This was a two-hour job from hell.

My first morning on the job, I picked up all of the tags

for a six o'clock wake-up and proceeded to walk through the porch, waking up the guys. Each guy got three wake-up attempts. After fifteen minutes, you returned the numbered tag back to the board in the hallway. If a brother didn't wake up in three tries, it was tough luck for the Rook Wake, who most often took the blame. So, the challenge became: Should I shake the living crap out of a guy and get beat up, or be gentle, as to run the risk of not waking him up, and get beat up as well? It was a lose–lose situation. A catch-22.

I was walking through the porch, waking up guys gently.

"It's time to wake up, *Brother Boner*. Wake up," I said whispered.

"OK. I'll get up."

Nice work, I thought. Easy and effortless!

"Brother String Bean, it's your wake-up call. Get up."

Brother String bean's long skinny legs hung to the floor. "Thanks, Kirby."

This all seemed pretty painless and easy—until I got to Brother Lurch's bed. He was given the name *Lurch* at his initiation because he was a giant, ugly ogre of a guy, about six foot eight. *That* was the spitting image of the butler from *The Adam's Family*. Everyone was scared to death of this guy.

The previous evening, Brother Lurch had reminded me, actually threatened me, "Kirby, if you don't wake me up tomorrow at six a.m. for my calculus midterm, I am going to *rip* off your head and *shit* down your throat." Bad image, I thought. So, I had best get him up for his exam.

"Brother Lurch, get up, it's your first wake-up call." No answer, no reply.

I'll be back in five minutes.

"Brother Lurch, it is your second call. It's now five after six. Please wake up?" Sweat was starting to trickle down my face; I fancied my head, didn't want my neck to be used as Lurch's latrine. Lurch did not budge, but did give a grunt, signaling he was *indeed* alive.

"Oh, Brother Lurch, WAKE THE FUCK UP, IT'S YOUR THIRD CALL. GET UP OR YOU'LL MISS YOUR CALCULUS TEST!" I screamed at the top of my lungs, fearing *decapitation* and immediate death. Everyone was now *yelling* at me—one guy pelted me with an alarm clock, and pillows from everywhere were flying at my head. Giant Brother Lurch now had me by the throat and was lifting me off of the ground. I thought for sure I was going to die.

In a low, gravelly voice he grunted, "Thanks Kirby, but next time don't yell. You *scared* the living crap out of me." Chuckling, he dropped me to the ground and left the porch to take a shower.

"Thank you, sir, may I have another." I recited this famous Kevin Bacon line from the movie *Animal House* in my head as I continued with my morning job. The Brother Lurch situation just about *sums* up what my life was like as a pledge in the Kappa House at Oregon State University: self-inflicted pain on a daily basis.

As I finished up my freshman year in college and become a *Member* and *Brother* of our house, I had officially become part of something much more superficial than I could have ever imagined in my life. We were young gentleman idiots, minus the gentleman part, of course. I began to drink *too* much. Drinking games and chugging contests, pre-functions, functions with sororities, massive keg parties and beer bongs were all weekly components of the sheer weekend madness inside the Kappa house. We were actually all alcoholics in *training*, and we didn't even know it yet. I *may* have thought about it for a minute from time to time, but I had another *drink*, diluting my worries.

Picking up girls became my other favorite pastime, especially when I drank several glasses of liquid courage. I was not a gentleman; I was rude, crude, self-centered, and I thought I was funny, which I was not. Well, maybe I was a *little* funny. I had no respect for women whatsoever. Maybe I was taking out my pent-up resentment and negative feelings about my *mom* on every female I met at Oregon State? This was a *real* possibility. I was the kind of young man you *wouldn't* want to take home to mom—in a catatonic, alcohol-induced state of denial regarding any of my awful behavior during this three-year period of my life.

My grandparents began to share some negative feedback on my living arrangements when they visited me on campus. After observing about an hour of our room parties one Friday night, my grandparents had seen enough and left in a huff to their truck parked out in front the house. This would be the first of many times my grandparents would try to dissuade me from being in my fraternity, and I would never pay any attention to their warnings.

"I don't like this fraternity idea one bit," Grandma commented.

"Give it a chance, Grandma, it's all for fun here."

"You've turned into a walking zombie with an alligator on your tit!" My grandpa said. By the tone and anger in his voice, I needed to bring out the *bigger guns* of bullshit here. "You guys are just seeing one side of the fraternity here tonight. The Greek system is all about building lifelong friendships, establishing networking opportunities, and participating in community service."

"That's a bunch of garbage," he lashed back. "You're living with a bunch of rich kids who think they're *better* than everybody else."

They drove off as I smiled and waved. At that moment, I thought them both to be *no* fun and *full* of crap. But they were right, and I was wrong. It would take me several years to figure that one out—probably twelve, when I *finally* got my diploma from Oregon State University.

(3)

Right after my grandparents left, I got a call from my mom. She told me that she had already arranged for me to go to work for my long-lost dad, D.L. Kirby, in Alaska this summer. She seemed excited about this idea, whereas I was definitely not. According to Mom, I was to learn the *art* of heavy equipment operating from the master teacher himself. My mom had already turned my bedroom into a *sewing* room and boxed up all of my belongings for the garage. There would be *no* place for me to stay this summer. I was to do this little summer job or else . . . "No college, no funds available." My mom was basically giving me the *boot*. *Her* parenting days were over.

"You need to make money for school and, oh! By the way, I have a new boyfriend. I want you to meet him before you go to Alaska. His name is Dick, and he looks *just* like Burt Reynolds." She was now giggling to herself like a smitten little schoolgirl.

"Great news." I hung up the phone, my hand now shaking. Holy crap, here comes Dad number four. My mom thinks she is marrying Burt Reynolds. Let's hope for the best? Fingers crossed? She's back in her Hollywood fairy-tale world *again.*

I got a chance to meet Richard "Dick" Willing at a Portland restaurant the night before I was ready to take off for my summer school adventure with D.L. There, I found that Dick was the perfect name for this wannabe Casanova. He was from Olympia, Washington, and had driven down to visit Mom for the weekend. They had met in April at a National Educators Conference in Anchorage, Alaska. My mom is not a slow mover; drinks led to dinner and dinner to who knows what else. She was now "in love." Dick was a high school counselor and had aspirations of being an administrator one day. He lived in a small house on the Puget Sound, had a boat and liked to go water skiing. My mom had been up to Dick's house the previous weekend to enjoy some boating together. They had been taking turns the past couple of months, driving to each other's places every other weekend.

Now, I had only been a frat guy for a year, but I knew he was a *dog* the first time I laid eyes on him. He was a lady's man, a *hit*-and-*run* artist. In short, I knew Dick was a dick. My mom, on the other hand, in her own little fairy-tale world, thought him to be a dreamy hunk.

"Be on your best behavior tonight, Mark. We want to make a good impression on Dick. He is a distinguished educator and a gentleman." A little pep talk before we entered TGI Fridays.

"Mom, let's go the movies like we used to and talk this over. I think you're rushing to judgement here on Burt Reynolds. He's really not a very good actor."

"*Nonsense.* I never *rush* into anything. You're overreacting."

During the entire dinner, Dick looked bored to tears. It was as if he didn't even really want to get to know me. Conversing with me would be too much work for him—a waste of his valuable time. The only time he got excited was when the cute young waitress came around. He knew her by name and would slip her silly little sexual innuendos from time to time. I was wondering now what else he had *slipped* her on the weekdays while my mom wasn't around.

"Could you get us some more of those *hot* buns, Tracie?" or, "I like mine *wet* and *juicy*, how about you?" He was smiling and winking at her right in front of my mom, talking about how he liked his steak—when it seemed he was really referring to Tracie's *honey badger*. It was so *in your face*, lewd, salacious, disgusting. I knew instantly that the guy was a *player*. He kept getting up in the middle of dinner to make "business calls." Soon, I figured I would ask him some questions to try and rat out this *rat*.

"Dick, I notice you're making a lot of calls. Trouble at the office today?" I knew the little weasel was a high school counselor, and that the only business he was probably into was in and around young schoolgirls' panties.

"I am working on a *business* deal, looking to purchase some land to build a bigger house on, and I'm talking to my real estate broker," he oily explained.

"Dick, do you like movies?"

"Nope, a *fucking* waste of time. I'd rather ski behind my boat."

He didn't pass the *sniff* test. I knew for sure now, Dick Willing was a complete *douchebag*.

"Dick is quite an enterprising guy, always looking to

make extra money," Mom *elucidated*.

The only *thing* that Dick is looking for is some extra *tail* to chase. He was already eyeing another young lady at another table. My mom was oblivious to all of this.

"Dick, tell Mark about your boat!" my mom suggested, looking at him as if he were a dream, rubbing his arm.

"NOT NOW! I got to make another call," he threw down his napkin and bolted from the table.

"Mom," I whispered, "this guy is no good. He is a player and he is playing you right *now*."

"Oh, what would ever give you a crazy idea like that?"

"Do you want me to make you a list of red flags on this stinking cocktail napkin right here? It's obvious he has interest in other women—*all* women, for that matter. Can't you see that?"

"You're letting your imagination get the best of you. That fraternity is putting dirty ideas in your mind."

"I see what's going on here, blaming it on the *fraternity*, eh? You have *many* more problems on your hands right now than your son being in a fraternity." As I ate my last few pieces of sirloin, I would have a moment of clarity for the first time in a long time. "It takes one to know one, Mom, and this guy is a lecherous ladies' man if there ever was one. If anyone knows this kind of *stuff*, it's *me*." As she got angry, she had nothing else to say.

My mom was right about only *one* thing that night. If you stuck a cowboy hat on Dick Willing, he would have looked just like Burt Reynolds in *Smokey and the Bandit*. He even had the same silly-ass laugh. My mom was back to her little *insanity* game again, doing the same thing over and over again and expecting different results. She would unload me on D.L. so she could be freed up to go *man-*

chasing again. She had done this throughout my entire youth and now she was doing it again in my college years.

While I was gone making money for college in Alaska, my mom would help Dick buy a new, bigger, better boat that *he* could not afford alone on a mere counselor's salary. This would become my mom's *new* tactic in every *new* relationship: Buy the *new* guy something *he* really wanted, go halfsies with him on it, create a little *business* partnership. She wanted her new *beau* to feel somehow committed to her, invested in their relationship. And voila, my extremely insecure mom had her *hooks* in the sorry *sucker* fish—for the short term, at least. So, while I was cast aside and sent to Alaska, my mom was hoping for a romantic summer on the lake filled with skiing by day and romantic dinners on their deck at night.

I had no time to dwell on my mom's love life, as I had major problems of my own. I was off to a lumber mill in Klawock, Alaska, on the Prince of Wales Island to work for D.L. Kirby. I could hear him now: "Pard, hold on to your diggers, we're goin' for a ride!"

(4)

After being near-killed on several occasions by my sadistic, alcoholic, heavy-equipment operator of a father over the summer—and upon returning from Klawock to the lower forty-eight with several uncashed paychecks in hand, I would *bury* all of my experiences of that awful summer with D.L. for more than forty years. Nobody would have believed me anyway, especially my white-privileged fraternity brothers at the Kappa house. One thing I knew for sure: I resented my mom more than ever for pawning me off that summer to the person I hated the most.

I was picked up by my mom at the Sea-Tac Airport. She had gotten *married* at Lake Tahoe to Dick Willing in July. What I didn't know was what had transpired the year before, while I was away at college. I had never talked to her privately before I flew out of Portland to Klawock; Dick was always around. She began to fill me in.

"You know we were engaged to get married in the spring, but Dick called it off because he got cold feet. Even after I went *halfsies* on that brand-new ski boat just to please him. "

"I didn't know that?"

"Well, I hate to bring this up, but Dick had been cheating on me for a year and a half, staying with me on the weekends at my place or his. "

"Yes, go on. . . "

"During the week, he was living with *another* woman in his house, behind my back."

"And you married him anyway!"

"Let me finish. She would pack her suitcase and leave before I would come visit him, and on one such occasion last April, I had found some of her makeup in the bathroom. I did some investigating on my own and found out HE was having an affair with a fellow teacher right under my nose!"

"You've got to be kidding me!" My acting skills still sometimes come in handy.

"And that's not all. I went to school and confronted her, we talked, and then I confronted *him*."

"And?"

"Well, he said he was sorry, but he still had *cold feet* and feelings for this other woman."

"You're *killing* me here, Mom."

"So, in July, I convinced him to marry me at Tahoe. Oh, it was a beautiful wedding in a garden—I have pictures at home I'll show you when we get back." She was so wrapped up in her own little make-believe, fairy-tale world, she had failed to make the connection that this guy was a complete loser and no good for her.

I was now dealing with the surprise that I had another dad—number *four,* for God's sake. Yes, the sleazy womanizer himself, Dick Willing. How could my mom be just plain stupid, I thought, as I tried to make sense of what she had just told me on our forty-five-minute drive back to Dick's place in Olympia. She had traded in Michael Melvin for a *Dick.* A Dick who didn't even like movies. What a *rat* bastard.

That night, as I looked at the wedding pictures, my mom all excited and giddy, I got this feeling that has popped up many times in my adult life in regard to my mom's misguided love quests. What could my mom possibly be thinking here? Had she completely lost her mind? The signs were there from the beginning, and she dismissed my warnings. In this particular instance, Dick confessed to her in April that he was seeing another woman and had feelings for *her.* Even *he* was warning her to stay away! I was now certain my mom had *lost* her way.

At that moment, almost to spite her, I let out the *secret.* That ugly shameful *tidbit* I had been holding inside forever.

"Mom, do you know why I hate D.L. so much, why I hate going to Alaska?"

"No, why?"

"He *molested* me as a boy, and I've been keeping this

secret inside me forever."

"Oh, my God! What?"

"You heard me. He molested me, abused me, all when I was *just* a little kid."

Silence.

More silence, and I stared at her. She started to cry.

"I don't believe it. When did it start?" She was now trying to retrace her life with her second husband.

"And at about four. Uncle Chester molested me, too!"

"How could I have been so blind to have not seen that happening right under my nose?" She sat sobbing.

"I wanted to tell you for a long time, but I just couldn't."

"Why?"

"Because D.L. threatened me and I was scared. Besides, I was embarrassed, ashamed for what I had done with *them*, you know. The *sexual* things. The older I got, the more I felt there was something wrong with *me*."

Fifteen minutes later, she was back obsessing over the "Dick situation" again. This would go on for hours. It's like the molestation of me as a boy was a *trivial* matter compared to *her* problems with Dick. My mom has been like this her entire life. It is *one* of her *major* character flaws. She will listen to other people's problems only as a way to get back to what she wants to do most: talk about *herself*. She is an emotional *cripple*.

(5)

I held anger toward my mom my entire junior year of college. I was also starting to form an overinflated opinion of myself. The combination of these two things, mixed with heavy dose of alcohol, made me a walking time bomb wearing penny loafers. I would re-invent myself into the biggest preppy idiot on the Oregon State campus. Like Melvin did at *Lifespring,* I drank the Everclear-laced Kool-Aid by the gallon at the Kappa house.

For two long years in the Kappa house, I lapsed into a submissive moral coma. I was like a modern-day pirate plundering parties, picking up girls and using only the pleasure-seeking portion of my brain. I thought I was so cool, living in the *best* house on campus, wearing my preppy pastel Izod and Ralph Lauren polo shirts, khaki pants and Ray Ban sunglasses.

I led and participated in various works of stupidity, some bordering on downright malicious acts toward other people. We spanked pledges with giant wooden paddles, drank enough ethanol to fuel a Nasa flight to the moon, and back-and-chained our Kappa brothers' boxer shorts to sorority houses to celebrate their birthday. The birthday boys had two choices: stay there all night with a bicycle chain wrapped around the front porch pillar of a sorority full of girls, or slip out of their cotton underwear and run naked through the campus. What fun we had at *other* people's expense. We never thought for a moment that this might be humiliating or embarrassing to the victim. "Happy birthday, dumbass!" we would all yell in unison as our petrified fraternity brother hobbled and ran through the streets naked back to our house. Oh yes, what excellent *brothers* we were.

The summer after my junior year, I was elected Rush Chairman of the house, which meant I would need to spend the summer recruiting high school seniors to join our house. I would be paid in the form of getting *half off* on my board bill the following year. This may have been one of the dumbest moves I ever made. I had no money for tuition and spent the entire summer partying. I chose not to go to Alaska, where I had a great job that could pay for my education. Still, D.L. had a lot to do with my decision; two summers had been enough, but *what* the *hell* could I have possibly been thinking?

I had squandered an opportunity to get a good education at a great school. I felt I had hit rock bottom. At least I was smart enough to remove myself from the situation before it got *any* worse: I left my senior year with about two years' worth of credits completed and an embarrassing 1.92 grade point average. It was time for a change. I had learned from my mom growing up that when times get tough, you need *to pull the rip cord* and *get the hell out of Dodge.* I did just that. I moved to Anchorage, Alaska, to escape my many problems.

To all the people who knew me during that immature period of my life at Oregon State University—as a wise ass, a skirt chaser, a preppy womanizer—I'm sorry. There was nothing I did during these four years of my young life that I am remotely proud of. Except becoming a pretty good dancer.

I had an "A" in ballroom dancing. This skill would help me navigate my way at wedding receptions and parities all the way through my twenties. Sadly, that is the *only* thing I learned in my first four years of college, how to dance. What a *joke* and what a *waste* of money. Arthur Murray dance lessons would have been way cheaper, and I would have probably learned a *proper* way to treat women. It would take me ten long years to return to Oregon State, finish up, and get my degree.

A FIFTH of Scotch

"Find your happy place," I said to myself over and over again. I was meditating, trying to get my elevated blood pressure to a more reasonable level. I was lying under another imaging machine table a month later at the cancer clinic, my doctor now injecting my urethra with dye to get a better look at my prostate and lymph nodes. I had just relearned five minutes earlier that my "urethra" was a more technical medical term for my "pee hole." I knew at that very moment that I should have paid more attention in my eighth-grade health class. I was none too happy at the thought of having some pretty young nurse inject my shriveled-up penis with thick purple sludge so the doctors could get a better look at my prostate. I can't take much more of this.

Daniel McCormick, my fifth dad, could probably relate with my current predicament more than anyone. Too bad he has been dead for over thirty years, taken by *it* long ago. Daniel was a good one, a distinguished gentleman. Tragically, he was only fifty-nine years old when he passed away. I am currently fifty-eight.

(1)

The Kirby kids were not doing well in school at Oregon

State. Gracie was running out of money and I was flat broke. We were both struggling academically. One more term on academic probation, and the school would show me the door out! I had hit rock bottom.

D.L. had dropped in unexpectedly to visit us during Father's Day, and my sister and I got the hairbrained idea over a couple of beers to hitch a ride with him to Alaska to find work. It would be the first time in my life that D.L. "lifted" me in any positive sense of the word. We took off for Anchorage up the Alcan highway in the Spring of 1982. Although we both despised D.L., we were desperate and needed to get out of Corvallis.

Here I was again, hanging out with my old adversary, D.L. It would be like this for my entire adult life. I would tell him to "fuck off" or "go to hell," but we would always keep in contact. This is the sorry-ass truth of it all; like a stray dog looking for a home, D.L. would always drift in and out my life. I don't think he had anybody else to turn to. I can't explain it, but I'm sure a good counselor could have explained my mental disorder in detail here. Maybe I was suffering from some bastardized form of Stockholm syndrome. I developed these psychological and emotional ties with D.L. after he had harassed, abused and threatened me over the years. It was strange, but who knows. It was the three of us again on an exciting trip to Alaska.

This was a two-week excursion from hell with a pickled old fool at the wheel. We rode side by side in D.L.'s Chevy pickup, pulling his brand-new, fifth-wheel trailer up the nearly 1,400 miles of mostly gravel road. Each night, we would pull off and camp. D.L. would make some deep-fried delicacies from his Presto Fry Baby deep fryer.

He would fix us beer-battered fish and chips and onion rings almost every night. Grandma Bonney would have been proud of her oldest son! And to wash this unhealthy food down, he would down at *least* one 12-pack of Budweiser each night. Gracie and I would then be forced to listen to two hours of D.L.'s mindless bullshit before retiring for bed. One of us kids usually had to tuck D.L. in because he had passed out in his chair in the middle of one of his drunken rants. Nothing had really changed since our bar-hopping days at Kito's Cave.

When we got to Anchorage, we all went our separate ways. D.L. went to work for an old friend in a lunch catering business. Gracie worked as an assistant manager at a small retail clothing store in the mall. She made some money for school and returned to Corvallis after only staying in Anchorage for six months. But I stayed in for two years, working several odd jobs before landing one waiting tables at a busy restaurant in the city. For the first time, I had a full-time, year-round gig and was making lots of money. I had hundreds of dollars of tip money in my pocket all the time.

(2)

During my two years in Anchorage, Alaska, my mom only reached out to me twice. The first time she called was about a year into my stay. She phoned to share that she and Dick were getting a divorce.

"He's back again to his cheating ways," she explained, "and I'm divorcing his ass!'

"Imagine that, now there's a real *surprise*," I retorted. I was going to tell her "I told you so," but I figured that would be rubbing salt into an open wound.

My first impression of Dad number four had been spot on, and it only took me one measly sit-down dinner at TGI Fridays to figure that out. Dick Willing was indeed a big-time *dick*. He was easy for me to *bury*. I blinked my eyes for three seconds, and he was permanently erased from my memory for good. I never saw Dick again.

I had saved up lots of money the past two years working in Anchorage. I had confidence again. I brought a brand-new 1984 red Mazda RX-7 sports car and felt for the first time that I had really made it. I really did not have a clue, as I was young and still immature for my age. I was only two years removed from my fraternity days, yet thought I had grown up and matured. Now, I thought it was time for me to return to Oregon State and get my degree. I had about $10,000 in cash and a brand-new car. I was *rich*. I was all set to take Corvallis by storm again.

As I was preparing to get my car shipped down to Seattle, my mom called me for the second time in two years. I wondered if she'd found another man as I answered and, God bless America, she *had*. Dad number five.

"His name is Daniel, Daniel McCormick! He looks just like Paul Newman in *The Verdict*!" my mom cried in glee.

"Is he an alcoholic lawyer?" I asked.

"How did you know that? Although I must say he is sober now."

"Well, you just said he reminded you of Paul Newman in the . . . Oh, never mind. I'm happy for you, Mom." But I really wasn't. I really just wanted to be left alone. My mom wanted me to jump on board the *Marilyn Train* and come down for her wedding. I would need a stiff drink or two. Or *ten*.

"Tell me this, Mom. Does he like movies?"

"He does. He took me the other night to see a double feature and took me out to dinner."

"Well, that's good. *Very* good."

"I'm glad you approve."

"Here comes the bride," *again*. This time, much to my shock and dismay, my mom was marrying the lawyer that had handled her divorce from her first husband, Skip, my real dad, way back in 1962. He was *the* young lawyer my mom had secretly been eyeing before she got married to D.L. Kirby. Daniel was married at the time, but twenty-four years later, my mom had tracked down the now-divorced elder statesman. They dated briefly, sparks flew, and my mom was now hopelessly in love. I was hopelessly ill.

Too many weird thoughts were now rattling around in my young brain about *this* one. The lawyer that handled my mom's divorce with Skip Barnes is the one she was eyeing right before she married D.L. Kirby—I felt like I was a character in some bad soap opera. For however twisted it seemed, I assured my mom that I would be there. Why? Because I can never say NO!

(3)

Daniel McCormick, a 57-year-old lawyer from Tacoma, Washington, married my mom in his big backyard in 1984. He would be my fifth dad.

All my relatives were there. My grandma tried to sing again, but fell down by the piano. Uncle Bill scooped her up for a swing dance right on cue. It had been thirteen years since my last garden wedding at Michael Melvin's house. My drink of choice in 1984 was gin and tonic, my staple, *cure-all* beverage for the next thirty years of my life. I must have drunk about twelve of those tasty thirst quenchers that day, and I needed many to *deal* with marriage number five.

Politicians, judges, lawyers and local dignitaries were all present, as the distinguished Daniel McCormick was a well-respected litigator. He held political clout in his community. Although a former partier, a *player* with the ladies, he was now clean and sober, having stopped drinking a few years ago. His drink of choice for forty years had been scotch on the rocks, downing a fifth of Johnnie Walker Gold Label a day. It was so *bad*, he had to handle at least one divorce a week just to support his extremely expensive drinking problem. Yet now, Daniel was head over heels for my mom, thirteen years his junior. She adored the attention she got from an older man. But, possibly convenient for her, they would have only two years together as man and wife.

(4)

I went to Oregon State for two terms and ran out of money again. I was paying rent, making car and insurance payments and *blowing* my money like I did in Alaska. Unfortunately, I was going to school now and did not have a job. I reentered the workforce as an insurance salesman for Colonial Penn Property Casualty Insurance Company. This was not my life's work. This was not my calling. But I needed cash, quickly. I worked out of a small office in the Fred Meyer store in Salem, Oregon. I was working in the city and going out every night to the bars, back to the same fun, single lifestyle that I had been enjoying in Anchorage. But lo and behold, without warning, my life would change in one chance encounter.

Barbara came in for a car insurance quote one afternoon on a tedious day at the office. Her friend had actually dared her to come in and talk to me. To sum it up, we began dating, *sparks flew* and, in one short month, we were engaged to be married in October.

"Mom, guess what! I'm getting married! And you're not going to believe this! She looks just like Farrah Fawcett!" My soon-to-be wife did bear a striking resemblance to the former *Charlie's Angels* television star.

"No! Oh, my God no, you're too young and . . . and . . . God, no!"

Here comes the bride. And this time, she was mine. Barb would be my soulmate, my wife, and the mother of my two kids for the next thirty-four years. It was by far the best move I had ever made in my life. But at twenty-five years of age, I was too *stupid* to even realize it yet.

(5)

In April of 1986, my son Bronson was born, beginning my life as a dad. I ached to do a better job of raising my son than my dads had done (collectively). I wanted to embrace the *messiness* of fatherhood.

I was a good father, but a lousy husband for those first few years of our marriage; my wife and I were struggling. I was not ready to be married, and she deserved better, much better. I just did not know what I wanted to do with my life. I was immature and selfish.

I had all kinds of different jobs in my twenties, none of which gave me much satisfaction. I worked at Pizza Hut, sold women's shoes, peddled men's suits, was a radio advertising salesperson, a car stereo vendor, a dishwasher, a busboy, a waiter, a nightclub promoter, a teen nightclub owner, an insurance salesman, and an outside sales representative for high school– and college-imprinted sportswear. I was like Schmelvin, hopping around from job to job, thinking *this* was indeed the next *big* thing. I had a bulletin board plastered with business cards in my office of all the jobs I had taken (and discarded) along the way in my twenties.

My worst career decision came when I took a job as a disk jockey at a busy Portland nightclub. Why did I make such a ridiculous decision? I was a bit of a showoff and liked performing in front of crowds. This job was fun, exciting and fed my ego like all the stupidity of my frat days at Oregon State. I had traded a frat castle, full of douchebags, for a giant dance floor full of partying, drunken, sexually charged hip-hopping fools in parachute pants. I would live in a haze of loud dance music, alcohol and late-night partying for two years of married life.

I would work in that kind of environment until I was thirty. This was not the lifestyle for me to have—I was yearning for a career that would match my desire to be a better husband and dad, one that would *fit* with raising a family. I needed to go back to school.

(6)

My mom and Daniel McCormick were beginning their lives together as husband and wife, too. Daniel worshipped my mom, and she was in love with him. He was mature, wise, and my mom did not have to babysit or mother him like she did with many of her former husbands. They were traveling and getting involved in politics together.

Daniel could have been an excellent role model to me in my mid-twenties, but I seldom saw him, and his time left on this earth would be limited. He did understand me, though.

One evening at a family gathering, he pulled me aside in confidence. "Mark, I'm sure you've heard that I am sick, so I will be brief," his voice cracking for the first time. I could see tears in his eyes. "First of all, you're a great kid. You remind me of me when I was your age. You know, you won't have your good looks forever. Look at me, I used to be young once," he reflected, bowing his head.

After a long pause, Daniel continued, "You've had a bit of a *rough* life here, lots of dads coming and going, popping into your life. Those guys will be of no help to you moving forward, *trust* me on that. Stop looking outward for guidance and start looking within yourself for strength. Trust in God. You are the dad now, and you can right all the wrongs in your life by being a good father to your own son. I have faith in you to do the right things moving forward. Stop fighting your marriage so much. *Relax and enjoy the ride.*"

I would never forget these words. It was the first time an older man had something positive to say to me since Michael Melvin. That was my last conversation with my fifth dad, a man who could have helped me so much more in my young adult years, but as fate would have it, our paths crossed for only an instant.

Daniel was diagnosed with a stage four variety of *it*. After fighting the battle of his life, undergoing radiation and chemotherapy treatments, he only lived a few more months and died in his sleep. A young man of 59, my age now. Kind, caring, loving, humble and selfless. He would be missed by all of us, and was laid to rest on November 21, 1987.

For the first time, my mom was left a widow. Now, her life was completely turned upside down. The harmony and balance that my mom was enjoying for only three short years was gone. She's a *survivor* though; she picked herself up and focused all of her energy and enthusiasm on her career that would pay her huge dividends.

Our whole family is full of self-centered survivors. We've really had no choice. If we had each purchased a ticket on the Titanic, we would have all found a spot on a lifeboat I'm sure. We would have pushed, elbowed, scratched, bitten, clawed and shoved our way to safety for certain. That is how we are hardwired. Every man and woman for him or herself!

My mom became a college administrator. And while she would *bury* herself in her career, I would *bury* myself in books for the first time in my life.

(7)

In May of 1990, my sister Grace married. No more *Gracie*, just Grace. The *amazing* Grace. She met her husband, Jack, while finishing college at Portland State. They formed a striking pair, and would make wonderful life partners and parents. My sister had learned so much from her childhood, determined not to make the mistakes my mom did. Grace had blossomed into a beautiful, dark-haired, tall and slender woman of over six feet. She could pass as a fashion model now, having swan-dived out of the gangly, awkward girl of her youth.

My brother-in-law Jack was six foot three. He was tall, dark and handsome. He was also an extremely motivated

Business major who worked for a major retailer just out of school. He would later make millions of dollars as a successful entrepreneur. He was driven, and would see to it that his wife and kids never had to worry about money. Grace would be a stay-at-home mom and devote her entire life to her kids. I would never have to worry about my little sister again; she would probably worry more about me. Her life was going to be *great* from here on out with Jack, and she deserved it.

I would give my sister away that day, the second time I would have that honor in my life. My sister was all grown up, and I thought she made a beautiful bride in her long, white wedding gown. At three years old, my son Bronson was the ring bearer. D.L Kirby was there that day, but did not participate at all. Grace had understandably left him out of the ceremony and wedding pictures. D.L. just sat in the back row of the church and took pictures. She now knew as an adult, her father was a pedophile. She *despised* him for this. He was back to his old hobby of photography, and I made sure that creepy old bastard took no pictures of my little boy that day.

After a few more group pictures were taken after the wedding, my mom came up to D.L. and said in front of her family very proudly, "Don, *we* did a great job of raising Grace, now didn't we." They hugged.

I whisked an unapproving glance toward Grace, and she reciprocated my disapproval with a giant scowl.

Later, at the reception, Grace would say, "What the *fuck* was that all about? Great job raising me? That is utter bullshit. I have never been so disgusted by a comment in my life—Mom is insane!"

"Don't worry about it, Grace," I said. "She is in

complete denial about everything, always searching for love in all the *wrong* places. We were always on the back burner growing up."

Grace would never see her biological father again. She *hated* her dad because of what he had done to me and other little boys; she would just *cut* him off. My sister has always been stronger than me—always with some of Grandma Bonney's toughness in her.

Moving forward, Grace would view ALL men as *creepers*. When she became a mom, she would never leave her kids at a birthday party alone. She would sit in the corner and watch, worried that someone's creepy uncle might crash the party and swoop up one of her precious little daughters in an instant. Seems like *helicopter* parenting to most people, but I get it—growing up with her and knowing our upbringing.

Grace and Jack have been married for thirty years and are great parents to their kids. My sister is *that* mom she always wanted to have as a child. Grace and Jack put raising their kids before everything else in their lives; they passionately raised two tall, intelligent, beautiful daughters.

D.L.'s life, from this day forward, would go the *other* way; his life would spiral downward. When the reception was close to over, D.L. pulled me aside and said, "Pard, I have this sore on my foot and I'm goin' to the doctor next week."

I did not think much of this conversation at the time, but this was an early warning sign of major health complications for D.L. down the road.

Adult Education

If you want a life lesson in humility, visit a radiation oncology clinic sometime. I met and talked to many courageous patients those two long months in the summer while getting my treatments. The actual treatments were a real bitch, though, no two ways about it. Some days my twisted and childish sense of humor was the only thing that kept me from psychosis.

I had to drive myself to the clinic every morning for eight straight weeks because my wife worked during the weekdays, and I had the summer off before football season. The clinic was in downtown Portland, about an hour away, me fighting morning rush hour traffic. My bladder and I were not seeing eye to eye on my commute each day.

The heavy dose of radiation, beamed squarely at my prostate, turned my bladder into a walking *time bomb*— ready to detonate in my boxer shorts at any given moment. Every day, I was required by the medical professionals to drink four-to-five glasses of water when I showed up at the clinic, before I got my daily twelve-minute treatment. Each day, I was reminded of this by the friendly staff at the front desk upon checking in.

"Good morning, Mark, make sure you have a full

bladder today!" If I had a dollar for every time I heard that during that summer, I could have treated myself to a lifetime supply of Depends adult diapers.

Dr. Johnson's rationale was, "If you don't want to be using a colostomy bag for the rest of your life, have a full bladder. Your well-fed bladder full of water will protect your rectum from the radiation."

The thought of using a bag to go the bathroom, and not being able to get an erection, seemed like the double dose of death to me. Needless to say, I drank water by the gallons, probably too much due to having the *bag* idea in mind.

Once I got to the clinic, the real challenge everyday became, how can I hold off urinating? All with a radiated bladder full of water, lying on a table for twelve to fifteen minutes, while radiation therapists carefully align your radiation target and laser beam over your rotten walnut. I tried everything humanly possible to not think about peeing or just urinating right there on that darned table. I felt like a little kid again, yelling more than a few times to the therapists, "How much longer? I HAVE TO PEE!"

I even tried to think about writing the next chapter in my book, but that didn't work. Coaching football? That was even *worse*. My mind would drift from players playing on the field, scoring touchdowns, to a water cooler full of Gatorade on the sidelines. Now I really had to relieve my bloated bladder. I tried counting, but that was no good either. Nothing seemed to work.

After two weeks of agonizing over the treatments, it just *popped* into my head. I began to recite this *damned* poem that one of my college professors, Dr. Goolsby, had made me listen to long ago on tape in his English

Literature class. I still could remember the whole darn thing from beginning to end. And by some miracle it worked. Every day for six weeks, I recited that poem in my head. Goolsby's damned poetry recording had finally come in handy:

When that April with his showers soote
The drought of March hath piercèd to the root
And bathèd every vein in such liquor
     ... Of which virtúe engendered is the flower

I could not get it out of my head; why that particular poem from that particular class?

(1)

My sister had inspired me to go back to school. I was running out of chances—thirty years old, wanting to do better for my family. College was much different this time around. I had a plan, short-term and long-term objectives, and I knew what career I wanted to pursue. I wanted to become a teacher.

I had seen the film *Dead Poets Society* that summer, and Robin Williams's character, John Keating, struck me. Engaging students, using unconventional teaching methods, standing on desks, using drama and theatrics in your daily lessons to inspire your students. I was *hooked*.

I left the theater saying to my wife, "*That* is what I *want* to do with my life. That is the kind of teacher I want to be. I want to go back to school!"

To reach my goal, I would need a bachelor's degree (in any old major, really) and a master's degree in Education to obtain an Oregon teaching license. I would work part time at Meier & Frank, a department store in Portland, for two years as the only straight male employee on the first floor.

To get started on my daunting academic journey, I took three fall classes at Portland City College. I had not been to school in ten years, but was much more mature than in my frat boy days of yesteryear. I knew I was ready to succeed for the first time in a long time as a student.

(2)

My first class at PCC was an English Literature course that I took at night. When I arrived at the school, I made my way up the tall and winding staircase to room 430. I opened the door and the room was empty, all fifty student desks vacant in a large, barren classroom. I thought I might have mistakenly made my way to the wrong room, but I double-checked my schedule and this was indeed the home of "English Literature 202-Dr. Dennis Goolsby, Instructor." So, I took a seat in the far corner of the room, not wanting to be one of those brown-nosing students who always sits up front, and waited patiently to see if anyone else would show up.

The clock arrived to 8:00 p.m., the starting time, and there were only three of us in the room: myself, a young kid who looked right out of high school, and a woman in her mid-to-late forties, who seemed more concerned about manicuring her fingernails than learning about English literature. We were all seated toward the back of the room, spread out, in our own little protective comfort zones.

The kid, who was a couple of rows in front of me but far to the left, suddenly whipped his head my way and whispered with a cupped hand, as if he was a spy with some top-secret information, "Have you heard about this professor?"

"No," I shook my head. A simple negative would have been sufficient here, but one of my major flaws as an adult has always been my propensity to share. "This is my first class here at PCC, I'm just getting back into school after a long time away." TMI, too much information in almost every possible adult interaction.

The kid continued, "Talked to my buddies, this dude is one step away from the *looney bin*. He got fired from being a full-time professor last year. Now he only teaches at night. I bet we are the only ones enrolled in this course—students are always dropping out of his classes. This guy makes Charles Manson seem normal."

"Is that so?"

"Trust me, this dude is a real *nut bar*."

I didn't respond, hoping the young kid would turn around and cease to add more stress to my first day back to school in over ten years. I grabbed for a pen in my backpack and took a deep breath. I knew I would have to *suck it up*. I was working at Meier & Frank five days a week and this was the only time I could take this class.

It turns out that this young kid's top-secret intel was right on the money. Goolsby was indeed a *mad*man—Edgar Allen Poe meets Vincent van Gogh; Jeffrey Dahmer meets Norman Bates. *Looney* meets *Tunes*. Two things became very clear immediately. Dr. Dennis Goolsby was not a very stable human being, nor a very good teacher.

Dr. Goolsby walked into the classroom an unfashionably twenty minutes late. He looked like he had been sleeping in a cardboard box all night. He smelled like it, too. I had already started to pick up my things, thinking the crazed mental patient had finally been committed. Goolsby placed his worn and tattered brown-leather satchel on the small wooden podium in front of the class, swept back his long, black, greasy, tangled and matted hair with his fingers, put his broken reading glasses on and looked up. This is the first time he had actually made eye contact with the mostly empty classroom.

He gasped like a man who was in a tremendous amount of abdominal pain, "Ooh, this is NO GOOD." As if we students were not there at all, Goolsby began to console himself like a mother would talk to a hurt child. "It's OK, it's OK, everything's going to be alright, Dennis. You will get through this, Dennis. Trust me, trust me." He raised his voice again, talking to no one in particular, "Two semesters ago, *fourteen*. Last semester, *eight*. And now only three, *three* lousy students. GOD HELP ME!"

Goolsby gathered himself for a moment, talking to himself once again, "What are we going to do, Dennis? Tell me, what are we going to do here? This is no good. No good at all. We have bills to pay. *They* are going to turn off our electricity, Dennis."

I looked over at the young kid and he could barely contain his laughter.

The professor looked up at Natalie, the woman filing her nails, and said, "What is going on here, uh, uh . . . Natalie?" Goolsby stared down at his sparse class attendance roster. "Why won't anyone sign up for my classes anymore, Natalie?" He started to cry a little, whimpering like a hurt puppy. Natalie said nothing, shrugged her shoulders and continued on her cuticles.

He looked at the young kid, David, and said,"Don't you have any friends who need an English credit, son? For God's sake, *help* me, son. Throw me a lifeline *here*. Can't you see I'm a *drowning* man?!"

We said nothing, too afraid of what Goolsby might do or say next. And I thought to myself—in too much fear to utter a single word out loud—well, the good news is it looks like I am going to get a great *deal* here. *Four* professors for the price of *one*.

Realizing none of his students were going to get sucked into his one-man pity party, Goolsby pulled out a giant book of poetry from his satchel and cleared his throat. He looked out at his audience of three, all spread about the room, and said, "This is no good, *no* good at all. All of you move up to these three seats in front of me. These are your assigned seats for rest of the term." We all rolled our eyes at each other, scurrying with our belongings to the three seats directly in front of his little wooden pulpit. The *bullied* pulpit.

Goolsby continued, now excited and animated, knowing he had a captive audience for the first time that evening. "I want you up close and personal. Yes, that's right, right up front! I need to feel the energy of my audience in order to get my creative juices flowing! Beautiful, just beautiful! Now I'm ready to teach! HA, HA, HA!"

Our crazed instructor began to read the poem, "To the Virgins, to Make Much of Time" by Robert Herrick aloud.

"Gather ye rosebuds while ye may,
Old time is still a flying
And this same flower that smiles today
To-morrow will be dying"

Dr. Goolsby then wandered over to the window, saw a tree swaying in the wind, and began to cry out loud, "LOOK, LOOK AT THAT TREE, ISN'T IT JUST

BEAUTIFUL! Look at the leaves, like they are being touched by God's loving hands ever so gently in the blowing breeze?" I glanced at the young kid, and we both started to laugh. I soon shut up when Dr. Goolsby shot us a glare. David kept on laughing—he couldn't stop.

Goolsby almost wept. "Stop laughing at ME, and quit making fun of me! Why are you still laughing at me, son?" Goolsby had both of his hands pressed against his cheeks, like his head was in a vise, now wailing.

"I was just laughing at you getting all *gushy* and crying at that tree over there," David clarified. The young kid had made his first and fatal mistake of the term, admitting he was indeed laughing at the fragile, tree-hugging Dr. Goolsby. David was right about one thing, though: our new English Literature instructor was indeed a complete *nut bar*.

Once Goolsby stopped crying and blew his nose in the dirty handkerchief he had pulled from his tweed jacket pocket, I could see that he was angry. From that moment on, he would *torment* poor David every week for the entire semester. Goolsby was *relentless*.

I never laughed. Instead, I made a *bigger* mistake; I *befriended* Dr. Goolsby. Believe it or not, Goolsby became sort of a *mentor* to me. I was desperate for an adult to guide me into the next phase of my life because, at the time, this was my low self-esteem talking; in my twenties and early thirties, my deep insecurity rested in not viewing myself as *smart*. I had completely screwed up college, and because I did not apply myself at school, I viewed myself as *dumb*, someone who didn't measure up intellectually to others. Most of my sense of humor, wiseass jokes and boorish behavior was just a way for me to mask my lack of self-confidence.

I also somehow felt sorry for this *fragile* human being Goolsby; he was like a sad rescue dog that needed someone to care for him. Goolsby would inspire me how *not* to teach. He was a deplorable teacher, but sucked me into his trap. I knew the guy was a weirdo from that first night, but I just kept coming back for more.

My first mistake was to offer to help assist him with his class. Goolsby was always late, and his breath often smelled of cheap whiskey. He had no car or driver's license. He rode the bus and he was never on time because the bus schedule didn't quite match up with the starting time of the class. Because he was always late, he needed one of us to get his class started with the warmup. That *helper* became *me*.

Goolsby was lazy and not very creative, so for the first half an hour of each class we listened to poetry on a small tape recorder. Why? According to Goolsby, "You will recite the entire poem to the class as your final project for the term, as well as turn in an eight-page analysis of the poem as your final paper." The memorization of the poem was the easiest part of this whole ordeal, as well as the most meaningless part of the project. The poetry analysis component, however, would be much harder for me to complete, and I would need some extra help and tutelage from Dr. Goolsby himself. This *extra* help would come at a heavy price, and I would learn one final time, now as a grown adult, to *never* trust adult males ever again.

(3)

Goolsby had given me the tape and told me to be in charge of getting the class started, which was simple, given there were only three of us. No one added the class after that first night, and we all needed a passing grade. So, we all did what we could to appease the *nutty* professor. By the time I finished that quarter, I could recite the entire thing from memory. In fact, I couldn't get that damned poem out of my head for the rest of my life. It would pop into my brain at all kinds of awkward and crazy moments in time—trying to remember directions to someone's house, taking an important test, or when making love to my wife. It was always there, this damned, disgusting little poem, just below the surface of my long-term memory.

"When that April with his showers soote
The drought of March hath piercèd to the root
And bathèd every vein in such liquor
Of which virtúe engendered is the flower

The second mistake I made was offering Goolsby a ride to and from school each Wednesday night of class. I knew the dude needed a ride, and that the tape and warmup thing was getting old, so I just offered one night after class. This is a sample of my *bizarre* behavior that would leave my wife shaking her head in disgust each night when I returned home.

"You don't know this man at all, Mark, and from what you've told me, he seems mentally unstable."

I also met with Goolsby occasionally at his apartment, where he would help me with my writing and teach me strategies in analyzing complex text, both poetry and prose. Goolsby was brilliant, and I had never had anyone take the time to teach me like this, in a deep, rich, purposeful way. He challenged me to think deeper and pull meaning out of the text I never knew was humanly possible. We had nothing in common beyond our teacher-student relationship and the weekly readings; I liked sports and he *hated* them. I liked to watch movies. Goolsby?

"I don't watch movies. I only watch *film*, cinematic *art*," he would say, scoffing at the idea of *Die Hard*. "You may as well put your head in a blender and turn it on *puree* as watch that mindless rubbish."

Goolsby did give me a great gift during this time period—maybe the greatest single gift any teacher has ever given me. He made me *believe* in myself as someone who was *intelligent*. No one had ever made me feel that way before. This time spent with Goolsby became my gateway to everything that is great about teaching, learning and literacy.

Goolsby had *other* ideas though—ones of which I had no idea were in store for me later on. He was a very *troubled* man.

The real trouble started for me when I let that crazy bastard into my home. I invited him for Christmas dinner. Why? I have no idea, really. It must be something in my DNA. Again, I felt sorry for the guy, but my wife was having no part in it.

Our family had spent Christmas morning opening presents. My mom, who was now single, was down from Tacoma. My wife's parents, Boyd and Melvina, were also there, having driven over the night before. Bronson, who was now in kindergarten, received his usual arsenal of toys from relatives—Legos, assorted Teenage Mutant Ninja Turtle figurines, Transformers, Robocop action figures and vehicles, assorted puzzles and games. Aunt Cathy gifted Bronson's favorite gift of the day, though, a bright-red battery-operated "voice changer megaphone," complete with several sound effects and ten voice settings. Cathy was the aunt who loved to give Bronson the noisiest toy on the market every holiday season; she thought this was simply hilarious. It became a long-running family joke, and this was the year of the toy bullhorn megaphone, the most annoying thing in the world!

(4)

I picked Goolsby up on Christmas afternoon and drove him to my house. Goolsby had been alone in his small messy little apartment, having drunk a bottle full of cooking sherry before I arrived. He was already in *rare* form and quite *pickled*.

"I am so *nervous*." He was staggering and almost fell on me when I opened his door. "I had to start drinking with my breakfast. The only thing I had in my cupboard was cooking sherry. I am so anxious about meeting your family, Mark. You don't know how much this means to me. You are a precious and dear friend to me."

I should have done a better job of listening that day. The "precious" comment was a bit odd. Well, I tried to sober Goolsby up with some coffee, but he was a drunken mess and smelled like fermented bacon and eggs and *sour* milk. I poured him into my car, and we were off.

Our first house on the east side of Portland was a small, modest, three-bedroom ranch starter home and was not ideal for entertaining a large number of guests, but we had several family members over for dinner that day, including my new mentor, Dr. Goolsby. Goolsby continued to drink throughout the day: wine, cocktails and champagne, and by the time we got to dinner, he was *three sheets to the wind*, SMASHED.

We were all sitting around the table, watching Goolsby. Why? Because he was making so much noise that no one at the table could eat.

"Oh my goodness, these green beans are simply heavenly! Oh, ah, oooh mmm good!" He sounded like he was making intimate and passionate love to each and every scrap on his plate. My father-in-law, Boyd, finally looked at him and said, "Are you going to eat those potatoes or screw 'em?"

We all laughed, except for Dennis. Dennis started to talk to himself like I had seen him do before in class. "It's OK, Dennis, it's OK. He is just a *mean*, insensitive man, a *bully*. You've met this type of guy before. It's all right, don't pay any attention to this man."

Boyd, in his younger days, would have probably reached over the table and *punched* him. But on this night in his mid-eighties, my elderly father-in-law decided against it. Still, the rest of the dinner conversation became strained and awkward as Boyd continued to *glare* at the fragile and already-intimidated college professor, who now ate more quietly: "Oh, ah, ee, mmm." I couldn't help but snicker in between my intermittent sips of wine. It was so silly, creepy and ridiculous, all at the same time, that my natural response was to laugh.

When dinner was over, Bronson took over the entertainment by bringing out his new megaphone. He went around to people, randomly shouting words that rhymed with their name.

"Dad smells bad, Dad smells bad!" He saw Dennis

sitting alone in the recliner and figured he was as easy a mark as he was. "DENNIS IS A WENNIS! DENNIS IS A WENNIS! DENNIS IS A WENNIS!"

You could see Dennis start to get agitated; with every "WENNIS," he grew more upset. He actually started pulling out his own hair, he was so frustrated by Bronson's cutting yet nonsensical words. Finally, Goolsby just snapped and yelled, "I AM NOT A WENNIS! I AM NOT A WENNIS!" He started to chase Bronson around the room like a giant drunken zombie, shouting, "I AM NOT A WENNIS!"

Unfortunately, the angrier Dennis got, the more excited Bronson got about yelling his poetry. We were all laughing hysterically.

When it was over, Dennis sat alone on our staircase, inebriated and exhausted from all the running around. He just sat there and cried, talking to himself, his head buried in his hands. "I am not a *wennis*. I am not a *wennis*. I am not a *wennis*." If it wasn't so damned funny, I would have probably been petrified by my college professor's nuclear meltdown.

I finally said, "Dennis, I think it's time to go home."

(5)

The following term, I started commuting two hours to school at Oregon State three days a week. I was focused, busy and motivated. I finished my bachelor's degree in two years, making the honor roll each term. I attended Western College the following year and received my master's degree in teaching. I had a 4.00 GPA there. For the first time in my life, I felt smart. It had taken me a long time to get to *that* place.

During my time at school, my wife and I had our second child, Destiny. Having my second child, a daughter, settled me down, made me grow up; I really started to *own* my life as a responsible adult and good father now. I seldom saw Goolsby anymore and *he* was not happy about this at all.

Goolsby began to call me in the early evening, inebriated and jilted by me because I was not visiting him anymore. At first, I didn't really get it. "Mark, why don't you call me anymore? I care about you and miss our times together." These random calls just before bedtime seemed innocent enough.

I would say something like, "Dennis, I have a wife and two kids now. I am going to school full time and student-teaching. I just don't have time to see you anymore."

He would cry and plead for me to come visit him. "Mark, just come see me one last time at my apartment for old time's sake. We can read some poetry together and share a bottle of wine." This was starting to get a little *creepy*, I thought. He started sounding desperate, and I started to fear that, somehow, he had gotten the totally wrong idea about where our relationship was headed. I viewed him as an older mentor. Maybe he viewed me as something else.

Then, his calls took a turn for the worse, and I felt like I was being stalked. He would call me at all hours of the night and early morning, screaming and crying into the phone. "Mark, I love you! I think about you all the time, I can't get my mind off you. I *want* you! I am going to USE the POWER OF THE PHONE, YES, THE POWER OF THE PHONE. YOU'LL SEE! YOU WILL SEE! HA! HA! HA!" He would laugh maniacally and then hang up. I started to ignore his calls, just simply not picking them up. This seemed to work for a while.

(6)

My advisor at college pulled me aside one evening and said two school security officers wanted to talk to me. I was led to a room where two men were sitting across from me at a long table.

"Mr. Kirby?"

"Yes."

"Mark Kirby?"

"That's me."

"Do you know a Dennis Goolsby?"

"I do."

"You need to call him and tell him to *stop* calling our switchboard operator at the college. He tied up our phones *all* afternoon today. Keeps shouting something about 'THE POWER OF THE PHONE!' He's looking and asking for *you* by name."

My head dropped and I looked down at the floor for what seemed like five minutes. I knew at this point Goolsby had completely lost it. Suddenly, one of the men interrupted my reflection with a question.

"Let me ask you this. How do you know this man, Mr. Kirby?"

"He was my Professor at PCC. I befriended him, and he is basically *stalking* me right now. Calls my home at all hours of the night."

"Is he mentally stable?"

"At this point, I would say *no.*"

"Mr. Kirby, you need to file a complaint with your local police. We will do so here."

"Thanks for your help, gentlemen, and have a good evening." I left the room, feeling like Goolsby had completely *violated* me that day, invading my workspace, crossing the limits of healthy boundaries. I now realized that my tactic of just ignoring Goolsby had backfired. Goolsby was now messing around with my college education and my potential livelihood as a teacher. *It* needed to be stopped.

The following morning, I called the Clackamas County Sheriff's Department, explained my situation, and they called Goolsby for me.

After talking to Goolsby on the other line, the officer asked me, "I'm sorry that I have to ask you this, Mr. Kirby, but did you have a romantic relationship with this man? He seems pretty distraught, says he *loves* you, always has."

I felt stupid and embarrassed by the officer's question. "Absolutely *not!*"

I never saw Dennis Goolsby again. I would finally stop looking to older adult males to teach me life lessons for good. It was my time to be the father I had always wanted in my life.

SIX Days Straight from Hell

After forty radiation treatments over my entire summer break from school, I would need to wait patiently for my two years of hormone therapy to do their job, and to contain *it* from spreading. I was definitely worried.

I naively asked, "If all goes well here, how much time do you think I have, Dr. Johnson?"

"I can't really say for certain," he declared. "Six years, six months, who knows for sure?"

"Well, at least you didn't say six days. My mom's *worst* marriage lasted for that period of time for God's sake. So at least I've got that going for me." I laughed nervously at my attempt at humor in this uncomfortable conversation with my physician. Dr. Johnson stared blankly back at me, having no idea what I was talking about.

I knew exactly what I meant; I was joking about my mom's sixth marriage, a six-day affair to Harvey Dingus, Father number six. 666? Totally *creepy*. Harvey was a crazy, bible-wielding, gun-toting, *born-again* Christian, a deeply sexually conflicted, creepy little cobbler. Goolsby was emotionally unstable. Dingus was mentally deranged, a complete psycho. Dingus would be the source of much of my comedy material at parties later on in life . . .

(1)

The two best decisions I ever made in my life were: (1) marrying my wife Barb, and (2) going back to school and becoming a teacher. I was ready to start my first teaching job at Renne Middle School in Newberg, Oregon. In three short years, my life had been transformed into something much better, as I had finally found that balance in life that I had always been looking for. Teaching would never disappoint me. As an educator, I could now be a positive male role model to kids on a daily basis, and this "life's work" was fulfilling for me.

I found out that, like parenting, teaching kids would never be an exact science. This noble and humbling profession was always full of unusual and sometimes shocking surprises. Just when you thought you got the whole figured out, a student with ADHD, hopped up on Adderall, *Mountain Dew*, and three bags full of *Skittles* would throw you an overhand curveball. Teaching sixth graders was like herding cats, chickens and greased pigs, while juggling butcher knives and chainsaws all in one small classroom at the same time for eight hours a day, five days a week. It was challenging work, but I absolutely fell in love with the profession. Ironically, I would spend the next twenty-five years of my life living in *that* wonderful world that I enjoyed the most when I was a teenager growing up with Michael Melvin, grades six to twelve. I was loving life once again.

For my mom, it would be a revolving door of losers from here on out, and the only thing I got from her boyfriends or husbands was a few laughs.

(2)

Speaking of laughs, I met Harvey Dingus only twice, both times at his home in Bainbridge Island, Washington. The first time I met him, he had invited several of our family members over for dinner. Before I came over, Mom debriefed me on potential husband number six. Notice that I did not say Dad number six. This complete goofball would never be a dad to me.

"Guess what, Mark, I'm engaged! His name is Harvey and he looks just like . . . "

"Let me guess, Burt Reynolds?"

"Goodness no! He's the spitting image of Tom Hanks."

"I'll bet he is." Tom Hanks in *Splash* or *Forrest Gump*, I snarked to myself, away from the mouthpiece of the phone.

"Harvey has impeccable taste, panache and a flair for interior decorating, but he is oh-so-sensitive. Be on your best behavior." She was advising a ten-year-old instead of me at my age of thirty-three.

I was not enthused; she had only been dating him for a few weeks. My mom's career was going great, and I thought she should heed caution when jumping into another marriage too quickly.

"How about instead of getting married, you just live with the guy," I suggested.

"Harvey is a proper Christian man, and he thinks that cohabitation before marriage is sinful," she edified.

Well, I just about threw up into the receiver at this new *major* warning signal. My mom was a not an extremely religious person, and she was certainly not a virgin. As far as religion goes, she was all over the map. She was a bit of a chameleon in regard to her affiliations, having converted to Catholicism after marrying Daniel McCormick. Michael Melvin was a Methodist, so we were all Methodists. Skip Barnes was a Lutheran, so she was Lutheran. D.L. Kirby drank on Sunday mornings, so she didn't go to church at all. Now she was jumping on the *born-again* bandwagon after knowing Harvey Dingus for only a few weeks.

But my mom was hopelessly in love and there was no stopping the *Marilyn Train* once it got rolling. Choo fucking choo, I thought, as I downed my second gin and tonic.

The night of the dinner, Dingus served us all at a long, formal dining table. He was a fabulous cook; we had roasted duck and potatoes, a goat cheese salad, and strawberry chocolate mousse cake for dessert. I couldn't help but notice that this guy had flowers everywhere.

Uncle Bill, who was there that night, picked up on it immediately. "Harvey, you have some fabulous flower arrangements here."

My mom quickly interrupted and spoke for him. "Harvey has all kinds of creative little hobbies like flower arranging—cooking, macramé, origami, woodworking. He even makes *puppets*."

"Puppets?" I remarked.

Harvey now spoke for himself. "I teach Sunday school and make puppets for little shows that teach the kids bible parables in a fun and engaging way. Would you like to see some of my *puppets* in my workshop after dinner, Mark?"

"Sure," I said.

"Before I show Mark my wooden puppets in the workshop, it's time for Harvey's dinner theater." Harvey and Mom were now clapping like a couple of little kindergarteners, all excited and annoyingly energetic for two people who had just consumed an elaborate meal. I was like all of the other guests at the table, stuffed and ready to relax. Well, not Harvey and Mom.

Harvey left for and swiftly returned from his study with a giant craft box full of art materials. "We are *all* going to make *me* puppets."

"Oh, Harvey, this is going to be just great fun," my mom gushes.

Harvey began directing us on this after-supper session of arts and crafts. "On the first day of Sunday school, my kids are usually reluctant to talk about themselves. So, we make *me* puppets. Here is a box full of the materials you will all need to design your puppet. Each of you is going to make one using a paper plate for the head, yarn for the hair, construction paper for the facial features and a popsicle stick to hold your plate up to your face. You're going to hide your face with the plate and introduce and talk about yourself to the people around the table."

"But we all know each other, Harvey," my cousin Jenny said, looking peeved by the whole "icebreaker" activity.

"Don't be a *party pooper*, Jenny," Harvey snapped back, already starting to get noticeably agitated by someone questioning him. "Look, there are cards in the middle of the table, and everyone will draw one. They have categories like family, hobbies, pets, favorite movies, and so on. Draw a card for a particular category and talk about that subject for one minute. I will time you. We'll start with a volunteer and then move clockwise from that person around the table. This is just going to be *super-duper* fun."

After about twenty minutes of frantic craft work, we were ready to begin. My mom offered to go first, as she was the most excited person at the table—besides Harvey, of course.

"My name is Marilyn. My card says 'family,' so here goes. I have two kids, Mark and Grace, and I am glad they are here to meet my Harvey. I love Harvey Dingus very much. He is so handsome, thoughtful, creative and special. He is a great host and cook. He loves his Sunday school kids and he makes me very happy. I hope my kids love him as much as I do, because he is my world. He is going to be my future husband one day." After this word-*vomit* fest, Harvey and Mom *smooched*, their lips puckered out for all to see.

"Very good, Marilyn. That was *super-duper*," Harvey said, kissing her puppet.

How bizarre this whole after-dinner scene had become; I thought I was in an episode of *The Twilight Zone*.

Now moving clockwise, it was Uncle Bill's turn. "My name is Bill, and my category is 'pets.' I used to have a pet cat, and he was white and warm, fat, loveable and fuzzy. I called him Stanley after Stan, my husband. But Stan left me three months ago for a young male waiter at Joe's Crab Shack, and he took Stanley with him. Now I've got no more *Stan* and no more *Stanley*. What am I going to do? I am fifty-eight years old, gay and all alone!" He put his face in his hands and began to cry.

"It's alright Bill, Stan sounds like a major-league *asshole* anyway!" Harvey comforted.

"Thank you, Harvey. He was, he is, but—oh, what am I going to do?" Bill continued to cry all over his paper plate puppet.

It was Grace's chance to share now. My sister is one of

the funniest people you will ever meet; she had developed a cynical, sarcastic sense of humor over the years, just like me, after living in a dysfunctional family for much of her life. It was her way of dealing with things, and I was curious to see what was on her mind. We had had so many *wannabe* fathers over the years, I was wondering what her *spin* on this whole wacky situation would be.

"My name is Grace and I am married to Jack. I am *not* picking a card. I know exactly what I want to say here." I *lean* in.

"I am first and foremost a mom, and I am always present for my kids. Jack and I only want to be married *one* time in our lives, not *five*. What guy would sign up to be number *six* anyway? Probably some crazy *bastard* who makes paper plate puppets! I'm out of here. If I want to see crazy shit, I'll buy a ticket to the freak show at the circus. Good evening to you, Harvey, and Mom, it's been real, it's been fun, but it hasn't been *real* fun." She squished her paper plate into a ball, threw it on the table, and left temporarily out the front door to "clear her head." That was awesome, classic Gracie stuff, I thought. Years of childhood frustration taken out on a paper plate puppet. Good for you, little sister, *good* for you.

We continued. Now it was Cousin Jenny's turn to share. Jenny is the daughter of my mom's sister, Linda. When God was giving out looks and personality, Jenny got handed the face of actress Jennifer Aniston, as well as an outgoing and fun disposition. I noticed her plate puppet had long, flowy yellow yarn hair and big, red, construction paper lips.

"I am going to go *off* topic her!" she exclaimed.

"You can't do *that*. It's against the rules!" Harvey

restrained himself from screaming.

"Watch me, you big party *pooper*."

"I'm not a party pooper, I'm Harvey!"

"Just sit back and see if you can guess who I am, Harvey! I am a 'Material Girl' who is just 'Like A Virgin.' I have a 'Borderline' personality disorder and I like to 'Vogue' at clubs!"

Everyone shouted "Madonna!" simultaneously, and Jenny began to sing the song "Lucky Star." The whole table was clapping and having a great old time until Harvey shouted, "STOP! This is not how you play MY game, you're breaking ALL the rules here!"

"Harvey, quit being such a PARTY POOPER," Jenny fired back.

This was the second time in two minutes that Harvey had been called a "party pooper," and he did not appreciate this one bit. He reached over the table and snatched Jenny's Madonna plate puppet from her hands, ripping it in two. "Cheaters never prosper," he said. We sat there, incredulous of the childlike behavior we had just witnessed from our dinner host.

Quickly trying to diffuse the situation, my mom said, "Harvey, we girls are going to clean up here—how about taking Mark out to your *shop* and showing him your wooden puppets?"

"All right then, all right" Harvey said as he led me quickly in a huff, walking with his butt cheeks clinched in *fisted rage* to the large room out behind his garage.

(3)

I was now in Harvey's workshop, being shown his hand-crafted puppets. I felt for a brief moment like a kid

242

again, remembering the time when Ankee had showed me how to make a whimmy-doodle out of wood outside of his hillbilly shanty up the McKenzie River.

"Tell me, Harvey, do you like movies?"

"Why *heavens* no. A waste of *time* and *money*. Most of them are *sinful* anyway. Violence, sex? All the *deadly* sins *squeezed* into two hours of craftsmanship by the *devil* himself. I like *making* puppets. For Sunday school children's theater."

Harvey Dingus had completely *bombed* the *sniff* test.

"Sounds interesting? Can I see a few?"

"Sure. This little puppet is *Jesus*, but he needs no further introduction, does he?" Dingus now *giggled* in a silly little way that I hadn't heard since the Uncle Chester days of yesteryear. He showed me a few more puppets based on characters from the Bible.

"What do you have under *that*?" I asked, pointing to the large white cloth on the other end of the workbench.

"Those are my *special* puppets," he said.

"What do you mean by *special*?" I asked.

"Let me just show you," he said, prancing over to the cloth and whisking it off the puppets, like a magician unveiling a trick.

I walked over to take a closer look at the *four* of them, just lying there, faces up, humming their silence back at me like a quartet of small corpses.

"Harvey, what's *this* one's name?" I was pointing at a male puppet in a three-piece suit with a giant scowl on his face.

"Why, for heaven's sake, that is *Miss Congeniality*!"

"Why is *he* scowling?" I asked.

"Because *he's* a little *bitch*." He was now giggling to

himself and fixing his shrunken tie.

"What about that one, Harvey?" I was now pointing to the rigid, stocky puppet in the military uniform on the end.

"Oh, that is *Captain Iron Closet.*"

"What's his deal?"

Dingus gets real close to me and whispers, "He is hiding his *true* feelings behind that manly uniform. That is why he is called *Iron* Closet."

I say nothing.

"You knew I was going to get to this sooner or later, Harvey, but what is the puppet's name with the enormous wooden, uh, *wiener* over there?"

"That is my special little helper, *Mr. Rumpy Rumpy.*"

"Uh, how does he help you?" I was now staring at the eight-inch wooden *member.*

"That's for me to know and YOU to find out," Dingus says. The little flaming puppet master now winks at me. I about got sick right there on Harvey's naked wooden sex toy, having heard *that* term, "Rumpy, Rumpy," when I worked in the men's clothing department at Meier & Frank. There, I was the only straight guy on the first floor, and on occasion we would go out for drinks. We had lots of fun, and a few of the guys would try to *shock* me with their slang terms, including "Rumpy Rumpy," which meant sex between men. I started to tremble, as I slowly realized my mom was oblivious to this part of Dingus.

"Let's call it a night, Harvey. It's been real," I said, suddenly wanting to shower.

I said nothing to my mom, and we all parted after a night cap of Grand Marnier in brandy snifters around a roaring fire. Harvey was a great host that evening, but he was not ideal marrying material for my mom. For my

Uncle Bill, maybe.

Mom had to call me the next day to get my opinion about Harvey; I was walking on eggshells here.

"What do you think?" she asked, ready to answer her own question. "Isn't he the greatest cook and host ever?"

"Mom, I want to be honest with you. I have my reservations about Harvey."

"What do you mean?"

"I think he likes you, but I don't think he *loves* you." I think of how to say it. "Mom, to tell you the truth, I don't even know if he likes women at all. Personally, I think he likes guys."

This was the wrong thing to say to my mom, as she now viewed Harvey Dingus as the ultimate challenge.

"Oh, we will see about *that*." She was off the phone in a matter of seconds, and I knew it was on her way to marry the *flaming* puppet master. It was only a matter of time.

(4)

Two months later, my mom married Harvey Dingus in an intimate backyard wedding at his place. It was a small gathering of family members: Cliff and Lavina dancing away; Uncle Bill minus Stan (who would die three years later from complications of prostate cancer); my wife and I with baby daughter, Destiny, and seven-year-old son, Bronson, among others. We ate Harvey's gourmet food, drank bottled beer and expensive wine, and played croquet in his big backyard. This was the ceremony for husband number six.

(5)

The following Friday, I was home with my two kids

when, at about nine that night, my mom called screaming and crying.

"He's gone absolutely CRAZY!"

"What?! Who are you talking about?"

"Harvey! As soon as we got married and I moved in with him last week, he turned into an over-controlling, crazy man! I thought he was going to *hit* me."

"I knew that crazy little bastard was *no* good. Settle down, let's talk about this. Where are you now?"

"I am calling from a payphone down the road. Can you come get me and help me move out tonight?"

"Holy crap, Mom, you've been married less than a week," I exhale. "I'm taking care of my two little kids this evening while Barb's at work. I can't come tonight." This was one of the first times I ever said NO to my mom, and it felt good. Can you drive over to your Union home in Tacoma tonight and spend the night there?"

"Uh—yeah, yes I can."

"Good. Go there tonight and in the morning, get some moving guys to come to his place and move you out. And Mom, don't go back there!"

"But, I—I *have* to. I've moved most of my clothes, some furniture, and other personal items into his house already this week. A whole U-Haul truck full."

"Will Harvey be away from the house tomorrow?" I asked.

"He has a job tomorrow until about four o'clock."

"Perfect. Meet the movers tomorrow and move out."

She moved out the next day, ending the shortest marriage of her six trips to the altar—six days to her sixth husband Harvey, the perverted puppeteer. We all wondered when she would stop her marrying madness once and for all.

I *buried* Harvey Dingus in a handmade wooden coffin, made by *him*, with all of his creepy puppets around him, deep in my mind that day. Farewell, sweet Harvey! You are the creepiest Sunday school teacher I have ever met, by far!

In her hurried frenzy to get the hell out, I had hoped and prayed that Mom had snatched *Mr. Rumpy Rumpy* by his wooden wiener and thrown the well-endowed puppet into her car trunk. That eight-incher would've surely made a better life partner then the next knucklehead she was about to bring into our family. It was about to get weirder, if you can believe it.

"Maybe you should just stay single . . . ," my sister advised.

"How about living with the guy first, you know, like a 'test drive' before you purchase?" I suggested.

But our advice fell on deaf ears, as my mom was bound and determined to find her *soul mate* one way or another. Her next trip to the altar would be her *costliest* one yet. My mom would finally *meet* her match.

SEVEN: Easily Divisible by Two?

After my radiation treatments were complete, my wife threw a party for me at a restaurant near the clinic. Friends and family showed up to celebrate the end of eight grueling weeks of my chestnuts roasting over an open fire. My grown kids were there, along with my two grandchildren. Curiously absent from this nice, intimate get-together was Mom; she texted me a week earlier and said she couldn't make it.

"I need to use my two-week time-share in Cabo, you know, the one I got in the divorce with Bob," she explained.

Bob was my seventh dad. He and my mom had gone through a messy divorce three years prior, ending in a split of their assets. My mom did not like to lose money. Whereas husbands were some sort of collectible item, money was a way for her to keep *score* of her life success. She had always made out well in her divorces. Yet, in this one, Bob had gotten half of my mom's properties and money. She despised him for this. She hated losing money more than losing husbands!

"Can't you come? I would really appreciate it, and so would Barb. It's been a long three months of tests and treatment and we haven't seen you," I texted back.

"If I don't use the time, I *lose* it," she replied. "I will *never* let Bob think that he got the *best* of me." This was my mom at her finest, thinking only of herself and of her miserable seventh marriage.

Bob D'Amato was a male gold digger. If he were at the party, he'd be looking for some way to pad his pockets. Oh yes—he would be here, all right, in *my* time of need, on the verge of death. His sole purpose, you ask? Try to figure out how *he* could get his slimy Sicilian sausage fingers on *my* life insurance policy. Once a conman, *always* a conman.

He would have said something like, "We are in this together, son. Sign this *change of beneficiary* paperwork so I can help you and your family, ease your burden in this time of crisis."

(1)

My kids were getting older, and I was loving being a dad. I had coached my son's little league baseball team every season, enjoying watching him play. And like Melvin, I always took my kids to the movies when they were growing up.

I started Bronson off at a very young age, going every Friday to the drive-in or one of the many indoor theater complexes in the Portland area. I took him to see the *Die Hard* trilogy with Bruce Willis, the Batman films, *all* of *The Terminator* flicks and the two *Robocop* movies. My wife was not happy and thought I was polluting our young son's mind. She was right. I was stupid.

"Mark, why are you taking Bronson to see all of these bloody, action, shoot 'em up movies? You're scaring him half to death and planting violent images in his head."

"Well, my dad took me see *The Exorcist* when it first

came out, and I *loved* it. Changed my life forever."

"But how old were you at the time?

"Fourteen."

"Well, Bronson happens to be *seven*."

My wife was definitely right. Again, I was a young, immature dad, and I hadn't received much quality parenting. When I was Bronson's age, I wasn't worried about what movie to watch; I was more concerned about being left home alone with my dad. I was probably trying to be Bronson's buddy. Never a good idea.

I must say, though, when Bronson's son comes to spend the night with his grandparents, he always reminds me, "Dad, only PG movies, no PG-13, got it?" I am sure he is sending me a message about *our* time spent watching *Die Hard*.

My daughter, Destiny, *mellowed* me out as a middle-aged man. She is seven years younger than my son, which probably gave me time to grow up and mature just a little. I was more thoughtful and sensitive, uninterested in shocking or scaring the crap out of her. I had evolved slightly. We went to all the Disney films together—*The Lion King, The Little Mermaid, Beauty and the Beast*. I took her to see all of the *Harry Potter* films. Why? She wanted to see them and knew I would pay for the film and concessions. I remember taking her to the second *Twilight* movie at a special showing at midnight, and to the debut of *The Princess Diaries*. As a grown woman, Destiny recalls fondly my willingness to share movie experiences and stories that *she* was interested in.

(2)

My mom was doing well in her career after leaving

Dingus in the dust. Without a man to hold her down, her life was flourishing in every way. For the past four years, she had served as the Dean of Instruction for a community college nearby. She had purchased a large, beautiful home on the Puget Sound, complete with a pool in the backyard. She also had a two-bedroom condo in Scottsdale, Arizona. She was making money, had invested wisely, had multiple properties, and was the perfect prey for a gold digger.

Along comes Bob D'Amato. I am being more than kind in referring to Bob as a "gold digger," because he was really a sociopath. He would be the second sociopath my mom would marry and bring into the family. I thought she would've learned, but my narcissistic mom would finally meet her match in this battle to the *death*. At least, that was Bob's plan.

Bob was not only a narcissist, but a cunning conman. He would sell himself to my mom like a sleazy, yet highly effective, used car salesman. Bob was probably just as bad as D.L. Kirby in his malicious intent; their motivations were just different. Whereas D.L.'s pleasure was young boys, Bob's was older women's money. Bob was not looking to *rape* your kid, but he was looking to *pillage* your whole financial portfolio. And I'm not talking some of your money here, but the whole pizza pie.

I met Bob D'Amato on a beautiful July afternoon at my mom's place overlooking the Puget Sound. We were watching the sailboats go by, both with our sunglasses on, our feet in my mom's pool, sipping on a tall, cool beverage. This was indeed "the life" I thought, taking this moment to grill my new potential father. Oh, by the way, he had already moved in with my mom. That took all of about two weeks of dating. And who wouldn't want to live in this beautiful place? Bob sure would, I thought to myself, as I took another soothing swig of my Tanqueray and tonic.

"Bob, how did you meet my mom?"

"I met at her at an 'Over Fifties' dance in Seattle."

"If you don't mind me asking, how old are you?"

"Fifty-four years young," he said.

I would find out later that summer that Bob had lied about his age to everyone. He was really forty-six years old. This *was* and *still* remains a major red flag—why would a guy lie about being older? Sounds like a gold digger tactic to me.

"Bob, I understand you're recently retired?"

"Yes, I used to be vice president of sales at Goodyear Tires, and after a corporate merger, I was given an early retirement severance package. I've been living off of it ever since."

"You mean you were fired, let go?"

"No, no, no, nothing like that, think of it as a *golden parachute*." Bob got all animated and started to *wave* his hands in the air.

"I'm not familiar with that term, Bob?"

"Let me explain, it's like this: When the company was taken over, I was asked to leave and was rewarded handsomely with a substantial package worth over six figures."

I said nothing, stared into the pool, and thought to myself, sounds like Bob got *fired*.

I learned later that Bob was actually an accountant for Goodyear, and that he was let go and under investigation for misappropriation of funds. Major red flag number two.

Last question, I thought—before I get another gin and tonic—"Bob, you got any kids?"

"I got two kids, but my ex is a cruel bitch and she won't let me see them. I haven't seen them in over ten years."

He now pulls out pictures of his kids when they were probably in their early teens. His daughter is in a dance recital outfit and his boy in a little league uniform. He starts to cry, and I am sucked into his drama. The questions are over for today. I find out later from my mom that he doesn't see his kids because he never paid child support. He is a *deadbeat* dad, just like D.L. Major warning sign number three—strike three, and you're out Bob!

But I was not dating Bob, my mom was, and *she* was hopelessly in love again.

I am skipping quite a bit of our conversation here, because the best quality about Bob, or any *con*man for that matter, is that *he* is a good listener. He will make you think that whatever *shit* you are selling is the best *shit* in town. Keep in mind, conmen don't have anything going on in their lives, so the more *you* talk, the less *they* need to *reveal* about themselves. They will ask you questions about your hobbies, your favorite sports team, your kids, and they will just sit and listen. Like a child molester, he is *grooming* you.

I wanted to learn more about Bob, as I was now rambling about the Pittsburgh Steelers, the "Immaculate Reception," and all kinds of other pointless things I am interested in that Bob was now drawing out of me with his many open-ended questions.

"Bob, where did you live before you moved in with my mom here?"

"I used to live in a nice two-bedroom condo in downtown Seattle," he continues his script. "I had a brand-new Trans Am, but I'm downsizing right now—sold all my furniture and my car. Bought a used pickup and here I am. I'm in this relationship with your mom for the long haul. *Trust* me on that."

Here you *are*, all right, I thought to myself—ready to *mooch* off my mom for who knows how long. In one afternoon, chatting with Bob, I was already concerned that Mom had made a BIG mistake with this guy. In all of her other relationships, the guys just left with pretty much their shirts on their back. My mom did receive home and life insurance from Daniel after he passed, but she had never been with a man who was interested in her for her money, because she really didn't have much. But now Bob was looking to snuggle up and eventually *cash in.*

Later in the evening, while sitting with my mom in her hot tub, I would find out that Bob's story was completely false. He actually lived in a one-bedroom rundown apartment in Kent, a seamy suburb of Seattle. When my mom went to retrieve Bob and his clothes from his apartment, she was shocked to find Bob in a compromising situation with another woman. She found an exotic dancer in a string bikini bathing in a kiddy pool, and Bob was straddling her and massaging her backside while sitting on his lawn chair behind her.

"Mom, did you ask him who the woman was?"

"Well, of course I did, silly. Do you think I'm a complete fool?"

I wanted to answer *yes* to her question, but decided to probe a little deeper. "Mom, why was he giving her a back rub? Doesn't that seem a little suspicious to you?"

"Not at all! Bob said she was the housekeeper and he was just massaging a muscle she'd stretched dusting the mantle."

"For God's sake mom, he lives in a one-bedroom apartment, he doesn't need a housekeeper!"

"I know that, you didn't let me finish. When I called him on that lame excuse, he said that she was a down-on-her-luck dancer who needed a place to crash for a week until she got her first check."

"Did you see Bob return any keys or sign any papers that day when he left? And why was he leaving while she was still there? Did you ever think that Bob might be crashing in her little apartment, because he was down on *his* luck?"

"Hmm, that never crossed my mind."

Bob had tricked my mom from that very first day he left his stripper girlfriend behind for the older woman with money. He tricked my mom into thinking that HE was in love with HER. He had offered a false background story, and she bought it. Even when she found out that he was lying, she made excuses for him. He seemed financially secure, but he was not. He seemed like an honest guy, but he was not!

Before I left my mom's place, I said, "Bob seems nice, but he's full of shit. I think he's worse than Harvey, who was pretty much the biggest piece of garbage ever." To sum it up, "Bob has NOTHING, and he is *using* you."

"He has just hit a little *speed bump* in his life—that's why he's *downsizing* to protect himself from *over*-extending financially," she clarified, still making excuses for her new man.

"Mom, you have to *own* things in order to *downsize*. Bob had *nothing* and still has nothing." She would not listen to anything I said because, for the seventh time in her life, she was *hopelessly* in love.

(3)

Well, a year had gone by and I was on another summer visit to my mom's beautiful place. She had just gotten a new job as president of a local college, and we were celebrating. Now she was really making the big bucks. Good news for her and *great* news for Bob. My mom and I were enjoying a couple of beverages at night at around ten in her hot tub. That tub must have had chlorine laced with truth serum because every time we were in it, she would slip me new pieces of information about Bob.

"Bob hasn't had a job for a year now. He's lazy, too. Doesn't do much around here except clean the pool and lay out in the sun. He spends a lot of time on the computer, too, almost the *whole* morning. The other thing that absolutely drives me crazy is he pays for *nothing*. Not one measly meal, no help with the house payment or utilities, *nothing*."

"What's he doing on the computer for all of those hours?" I asked.

"Bob said he's checking the stock market and investing his money every day—you know, moving it around and making money."

We would all find out much later, but Bob had no money to invest; instead, he liked movies. Internet porn, and was *addicted* to it, spending hours at a time on various sites. But we wouldn't find *that* out until my mom would confiscate his computer while he was golfing, and a private investigator would check his *hard drive* to find a trail of porn sites thousands of hours long.

This kind of insanity would go on for twelve long years. Bob would be caught in a myriad of lies and deceitful behaviors; he would give some lame-ass excuse, and she would believe it. I warned my mom from beginning, but she never wanted to believe me. It was beyond frustrating, and my grandparents just didn't want her to get married again at all.

"You're doing so well on your own, and Dad and I are so proud of you. Why in heaven's name would you get married?" my grandma asked.

"Don't worry, Mother, I will never get married again as long as you're alive," she promised. It would be a short-lived promise.

(4)

Grandma Lavina took a fall and broke her hip while vacationing in Hawaii. She died later that same year. Grandpa was alone, for the first time since his early twenties, and was lost. He got sick and died the following year of lung cancer. The guy could never stop smoking.

I lived out my forties healthy and happy, but often thought of my grandparents while raising my kids. I had actually taken up long-distance running when I was thirty-nine years old, and I ran every day for eight straight years. I wasn't talking any days off and was in shape, confident, never sick, and always busy, healthy and loving my life. When I ran, I often reminisced about the many fun times I had had with all of my grandparents. My life was in perfect balance. I was thankful for my life and for a great family.

I had moved to a different middle school in my town, and taught eighth grade for fourteen years there. My kids were going to school in the same school district, and my job was more than work; it was a *lifestyle*. Our family was living the kind of life that I had for two short years as a teenager, with Michael Melvin in Albany. My kids were thriving in school and in sports, involved in many extracurricular activities. My son and daughter would not move from school to school like I did, and we would live in the same house for twenty years. This stability that my wife and I created for our kids might have been our greatest subtle achievement as parents. It allowed my children the opportunity to *just be kids* and flourish in our small, close-knit community. They never had to worry about getting the rug pulled from under their feet. They were both confident and self-motivated, played sports, and got good grades.

For the first time in my adult life, Destiny began to bring family pets into our home. She would see litters of kitties in boxes in front of stores, fall in love with one of them, beg, plead, and give me a sweet, pitiful, innocent little look. I could never say *no*. She loved her cats and we ended up taking in four: Jackie, Jenny, Romeo and Chloe. For a few years, we had three of these friendly, frisky furballs living under our roof at the same time. They would all bring chaotic, frenzied energy to our house, but provided much joy and happiness as well.

One day just before Destiny's eleventh birthday, she approached me about a *present* idea. She knew I was the *softy* of the family, and intuited that I could never say *no*.

"Dad, could we please get a puppy for my birthday?" She looked up at me with those innocent baby-blue eyes, and my heart melted right there, all over the kitchen table.

I fondly remembered my two favorite birthday presents growing up, my puppies Misty and Waddles, and said, "Let me think about it." The *thinking* didn't last very long.

My daughter really began her assault on my inner child. "Dad, I saw this cute little white-and-black puppy over at the pet store by Safeway. It's a Chihuahua, I think. It is the *only* thing I want for my birthday."

"Well, let me–" I couldn't finish my sentence, as my daughter was about to pull out the *big guns* now.

"Pretty please, I will take good care of her, clean up after her, and do extra work around the house," she pleaded.

She had done it—moved me to action by touching my heart. I said nothing, grabbed my car keys, and we were off to the local pet store to buy my daughter a puppy. The little pooch was still there when we arrived at the store, and she instantly jumped up on her hind legs, pressing her little black nose against the glass.

My daughter was right about one thing: that was the cutest puppy I had ever seen. Four hundred dollars later, we were driving home with a tiny black-and-white Chihuahua and terrier mix, our new furry family member. My daughter would name her *Chiquita,* meaning *little one* in Spanish.

(5)

"I want to bring a little bit of stability to my life by marrying Bob," my mom declared on a phone call one evening. "Besides, he reminds me of Robert De Niro, you know—an Italian-mafia bad-boy type. That kind turns me on. Besides, I love the *rough* stuff."

Bad idea, I thought, very *bad* idea. Bob had been *grooming* my mom for two years now, and had convinced *her* into trusting *him* by selling her the idea of *we*. The man was cunning, conniving and ruthless; my mom always underestimated the lengths he would go to get her money. Why? Because she truly believed he loved her. She wanted his love so badly, she would make excuses for him all of the time. It was tragic, really. It would be the battle of the two narcissists to the death. Bob would send my mom to the brink of madness.

"We are in this together," or "Trust me, we are in this thing for the *long haul*," he would say to my mom, *grooming* her for the ultimate end game.

But what was *his* end game? I believed that, best case scenario, he was hoping my mom would die, and he would get *everything*. Worst case scenario, he would get *half*. It was that simple, and *that* terrifying.

Bob and Mom got married in June in an extravagant affair in a downtown Tacoma ballroom. My mom was well connected and involved in city government. She kept her *McCormick* last name because it was known and respected in her community. She was all about being *recognized* as *popular* by other people, and would later become an elected official of her town. She would *cherish* this position of *power*; she loved being *important*. So, not surprisingly, many local and state dignitaries were invited. Bob was along for the *ride*, smiling and loving all the newfound attention.

The *Marilyn Train* was pulling out again. Choo choo! Final Destination? Halfway, *right down the middle.*

(6)

There are two kinds of people in the world, *workers* and *nonworkers*. My mom, a *worker*. Bob D'Amato, a *nonworker*. this simple truth and difference is what I believe caused their eventual divorce. Besides all the other drama and nonsense going on in this relationship, it really *blew* up when my mom tried to change her nonworking *conman* into a worker.

Bob D'Amato was a different breed of *cat*. Outwardly, he seemed polished; inwardly, he was like an *alley cat*, street smart and calculated. He was not a *worker*, though, yet still desired to be a *kept* man. He would be this kind of guy for most of the years he was married to my mom. My mom fed into Bob's laziness and enabled him in every way possible the first several years of their marriage. Bob was a spoiled, petulant child. My mom paid for everything, including: Bob's expansive, expensive wardrobe; all his dry cleaning; manicures and pedicures; tanning; dining; a country club golf membership; and all vacation expenses incurred. He had two credit cards, which she paid every month. If he didn't get his way he would pout and stay in his office *surfing* the internet. As a *president,* my mom expected her husband to be presentable.

"Bob looks pretty good as a *president's* husband, don't you think?"

"Yep," I would answer, almost throwing up in my own mouth.

My mom sold her beautiful home on the water. Bob had convinced her that it was "way too much work to maintain." They traded it in for two new homes easily divisible by two: one in town, and one in the country by the water. They were *both* in Bob and my mom's names. She called to share the exciting news.

"Bob and I just bought place on the water!"

"It's only in your name, right?" I asked, afraid of the answer I might get here.

"Why, no. It's in *both* our names."

"What in the hell are you thinking, Mom?"

"Well, it was Bob's idea. I am letting him handle *all* of the finances now. He is better at that sort of stuff anyway—he did that kind of work at Goodyear, so he's an expert."

"He's an *expert,* all right—an expert at sponging off. And he's about to *take* you to the cleaners."

By the end of the decade, Bob would have convinced my mom to have *two* homes in Washington, *two* in Arizona, and *two* timeshare properties in Mexico. I am no mathematician, but it seemed as though everything they owned was now easily divisible by TWO. Bob had done what he set out to do in the beginning; now he just had to wait for my mom to die.

I will say, during this marriage to Bob, my mom and I got close. I would call her all the time to check on her. Why? I was constantly worried and knew Bob was only in it for the money. But I still found him fun to be around; we got close, but not too close. I never trusted the man.

For the first time in a long time, *we* were taking vacations together. Bob had encouraged my mom to get four time-shares (easily divisible by two, by the way), and we were always going to fun places as a family. We traveled to Las Vegas, Honolulu, Maui and Cabo San Lucas. *We* were all having the times of our lives and I enjoyed being in my mom and Bob's company. They were fun to *hang* with and seemed to be having fun together. *We* were indeed living the good life. Bob's *grooming* of our family was now complete.

I even introduced Bob as my *father* to some friends at dinner one evening. That must have been the *kiss* of death for good old Bob. I found out one week later from my mom that things were not going well between them.

(7)

Toward the end of their marriage, my mom and Bob were living in separate houses. My mom was still footing the bill for everything and, much to the disappointment of Bob, she was still alive. This was not part of Bob's plan. Bob wanted the whole calzone to himself. To make matters worse, my mom *grew balls* one summer day in August and cut Bob off. He had jacked up both of his credit cards, and she was wondering what kind of hanky-panky her husband was now involved in.

No more money, no more country club membership, and she gave Bob a loan to buy a crappy old car to use in his new job as a newspaper delivery person. He would now have to *work* to make spending money, and Bob was not happy with this. The life of a tan, well-dressed, manicured paper boy was not what he had in mind when he signed up to be part of the *Marilyn Train* twelve years ago. Bob, after all, was a *parasite*, not wishing to work for long hours and little pay. In the beginning of their relationship, Bob had a *huge* ego, with a *huge* list of accomplishments, and a *huge salami* tucked inside his pressed Italian slacks.

I would've rather not known about that last tidbit, but sadly my mom has always had *boundary issues* when it comes to revealing information about her *sex* life. In the end, Bob was a *colossal* disappointment to my career-climbing mom. She would browbeat Bob constantly, just like she did with *Schmelvin* back in the day. Bob confided in me on a family vacation to Hawaii that he felt *emasculated* around my mom. Bob was on borrowed time.

I believe Bob went to *plan B* when my mom outlived

plan A. He took a stick of dynamite and just *blew* his marriage up, sabotaging it by getting caught posting naked pictures of himself for *men* on the internet. Bob *wanted* to get caught.

Was he a closeted gay man?

My mom said, "Hell yeah!"

I say, "Absolutely not!" It's just that he would do anything to get my mom's money.

Bob was *done* with *this* marriage and wanted to end it *once* and for *all.* He wanted a younger woman anyway—he had told me so over a couple of cocktails in Maui. Frustrated and tired of delivering newspapers in his crappy old car, he was happy to settle for half of my mom's stuff—even if that meant *showing his hairy ass* on the internet to other men for a few days. This makes complete sense to me.

Besides, Bob would be moving to beautiful and sunny Boca Raton, Florida, in a few short months. His *new* thirty-five-year-old girlfriend was already there waiting for him, keeping the bed warm. She was in it for the money as well.

It took about two years to settle this one, with lawyers from both sides hauling in a pretty penny. Bob got one house, a time-share, and some cash, and neither party was very satisfied with the deal in the end. It became *all* about *the money.* So ended marriage number seven for my mom in a bitter, nasty divorce with Bob D'Amato. I buried Bob with his heinous naked photos, erasing the hard drive from my brain and not allowing his hairy ass to haunt me in my sleep.

My mom would remain bitter for the next three years. She vowed to *never* marry again. She also vowed to *never* let a man get *his* hands on *her* money and property again.

But my mom wasn't wired to grow old *alone*. She needed to *snag* another man just for the *sport* of it. She would have to go to the body shop this time for a little tune up.

My mom slapped down twenty thousand dollars in *cash* for a face-lift from a renowned plastic surgeon in the Seattle area, and voila, and she was ready to enter the marketplace once again, looking twenty years younger. The woman was relentless. I couldn't bear to watch. I just didn't have the stomach for *it* anymore.

(8)

After a few years of struggling mightily after her divorce from Bob, my mom found husband number eight on an internet dating site, Ken Olson, a retired small-business owner. Destiny and I had helped her make a not-so-self-centered dating profile. Her previous profiles made her seem like a narcissistic, ball-busting, power-hungry real estate tycoon. We encouraged that she eliminated the braggadocio and add some *real*ness, even though her initial profile was probably more fact than fiction. Her old touched-up studio picture showing her in a black business suit was replaced with her in a bar with a cocktail, wearing a low-cut blouse. She had always been blessed with large "*thunder buckets,*" and her new profile appealed to a target audience of men who hadn't had a hard on since the Reagan administration.

The new suggestive profile worked and, after dating a few *duds*, my mom met Ken. I was happy for her, I guess. Hopefully this would be her last husband, but I made sure that there would be no need to bury Ken if this marriage ever went south; I would *refuse* to get close to him. Eight dads are more than enough! This was another car wreck waiting to happen, and this time I would just speed by the crime scene, living my own life and not looking back at the damage incurred. This was another marriage based on the values of . . . ? Hell, if I know!

Wait, I actually do know, now that I've thought about it for a minute. It goes something like this . . .

It was a match made in . . . heaven? Although all of my mom's marriages seem to start in the penthouse and end in the outhouse, knee-deep in shit—Ken would get everything he had longed for in life after his first and only wife had passed away from a long battle with *it*. I felt for the guy, actually had empathy for his situation in life. Ken created a profile on a free online dating site, hoping to get married once again. And this time, Ken was looking for a life partner with money; he dreamed of a retirement with luxury cars, travel to exotic places, cruises. He wanted to live out his retired years in a big house in Arizona with a giant man cave in which he could entertain guests and watch Seattle Seahawks games with a fully stocked bar of fifths of *top-shelf* alcohol and bottled IPA beers. He had always wanted to travel to the National Parks across America in a brand-new, customized motorhome that he had already sketched out on a cocktail napkin while drinking with his buddies after a round of golf.

He told his friends after a few Bud Lights, "You know, fellas, a diesel, customized motorhome just like the one the casino band guys drive around in—that's what I really want!" And with that, they all toasted their bottled beverages, just like buddies in beer ads. Ken would hit the lottery—he would find a woman that would fulfill all of his dreams and then some.

My mom was so intent on harpooning another man,

she would have paid almost anything to get hitched one last time. Like Ken, she went online looking for a life partner. Her motivation was a bit different than Ken's, however—she was looking for a man who could finally fill that giant hole in her heart, the one she had always tried to fill after her dad left her as a little girl. She could have chosen any platform—Plenty of Fish, eHarmony, Christian Mingle, Hot or Not, OK Cupid, FarmersOnly.com, or even Craigslist. She chose the same site Ken did, *Seniors People Meet,* because it was free. Baby boomers like Ken and my mom are thrifty and like stuff that's free. Except for that $20,000 face-lift, of course.

This would set these two geriatric lovers on a collision course of dating, hot tubbing, romance, sex and marriage, all in the matter of months. My mom was not as particular as Ken. She was looking for any man, really, with a search ethic akin to that of car shopping. That is, her future soulmate could have been new or used, broken down, damaged, rusty, black, white or blue, lazy, good for nothing, with nothing else to do.

In retrospect, I must say that my mom's marriage career is quite impressive! She married once in the nineteen fifties, once in the sixties, twice in the seventies, twice in the eighties, once in the nineties and once in the twenty-first century. Her romances went from love letters, soda fountains, and swing dancing to internet dating, Viagra, and swinging. In a twisted way, I have come to admire my mom for always trying and never giving up on the idea of finding her one and only. I hope she has found that person in Ken. I know I have found that person in my wife Barb.

My mom would survive—she always has. She is

presently living in a big home in Phoenix, Arizona, with a giant man cave for her dear Ken and his trailer park buddies. Beer flows like wine in the Olson household every Sunday during football season. Mom and Ken take exotic cruises every year and travel to National Parks across America, cruising down the highway in their new customized motorhome. They feel like rock stars, and more than surviving, my mom seems to be thriving.

(9)

My wife and I decided to sell our house of twenty years, hoping to move closer to her work. She had spent the entire time our kids were in school commuting over an hour, so, one day, we just stuck a sign in our lawn and somebody knocked on our door and bought it. We then moved to a beautiful home in Happy Valley, Oregon, *the happiest place* in Oregon, only thirty minutes from my wife's work. Our kids were full grown and out of the house.

Two weeks after the move, we were walking the track at Mountain Heights High School, a few blocks from our new home. The backdrop of the football field is the majestic snowcapped Mount Hood, the largest peak in Oregon. Staring at it as we walked around the field just took my breath away. The combination of the new school building, the tremendous athletic facilities and the scenic view made me want to teach and coach there.

"Wouldn't it be cool to work at this school? It's only two blocks from our new house. I could teach and coach here. I've always wanted to teach older, more mature kids. I could walk every day to work."

My wife agreed, "It's a beautiful school. I just love the

view of the mountain."

At the time, it was probably more of a joke or wishful thinking, but I could see myself there. It was a vision about my future that was as clear as could be. Usually, if I see something that clearly in life, I can do what is necessary to get there.

A job for an Economics teacher at Mountain Heights was posted online the very next day. I sent in my materials, wrote a thoughtful cover letter, was called in for an interview, and got the job that very same day. After twenty years of teaching middle school kids, I moved to the high school where I would teach economics to seniors.

(10)

Our first summer in Happy Valley, one of our cats, Jenny, just *ran* away. We never saw her again and have no idea what happened to her. Cats hate change, and Jenny may have tried to get back to our old house on the other side of town. We will never know for sure.

Our other cat, Chloe, died two months later after a battle with leukemia. The veterinarian drove her mobile hospital to our house and, on that October morning, Chloe was put to sleep.

The following summer, Chiquita became ill. She was diagnosed with *it*, which had invaded her stomach and gone to her lymph nodes. We tried surgery, but afterward, our veterinarian said, "I'm afraid we didn't get *it* all. *It* may come back."

It did. Chiquita died three months later. She was in so much pain at the end of her life that, in one of the hardest decisions my family has ever made, we had the veterinarian put her down. We all cried buckets of tears that day.

The following summer, as fate would have it, I guess . . . I got sick.

Maybe there was *something* in the water? Too much Round Up used on my lawn? Something toxic in our new home, asbestos, paint, carpet, other harmful chemicals? Are we living too close to power lines? I wondered. My wife even tried to blame *it* on the leather interior in my brand-new Honda Accord.

"Maybe they treated your leather interior with some chemicals you are allergic to. I think I read that somewhere," she hypothesized.

"Probably not."

The reality was, Happy Valley was not turning out to be such a *happy* place after all.

It's Back?

It has been a year and a half since my radiation treatment party. I have one more hormone injection and then am hopefully done with the *hot flashes*, the erectile dysfunction, the muscle loss, the "man boobs." I am hoping and praying for a total remission here. I don't worry about my many fathers anymore. The only father I worry about now is *father time*.

I remember the worst day of my adult life—so far, that is. It was about a year ago to this day, and I had been experiencing lower back pain for about two weeks. I've had some back pain over the past several years, but this was different, and it seemed to be getting worse.

My wife had left on vacation to Disneyland with Bronson and his wife and their two kids. My wife wanted to spend some time with her two grandkids at the happiest place on earth. Unfortunately, I couldn't get the time off from work. Bronson, now thirty-one, had all the time in the world. He happens to be a well-to-do businessman. He currently has money *shooting* out of his ass like a giant leaf blower. He is doing so well that his wife, who used to be a teacher, doesn't have to work anymore.

Don't get me wrong here; I am proud of my son, but I was feeling a little bit sorry for myself. Everyone else in my family was going on vacation, but I was a teacher who actually had to *teach* that particular week. Everyone got to go to that damned Disneyland except for me. I was beginning to feel like a poor, overweight fifth grader once again, left out of all the fun.

Because of my tremendous back pain, I became consumed by thoughts and worries about *it* returning. I had terrible nightmares each night and would wake up screaming in a cold sweat. It would take me several hours to calm myself down. By Friday, my back pain had gotten so severe I went to urgent care that evening after a long school day of teaching. I knew something was terribly wrong, and every time I saw a doctor these past two years, it always led to bad news.

I called my daughter. She was always a real *sweet* kid. She had graduated from the University of Oregon, like her older brother Bronson. I am convinced they both made the decision to be *Ducks* just to do the opposite of their father. I was of course an Oregon State *Beaver*.

Well, Destiny was now a successful Social Media Director for a small company in Portland. I had counseled her as a middle and high school student to "stay off that *damned* phone," and of course, she had turned her hand-held device into a well-paying job. Millennials, go figure.

Destiny, now a grown woman of twenty-four, came to sit with me in the waiting room of Sunnyside Kaiser Urgent Care after I had called her on my *damned* phone. I am a baby boomer and would like to take my annoying piece of shit cell phone and *chuck* it into the Pacific Ocean. *They* are the biggest distraction to a good learning environment in my high school these days. Kids are addicted to them; they are *worse* than crack cocaine. I know I'm sounding like an old fart here, "OK, boomer," but I remember back in the day when we used to call a girl on a *landline* to ask her out on a date. Now you can just text someone to break up with them.

My loving millennial daughter was there in a flash, smiling with a deck of cards in hand and her precious cell phone pressed against her ear. She gave me a great, big, one-armed hug, clutching her iPhone with her other for dear life. I almost started to cry.

"It's going to be all right, Dad," she reassured.

Those were the only words I needed from her to calm me down. We played cribbage and waited patiently for two hours in the large waiting area on a chaotic Friday night at the urgent care wing. I had handed down all of the card games I learned as a kid from my grandparents to my own kids, and we loved playing.

I saw two different nurses, both of whom probed me about my health history and took my blood pressure. The first time my blood pressure was *sky*-high; the second time, it was *normal*. Being in a hospital always makes my blood pressure go *way* up.

I was called back again to a small room where I waited on a table—another hour alone with my thoughts. A young, dark-haired doctor came in, said, "Hello," and shook my hand. She asked me my name and birth date and began to look at my expansive health history over the past two years on her computer. She double-checked my medication. I currently take about twenty pills a day, mostly for hives. My immune system has been compromised the past few years, thus the random itchy rash all over my body from time to time. To think only a few years ago, I had never been sick a day in my life. I've never even had a cavity before. Now I was one of Kaiser Permanente's best customers, a *pill-poppin' junkie* in my late fifties.

"So, you *had* prostate cancer, I see in your health records here, Mr. Kirby?"

I lowered my head, paused for a *long* moment, lifted my head up and said in a moment of total clarity, "No, I *have* cancer. I had forty radiation treatments and am currently getting hormone treatments." There, I finally said *it*. I *HAVE* CANCER.

"Hmm, I see. You are here because of lower back pain, correct?

"Yes, that is correct."

"Let's check your back."

She laid me down on the table and began to poke and prod at my back, contorting my body like *Gumby*. She touched my stomach, kneaded my back, grabbed my *love handles* and even *felt up* my *man boobs*. At that very moment, once again, I knew God in his almighty wisdom was punishing me in my later years for my past transgressions and awful treatment of women in my twenties. I had sadly conceded once again that he had sent out yet another young, beautiful, female doctor to *violate* my old flabby body, humiliating me behind closed doors.

"Does it hurt there?"

"Yes."

"How about th–"

"YEEES!"

"Hmm. I am very concerned here, Mr. Kirby. Prostate cancer sometimes likes to *move* to the spine. That does concern me quite a bit," she repeated. "This is out of my specialty area. I'll need to consult another doctor. Be back in a flash!" She pointed her finger to the ceiling, flashed a broad smile, and she was gone in an instant. And there I sat, for another hour on that same table, this time thinking that I may indeed have cancer now in my spine. Holy shit, I thought. I'm a dead man walking.

She finally returned. "Mr. Kirby, we are going to have you get a CAT scan here tonight and will have the results for you later this evening. If the cancer has spread to your spine, rest assured that the images will let us know for sure."

I was led to a small waiting room area with lockers. I exchanged my clothes for another *damned* patient robe. I sat there alone, waiting. And waiting. And waiting. My thoughts and worries now almost *paralyzed* me. A nurse finally came with an IV for my arm to fill my body with imaging dye to get a better look at my spine. I was led to the machine and strapped in; it took a mere ten minutes of my life to see if my cancer had indeed spread.

I changed, went back to the doctor's office, and was told by that same doctor, "Mr. Kirby. We will let you know in about an hour whether your cancer has spread."

"Should I wait?" I asked.

"No. Go home and relax. Tell you what, I will personally call you in about two hours."

Relax? How the hell am I supposed to relax? I thanked the doctor for her time, flashed a fake smile, shook her hand, and vacated the premises in haste. My daughter pulled up the getaway car and we were off. I arrived at home at one in the morning, my daughter dropping me off.

"It'll be all right, Dad. Don't worry about it!"

As I got out of the car, I gave my daughter two thumbs-up, flashed another broad, fake smile, waved to her like I was on a float in a parade. My one and only precious daughter drove off into the night, and I was alone again with my thoughts. After entering the house, I proceeded to my office, sat down, and placed my cell phone on the desk. I leaned back slowly in my leather chair and tried to relax, but just couldn't.

The thought of dying scared me to death. In those two *long* hours of unknowing, I was petrified my cancer had spread to my spine. If that was indeed the case, my days would be numbered on this earth, and I was a paranoid little boy again, wondering when *he* would come to *bite* me.

I thought about my life with D.L. once again. It had just occurred to me, in my moment of despair, that D.L. was much like a *cancer* to me all my life. He was a monster, a random aggregation of nightmares, that I could never totally get rid of. When my mom divorced D.L., I vowed to myself as a young boy that I would leave *It* behind for good. Little did I know that he was an old *boomerang*. Every time I would try and *throw* him *away*, he would *come* back.

Cancerous thoughts of my youth began to invade my brain once again; that damned lumber mill in Klawock and that *other* poor little boy, Shawn. Some of these things I hadn't thought about for forty plus years because I had buried them. I had to compartmentalize them, it seemed, to move forward. But now, I had to revisit the *darkness* of D.L. Kirby once again.

(1)
I drifted off; my mind went back to that summer *from*

hell, the one after my freshman year at college, my time once again spent with D.L.

We were in a lumber camp in Alaska while my mom moved into Dick Willing's place for the summer. I was hurt and felt abandoned. Lost at college. Too much partying, not enough studying. I had no place to go. Dick didn't like kids (even though he was a high school counselor), and my mom seemed to have forgotten why she had kids in the first place. I couldn't even see my dog Waddles, and she would never be *my* dog again. She would now be Dick Willing's *little* pet. I blamed my mom.

I had blocked this memory out of my mind for over forty years; it just *hurt* too much. I had no one to talk to as a nineteen-year-old frat boy. No one would've believed me anyway.

D.L. Kirby was now living and working in a lumber mill in Klawock, Alaska, a tiny village of mostly Tlingit natives on Prince of Wales Island. It had been years since my mom had let me visit him. He had been a deadbeat dad for a very long time. But she was now busy with Dick Willing, and *they* decided I needed money for college.

D.L. was building a steam-powered plant for the Alaska Timber Company, a proposed three-year project for mill owner Ed Head. I would live in a trailer for the summer directly on the lumber mill property with D.L. and Chief Financial Officer Steve Westwood. D.L. and I would share a small room with twin beds. It was bizarre to me that I, a young man of nineteen, was now bunking with a man that had chronically molested me as a child. Was this allowed to happen because I had never told my mom *the secret*? Probably so. I was being a victim here. Not fully owning my life as a young man. Not speaking up to my mom or the police long ago was catching up to me. How was she to know that I was being sent off to *summer camp* with a sexual predator? They had settled things on the phone, and it was to be the former *Rotund Buffoon* and me as bunkmates for the entire summer in southeastern Alaska.

D.L. would spend the rest of June planning the first phases of power plant construction, so he would not need me to assist him quite yet—he had bigger plans for me later. In the meantime, anyone at the mill who needed help could use my services. That first month, I would have many teachers who would share their craft and teach valuable life *lessons* along the way.

My first day on the job, I was assigned to be a *gofer* for Ed Head—the boss, "the old man," as D.L. referred to him in private. Ed had started in the lumber mill business in northern California in his thirties and had served as a boiler engineer on the same PT boat as John F. Kennedy in WWII. He was a grizzled *old coot* now in his late fifties, looking more like seventy or eighty. I had been around lots of *rough-and-tumble* elders growing up—just think of my two grandpas and my grandma Mel. So, the first sight of him did not alarm me at all. However, the tone in his voice and the way he spoke did, as I was to meet him in the boiler room at 8:04 a.m. sharp! You see, the *boss's* special skill was *yelling.*

"*God, dammit!* You're late, it's eight oh five! Can't you *fucking* tell time?"

"Yes, sir, I mean no, sir, I mean . . ." I was in deep trouble five minutes into the job.

"Get me a *goddamn* pipe wrench from my toolbox next door *now*, and make it *snappy.*"

I started to walk, and he yelled, "Run, *God dammit,* run!"

Holy crap, I bolted out of that room like I was *shot* out of a cannon. In one minute, I had learned that anytime Ed asked you to do anything, you *ran.* He expected it and I delivered a *dead sprint* on cue hundreds of times that summer. What I *didn't* know was anything about tools. I couldn't tell you the difference between a *standard* screwdriver and a *Phillip's* head screwdriver as a frat guy. So, I pulled out what I thought to be a *pipe* wrench bolted back to the boiler room.

"That's not a *fucking* pipe wrench, it's a *crescent* wrench for *Christ's* sake." He *threw* the thing at my head; I *ducked* and it hit the wall. That was a close one.

"Now, run and get me a pipe wrench this time."

I ran again to the toolbox, this time throwing aside the *monkey* wrench. This is one of the only tools I knew because Michael Melvin had used a *monkey* wrench to fix the toilet long ago during *Operation Shitty Perm.* I grabbed what I thought was a *pipe* wrench and returned, panting.

"*Holy Moses,* you don't know shit about tools, son. Follow me."

We charged to the toolbox in the other room, and Ed pulled out a *pipe* wrench and *stuck* it my face. "This is a damned *pipe* wrench, *got it?*"

I got it, all right. It was that stupid old *monkey* wrench I had cast aside, the only tool I knew in the whole darned box. Boy was I stupid. But I would learn plenty on the job that summer from Edward Head. Day one, I learned three things about my new boss: he likes to yell; run like *hell* if he asks you to get or do something; and this wrench has at least two names.

279

That evening, over a couple of beers and a shot of whiskey, Ed told D.L., "Your boy don't know *shit* about tools, have him take a nap and report to *Old Bill* at eleven sharp tonight, by the *head rig* in the mill."

D.L. had to explain to me what a *head rig* was, of course. "It's the *big saw* at the entrance to the lumber mill that makes the initial cut in the log," he explained as he guzzled his third shot of whiskey. "The *sawyer*, manning the *head rig*, turns the logs into *cants*, or planks of wood."

I was at the *head rig* at eleven on the dot and no Old Bill. By about eleven forty-five, though, he came weaving and wobbling his way through the mill's back door, drinking from a tall silver thermos and eating a baloney sandwich. He started to laugh out loud. "Boy, I'm glad you made it! My name is Bill." He stuck out his big old meat hook and shook my hand.

I could smell alcohol on his breath. D.L. had warned me that Old Bill was "strange but harmless." Old Bill used to be a master welder, but several years ago, a bulldozer accidently pushed a giant shovel of bark chips on top of him, burying him alive for several minutes until he was dug out by coworkers. After the accident, he was never quite the same in the head, and his hands shook constantly. Ed felt bad for him, so Old Bill had become the night watchman. It was a job that Ed had graciously created for him. So, what did the man watch all night? While Ed would say, "To keep *intruders, thieves* out of my mill," Old Bill would say, "I'm watching for *alien spaceships.*"

No more than five minutes into our evening, Bill lays out the expectations for tonight's graveyard shift as his new "little helper."

"Take this here flashlight boy, and keep it pointed down—the *aliens* will get *spooked* if you beam that thing at their headlights!"

"Spaceships have headlights?" I asked politely, playing along with the old man.

"You betcha they do, you betcha!" He laughed wildly and took another swig from his gargantuan thermos.

"Have you ever seen any *aliens*?" I asked.

"Seen 'em? Hell, I *help* 'em! *All* the time!

I was now intrigued. "How do you help them?"

"See this here tool belt?" Old Bill wore the same denim overalls always, along with his black boots and red-and-black flannel shirt. At night, he strapped on his "magic tool belt," as he called it. He was pointing at his fifty-pound belt of pride and joy.

"Yeah, I see it, *so*?"

"So? This here is my 'magic tool belt!' I carry special intergalactic tools on it given to me by aliens on their many journeys to see me."

I was trying to find a line in his story here. "So, let me get this straight—you're really an alien spaceship mechanic?"

"Damn straight, now you're catchin' on!" He took a hard tap off his thermos and belched.

Of course, we waited around all night for them to show up. I fell asleep up next to a pole for about a half-hour, and upon waking up, found Old Bill grinning from ear to ear.

"They came in their spaceship and I fixed it, sent 'em on their way. I was gonna wake you, but you looked so peaceful restin' there."

"Nice job, Bill, way to go!" I cheered as much as I could, nodding back to sleep.

I had several other *life teachers* that first month at the mill. Some of these guys reminded me of older, creepier versions of my Kappa frat brothers back home: they looked twenty years older than their age, had missing teeth, were deadbeat dads, alcoholics, and were *all* looking to escape some problem in the lower forty-eight.

Bobby *Bean* Johnson, a camp carpenter, told me, "You know, you've never really made love until you've had sex with a *fat* woman!" The guy was rail thin, about six foot three and one hundred forty pounds, and missing his two front teeth. I tried to block that image from my mind the rest of the summer.

Virgil Gill, the shop foreman, who liked to get drunk and sing with the band on Friday nights, advised me to "*never* get married, kid. Why would you ever want to take a tuna fish sandwich to a banquet?" He had several girlfriends that summer, and they all looked like garden gnomes with wigs.

And finally, Walter *Whimpey* Watson, a millwright who I was job shadowing, showed up drunk his first day to work and fell into the *debarker* machine. This was a dangerous shredding machine with sharp blades that remove the bark from the logs. Luckily for *Whimpey*, the *debarker* was off.

He left after only three hours on the job, beat up and badly bruised. As he left to catch his seaplane to Ketchikan he said, "Kid, stay away from 'the sauce,' it's the devil's *Kool-Aid!*" I probably should have paid more attention to that succinct piece of advice from the skinny old millwright; it would have saved me all sorts of pain, heartache, and *hangovers* down the line.

(2)

My first month went by quickly, and it was time to go to work for D.L. My former father, master heavy equipment operator, had one goal in mind for me that summer. He was going to transform me from a *Candy Ass* to a REAL MAN, like him. I was to meet him in the morning at the "back lot" where all the work vehicles were parked at eight. When I arrived, he was sitting on the track of a crane, smoking a cigarette.

"Glad you could make it, Pard, you're mine now!" he said, puffing on his Marlboro.

"Good morning," I saluted. "What are we doing today?"

"You know, Pard, your mom and pantywaist stepdad had no clue how to raise you kids!"

"I think they did a pretty good job."

"Really, what do call a dick with an Afro?"

"What?"

"Michael Melvin!" He still knew how to crack himself up.

"Not funny."

Now D.L.'s jokes were more cutting, and revealed the rancor he held for the people who pushed the state of Oregon to garnish his wages for unpaid child support.

"Your stepdad is such a pantywaist, he sat on a Cheerio and it turned into a Froot Loop."

"What ARE we doing today?" I repeated, trying to get him to focus on the day.

"Behold, my boy, these are the rigs that I will teach you to operate this summer!" He was now strolling down the line of machinery like a military commander inspecting his troops.

"Pard, this is a D9 Caterpillar, here's a D8 Cat, we got a 988 Front End Loader, a Case 450 Backhoe, and of course my little beauty here, a 1971 American Crawler Mobile Crane. You will learn how to operate all of these 'bad boys' this summer!"

"How in the heck am I going to do that?"

"Well, I'm going to teach you, of course!"

"How stupid of me to even ask."

"For the next couple of weeks, we are going to be clearing some heavy debris from the power plant worksite, and I'm going to teach you how to be a *rigger* while I operate the crane."

"What will I need to learn?"

"You will act as my eyes and ears on the ground, learn to secure loads safely, and I will teach you the signals you will give me when I'm in the crane's cabin."

The first week, D.L. did deliver on his promise, teaching me most of what I needed to know to clear the work site with the crane. The problems came in week two. D.L. had been on his best behavior the first month while staying in the trailer and drinking only a few beers and or shots of whiskey. Part two of his education of the *Candy Ass* involved teaching me how to "drink like a man." I call this *night school* portion of my summer adventure *Kito's Cave Volume II*.

During month number two, we would take the short, seven-mile drive to Craig, Alaska, and bar hop. The two local watering holes in Craig were Hill Bar and The Craig Inn, and D.L. would pay to get me "loaded up" with liquor every night after work. The drinking age in Alaska was nineteen, so I was old enough to partake in all the alcoholic hospitality that Craig had to offer. This was not the *child's play* of my fourth-grade bar-hopping days of Roy Rogers and Oly beer four dotters at the Petersburg bars with my sister. This was *bellying up* to the bar with the *big boys* and downing some whiskey every night! D.L. and I went out together to the bars forty straight nights that summer.

Now, I can assure you that this binge drinking affected our work in every negative way. Much more so for D.L., as he could down three times as much alcohol as I in any given social setting. He started showing up to the job site either hungover or still drunk from the night before. One day he almost electrocuted himself by swinging the giant crane boom into a set of low-hanging power lines. Luckily, I had given the signal for *stop*, or he would have been *dead on arrival* at the Craig hospital that morning. Another day, he walked right off the crane without using the ladder, falling to the ground and breaking his foot. Now he limped to the bar and the job site with the aid of a walking cane.

That summer he taught me how to run all the equipment, except for the crane. He taught *me* to run this equipment for *him* because he was too hungover to do the work *himself*. This was scary because he would give me a two-minute tutorial and I would climb aboard the big machine and learn by trial and error. This was not safe, and I'm lucky I didn't die that summer.

"Pard, these are the foot pedals on the D9 Cat, you go like this, see? And these are the hand levels to steer and use the blade, see? Now get up there and letter rip tatter chip!"

It was a life lesson of character and courage, each day I stepped on one of those expensive pieces of equipment and took command of the job at hand.

No day on the job would have been complete without a little hazing by the washed-up heavy equipment operator. We would attach a small wire basket onto the crane hook and D.L. would hoist me hundreds of feet in the air and then swing me about wildly. I crashed into more than one structure that last month. When he was really in a mood to mess with my mind, he would push the crane lever down, letting me free fall a hundred feet, and STOP *just* before I hit the ground. It was a *white-knuckle* ride from hell, just like our days together on the Ferris wheel.

For the first time in my life, people were starting to notice something was not quite right with this father-and-son relationship.

"Quit *riding* your boy so hard," Ed would say on a weekly basis.

"I *hate* the way your dad is using you at the power plant site, he's dangerous and unsafe," Bean Johnson observed.

I had had enough of *hazing*. The other mill workers in my ear had granted me confidence as well. For the second time in my life, I confronted my second dad after he swung me into a giant steel beam hundreds of feet in the air. I almost flipped out. I told him to immediately "STOP!" This time, it would be a toe to toe, in your face showdown.

"Geez, D.L. Stop this shit right now. You're going to get me *killed*."

"Don't be such a candy ass, like your goofy pantywaist stepdad, Pard." Always was so creative with the names. "You know, Pard, life's a bitch and then you *die*." He looked at me and just laughed out loud, bullying me, taunting me to say something back.

Hearing these words from my childhood, seeing that evil smile hearing that demented laugh—it all just made me snap. "*Fuck you*, D.L., you are a miserable old son of a bitch. *Stop* harassing me or I'm going to *knock* your *fucking* block off!" I was as tall as him now—younger, stronger, and in better shape. I was glaring at him and he knew I meant business. He had seen this hateful glare from me as a nine-year-old boy. I could again see the fear in his eyes. He knew I had called him out on his abusive behavior again and he was *afraid* of what I might do next.

After several seconds of staring each other down, he backed away, took a few slow steps backward, bowed his head, and began to cry like a baby. "Imma sorry, Pard, I'm a drunkin' old fool and I luvs ya. I just don't know how to show it. I learned how to be this way from my own dad. He was a mean old son of a bitch. He used to burn my arms with cigarettes and whip me with an old hickory switch and other cruel stuff. Twisted, evil crap I had to endure as a kid."

"Fuck you D.L., I should have told my mom *and* called the police that night. But I didn't. You are a *coward* who abuses little kids. I know what you *did* to little Shawn in your motorhome. How many other kids have you *fucked* over the years? You are an *evil, disgusting*, child *molester*, probably just like your own dad. You should be in jail with all the other rapists." He said nothing, turned and walked whimpering to his trailer for the rest of the day.

I was in no mood to feel sorry for the old man. I could have put my arm around him before he left and said, "It's OK, D.L. I understand," but I didn't. My contempt and hate for him ran too deep. I turned my back on him and walked to the mill to finish my day of work on the power plant myself. I made a vow that day that, if I ever had children of my own, I would stop this family cycle of abuse and be a *good* father to my own kids. I hoped I would one day be a dad like Michael Melvin had been to me. Why had my mom left Melvin and continued to pawn me off on D.L. Kirby? It was about time for me to have a sit-down, heart-to-heart talk with my mom. There were things I needed to finally get off my chest. She needed to know about *the secret*.

I had survived the summer, despite D.L.'s careless and reckless antics.

(3)

I would go back for a second summer to Klawock to make money for college. I had no other choice and no place to stay in the summer once school was out; the fraternities were closed for the summer. My mom was immersed in her Dick Willing drama, and she had a very short memory of that tidbit about my childhood abuse that I shared with her last fall. It was like it *never* happened, and I was evidently not welcome to stay the summer at *Dick's place*.

"Dick doesn't want any kids around in the summer, Mark."

"But, Mom, I won't be a bother. I will find a job and could crash in your basement with Waddles—I can pay rent—"

"You're not getting the idea here. Dick spends the entire year with kids and needs a break. Besides, Dick never wanted to have kids of his own and he certainly doesn't want to have any *step* kids hanging around. He says it would make him feel old. I don't want to make Dick angry."

"I get it, but it is *your* place, too."

"Why don't you go back and work for your Dad. It will provide the both of you an opportunity to *mend fences.*"

"*Holy crap,* Mom. You're the one who doesn't *get it.* You *never* have." *Mend* fences? That *fence* had been torn down long ago.

"You know, young man, if I had to do it all over again, I probably never would have had kids in the first place either. I could have finished college and focused on my career earlier."

"Bye, Mom. I'll see you in the fall." I hung up the phone, and that was that.

I was *pissed.* Do I have to explain why? I now know for certain that she only cared about herself and not her kids. That she never wanted to be a mom. That she never wanted me in the first place, and I was probably a mistake. She only brought my sister into the world to please D.L. We were always on the back burner. She was now desperately trying to save her fourth marriage by doing whatever the selfish Dick wanted. I knew this bond of unholy matrimony would ultimately end like *all* the others. So, I was off to Alaska for one more summer with the sadistic heavy equipment operator.

This time, things would be different in Alaska. D.L. would get fired for being drunk on the job within the first two weeks of our second summer together. I barely saw him for my entire stay there. He parked his motorhome at the bar in town that summer and almost drank himself to death. He had become the *town drunk.* I, on the other hand, for four hundred bucks a month, lived in a tiny room in the lumber camp bunk house. I worked sorting lumber the entire summer and loved it! I was on my own, working hard, building muscles, making lots of money—I enjoyed being part of my *new* family at the mill. But D.L. had become a source of shame and embarrassment, and would sadly remain part of my life.

(4)

About a year into my stay in Anchorage after dropping out of college, I had strange and frightening chance encounter with Shawn—the little boy who visited our house on the motorhome trip with D.L. He recognized me right off.

It was well after two in the morning on a Saturday night of partying; the bars had just closed. My best friend, Perry, and I were walking out of a bar on Spennard Boulevard, a seedy part of the city where vagrants and prostitutes dwelled. Why we had drifted to that part of town—it had to do with two women who would end up leaving the bar for a couple of biker types. We were now extremely intoxicated and making our way back to our car a few blocks away. Mid-stagger, down the dimly lit street, Shawn jumped in front me, drinking a pint out of a crinkled brown paper bag.

"Hey, are you Mark, D.L. *fucking* Kirby's boy?"

The skinny street dweller took me aback—a small "yes" was all I could muster. His hair was long and dirty, smile missing some teeth. He wore torn jeans, a dirty white T-shirt, and had a lit cigarette in his mouth. I thought he must be shaking me down for money. Perry, who didn't mind mixing it up on occasion, especially after drinking a few, stepped in between us.

"What the hell do you want, punk?"

"Hey, it'sh me buddy boy, Shawn!" The boy of about

eighteen peered at me over Perry's shoulder. "I met you when you were a teenager in Oregon, remember me? I was your house guest for a couple of days' way back when with D.L. Do you remember me?"

"I remember you, Shawn," I replied, recalling for the first time that night long ago, which I had pained to forget. My endless nights of partying the past several years had done a nice job of suppressing those dark memories from my past. "What are you doing here?"

"Ah, I'm in between jobs, doing a little 'tough guy boxing' at a bar on the west side of town—Gussie Lamoure's, ever heard of it? Won me fifty dollars last week, but got my face tore up pretty bad, ya see?" Shawn had two black eyes, a cut nose and a fat lip. He looked like he had recently been in a head-on collision with a cement mixer.

"I know the place, home of the twenty-five-cent drink, right?"

"That's the one alright!" Shawn staggered, either intoxicated or high or both. He grabbed my hand and squeezed it, glaring at me with desperate eyes. I could see the needle marks all up and down his skinny, dirty arms, and knew Shawn was in bad shape. He suddenly turned white and started shaking. Looking around in all directions, paranoid, he said, "Your dad's not with you, is he?"

Perry, not knowing our history, said, "What's wrong with you man, you look like you've seen a ghost or something."

"I've seen that son of a bitch D.L. a few times. Down here in fucking Spennard, you see, going into the liquor store to buy his booze, to get liquored up and probably play with little boys. But he never sees me. I make sure of that. No way man! I would never let that *fat fuck* see me or touch me again. No way, no how! He used to call me his *little pard*. Man, I was just a little kid. I can't get those damned nightmares outta my head man. Please help me *get rid* of them, dude."

He was pounding the side of his head with both hands in frustration like a *mad man*, and began to cry, getting angry angrier the more he talked to us, now shouting, "If I had me a gun the last time I saw ole D.L., I would have shooted that old perverted bastard right in the nuts! Taken away his miserable manhood for good! He took away my innocensh as a kid, yeah, my innocensh. What a twisted fuck, that guy! I hate your dad, I hate him, with all my might! He is a monster! I never could get my shit together in school after that, that trip! I was a mess, a fucking basket case! I could never focus in class, never learned to read or write when I was little. I was always behind the other kids in class and hated school. Pissed my pants right in the middle of reading class in second grade. Kids never let *that one* go. I was humiliated, man. I skipped school, got into fights, punched my history teacher, got kicked out of my high school here in Anchorage when I was sixteen. Went to *juvie* for two years and here I am, out on the street. Either you guys got a fucking light, man? I am fucking wigging out here."

Shawn looked exhausted, absolutely *spent* after ranting on and on for minutes. He reached in his back jeans pocket for another cigarette.

Perry and I looked at each other not knowing what to say. Shawn stared back at us, hoping we could somehow save him from his despair. I pathetically responded to his cry for help, not knowing what else to say, "Do you need some money, Shawn?"

"Thanks, man, I appreciates it, I do, anything would help me, man." He stumbled to the side, almost falling over in a heap on the sidewalk.

I pulled out twenty dollars of my tip money from my wallet, gave it to Shawn, and he was off in an instant. Twenty measly bucks. That was all I could give a kid who needed so much more from me in his desperate time of need that evening. He left us that night as a hopeless young victim of child abuse, an addict who was mentally unstable. He was a young man living on the street who was drowning himself in drugs and alcohol to kill the pain from his past. Pete and I saw him head directly for the liquor store for another bottle of booze. I had given him a temporary twenty-dollar distraction from his problems. I did not feel good about it.

As I watched Shawn lope away to liquor store, I saw a young man who was definitely broken and never fixed. He had let D.L. get the *best* of him. I was *pissed* at D.L. Even more so at myself. I realized at that very moment, Shawn and I were different, but we were the *same*. My guilt was heavy. I could have done so much more to help the boy back when he visited our family in the motorhome. I could have told my parents about the *secret*. But I was too *weak* to help him. I owned my culpability, but it was *way* too late. That was the last time I ever saw Shawn. I wondered why I had dealt with my abuse better than Shawn had as a teenager? Or had I? It was obvious to me, we were both self-medicating our trauma with alcohol.

Perry and I walked that night at least two miles back to my apartment, too drunk to drive home. At least we hadn't been stupid enough to get behind the wheel that evening, although the encounter with Shawn had sobered us both up a little. I knew at some point I would have to quit my partying ways and grow up. I needed to go back to college, finish what I had started and get my *shit* together. Like Shawn with his twenty, I was using the partying as temporary distraction.

On our walk home, Perry asked, "What in the *hell* was that all about?"

I told Perry the whole incredible and almost unbelievable story of my second dad, D.L. All of IT. The ABUSE! He found it hard to believe as he had met D.L. on a couple of occasions at a local bar I had taken him to.

"I thought D.L. was just a funny, lovable old teddy bear," Perry said.

"That's what everyone usually thinks when they meet him," I said. "It makes what *HE* did to me as a kid even worse in my mind now, as people think he is somehow a good person."

Perry would be the only friend that I would share my childhood secret to, the only male adult I would ever trust enough to share this secret with, and we would be friends for life.

(5)

D.L. was never really part of my life when I left Anchorage. I had only seen him when he crashed my sister's wedding. D.L. had called me from Alaska twice during this time period, once to tell me he had diabetes. The second time to tell me he had his right leg amputated just below the knee. This was his second operation already on that leg.

"Have you stopped drinking?" I asked.

"Not yet, Pard."

"You better stop now or you're going to kill yourself!"

"I know, Pard, I know. It's been real tough for me lately. Been really hitting the ol' sauce. Did you hear about Shawner?"

"You mean Shawn? No I didn't."

"He was found last week, dead in his apartment. Put a gun to his head and shot himself."

"No *way*." I about dropped the phone and my feelings of sorrow for D.L. Anger was the only way, now, through which to deal with this cancer of a man.

"Get your life together, D.L., and stop drinking. And quit *ruining* other people's lives." I hung up on the drunken bastard after listening to ten more minutes of his incoherent blubbering.

My former father would not listen to my warnings. D.L would have four more operations on both of his legs and be a double amputee before the decade was over. He *finally* stopped drinking once he lost his second leg.

(6)

When my son was a sophomore in high school, *he* came back one *last* time to *haunt* me. It would be the last time I would see him—*alive,* that is. D.L. came to visit my family for the first time ever. I had not seen him since my sister's wedding twelve years ago. Now that I was a father of two kids of my own, I wanted to put all that childhood *crap* behind me.

He called on the phone and asked me if he could stay for a week; through my teeth, I said yes. He had called Grace as well, but she declined. She had completely *cut* him *off* and would *never* let her father around her two daughters. I respected Grace greatly for making a stand. Why in the *hell* did I say "yes" to the *disgusting* old codger? Maybe I wanted to show *him* that despite all his abuse over the years, I had turned out just *fine*. I wanted to prove to him that I was a *good* dad.

My son was aware of the abuse I had suffered at the hands of my second dad; my daughter Destiny was not. She was a third grader at the time.

Barb was very aware of my upbringing and was none too happy when I shared who was spending a week with us. "You are letting a child molester into our home," she said.

"It's all right, I will watch him. Besides, he doesn't drink anymore and is missing both of his legs," I assured.

Now I found myself making excuses for D.L., and I couldn't figure out why. I should have just said *no,* just like I did when I was a kid. But D.L. and I had a history together. I would put up with him again for one more week, I thought, and then we would be done, *finished.*

Uncle Timmy was probably right that while ago: My first name was *Hairy* and my last name was V-a-g-i-n-a, *Vagina*. I hadn't checked my driver's license for a while, but I am almost certain *that* was the name on the DMV-issued card, as I listened to my wife tell me what a fool I was for letting D.L. into our home. I deserved the tongue lashing; I shouldn't have been such a coward and said yes. I felt sorry for the guy, probably burying a lot of my ill feelings and hatred toward him in the back of my mind for the past thirty years. That hatred would come out in the next couple of days in a rather vindictive way.

Not since my trip up the Alcan highway had I spent

any significant time with D.L. He was now to enter our family home as *half* the man he used to be. D.L. did not drink anymore and his demeanor was definitely more laid back. I was *halfhearted* about seeing him once again. With the loss of both of his legs, he came across as a poor little puppy dog who had lost his way. My *half*-father entered our home aided by two prosthetic legs and crutches. For the first time, I noticed he was humble and did not have to be even *half* the center of attention. What he was looking for from us was a place to stay and people to take care of his needs on a daily basis. This was his *half*-baked scheme. But my wife and I would have none of that.

"You got a nice comfortable place here, Pard. It ain't *half* bad. Looks like you have some extra room?"

Half bad, eh? You are the one who is *half* bad, I thought to myself, chuckling out loud. I tried to instantly discourage D.L. (the now Delusional Legless) limper from getting too comfortable in his new surroundings. "Not really, Barb's mom stays here quite often, and the extra room is for her."

"I only take up *half* the room now!" he laughed. It gave everyone in the room the creeps—even me, although I was crafting similar puns in my head. The awkward silence turned into everyone staring at me for a reasonable response to the *half*-witted old man.

"D.L., we just don't have any room. Sorry. Don't start getting all *half*-cocked here." My wife and son laughed at my quick rebuttal. Now, we had room, but I did *not* want D.L. bunking with us for more than a week. I had had plenty of *intimate* bonding time in my past life, and was looking for no more life lessons from him. Still, I did have an idea up my sleeve for the former "Rotund Buffoon," and had been waiting patiently all of my life for such an opportunity to come.

"Hey D.L., you probably noticed we had a ski boat parked outside in the driveway. Are you interested in coming to the lake with us tomorrow?"

"Sure, Pard, that would be great. We used to have some great times up at Loon Lake when you were a kid. Do you remember those fun times we had?"

"I remember, I remember." I was now thinking back to all of the mental *hazing* D.L. had inflicted on me as a young boy on our many trips to the lake.

We awoke the next day to find the *half*-asleep D.L. the first one up. In the old days, he would have been finishing off his third Bloody Mary by now. Today, he was sitting in a chair with his prosthetic legs off and at the foot of the kitchen table, eating some oatmeal and blueberries, washing it down with some orange juice.

"I see that you're eating pretty healthy these days, D.L.?" my wife inquired.

"Ever since I found out I had diabetes, I changed my eating habits and stopped drinking."

This was *a half*-truth. It took him several years to change his habits, and he only quit drinking after fearing he might lose his second leg. Of course, it was too late.

"I understand you used to be a pretty big drinker?" my wife asked, now pouring him a second glass of orange juice.

"Not really, I only had a few beers on occasion."

I laughed out loud and said nothing. That was the most ridiculous, lame, *half*-assed thing I had ever heard.

"Let's get ready to go to Hagg Lake!" I enthused, refusing to hear more of his bullshit.

As we got ready for the trip, D.L. stayed on the periphery of the "loading zone" taking pictures. He did not joke anymore, and he wasn't his old drunken boisterous self. I asked him to be selective on his picture taking without being *too* rude.

"If you take any pictures of my kids today, I'm gonna throw your camera into the lake."

"Yes, Pard," he responded all sheepish, bowing his head and hopping away from the boat, as he used his crutches to get around.

D.L.'s *Mad Men* days of yesteryear—pinstriped Brooks Brothers suits, fashionable skinny ties, and matching pocket squares—were ancient history now. He was not a *mad man* but sad, sorry, and broken. He had become a pathetic, crippled, shell of his former self. Even the *Rotund Buffoon* act he had perfected when I was a boy was distant memory now. The one-liners and tasteless jokes were now replaced by the words and demeanor of a *lost soul* who was overwhelmed with the sorrow of a once-promising life gone chillingly wrong.

We all piled in my white Ford Expedition, the perfect family vehicle for this kind of trip. *Chiquita* was the last one to get in the car. She sat on Destiny's lap as always; she loved to ride in the boat just like Misty did when I was a young boy. I had a little plan for this day *up my sleeve*, and I was snickering to myself the more I thought about. *Karma* would be a *bitch* for good ole D.L. on this day. It couldn't happen to a nicer guy, I thought. We took the one-hour drive to Hagg Lake and put the boat into the water. As I pulled out of the water, I parked my vehicle and boat trailer in the parking lot and made my way back down the boat ramp by foot.

D.L. was on the boat with my wife and kids and was yelling and waving his arms to get my attention. *"Pard,* I left my legs up in your car, can you get them please?"

I retrieved his prosthetic legs with his hush puppy shoes attached, and was now lugging each of them under my arms and around my hips. I started to laugh while imagining the sight of me, carrying those two artificial limbs down the boat ramp. I felt like an old gunslinger from the Wild West, my six-shooters in each hand, ready to take on my sworn enemy, D.L. Kirby. It was *high noon,* and I was ready to *shoot it out* with the old codger right in the middle of Hagg Lake.

Everybody took turns either skiing, wake boarding or inner tubing that morning. Destiny was the last one on the water with the tube, so the yellow flotation device was already hooked up to the boat when we pulled her in. This was where I would make my move, the moment I had been waiting for since I was a kid hanging on to D.L.'s shoulders for dear life as he skied around.

"D.L., it looks like you're the only one left. How about a ride on the *old tube?*" I was chuckling to myself in anticipation of some great fun at the creepy photographer's expense.

"I don't know, Pard?" he paused, trying to make an excuse. "I haven't been out in the water in an awfully long time."

Now everyone on the boat was egging him on. "Come on D.L., you can do it!" my kids were shouting in unison.

The old *gas bag* couldn't resist the temptation to show off in front of an audience.

"I'll do it, Pard, *throw* me a life jacket."

The only life jacket that would fit him was one of the

old orange kind that slipped over your head. I must say, he looked like a *rotund buffoon* with one of those on, more like a bib on his fat torso than a life preserver. D.L. did a *half*-gainer off the side of the boat and frantically paddled his way to the inner tube. We were all *half* ready for some real fun now. *Game on,* I thought, pulling down on the throttle to move away from the tube with D.L. now squarely in it. I knew he would have less than *half* a chance to survive this soon to be summer ride from hell.

I yelled, "When you're ready, give me two thumbs-up and say, '*let er rip, tater chip*'!'"

I could barely contain myself. My kids thought the *tater chip* battle cry hilarious.

"Are you ready, D.L.?"

"Ready," he said, sounding for the first time scared to death, his enormous fat torso looking like custard, *oozing* out of the middle of a jelly-filled donut.

"Give me the signal!"

"*Let er rip, tater chip*!" His high-pitched squeal sounding more like a pig getting castrated on a farm than a grown man screaming.

I pushed down on the throttle, and D.L. nearly flipped out of the back of the inner tube. He was now holding onto the side grips with both hands and *squealing* like the swine he was. Chiquita sat next to me, enjoying every minute of this aquatic sideshow. My kids sat up in the bow and were laughing and waving at the geriatric, gray-haired, no-legged, tubby tuber.

"*Slow down, Pard*! Slow *down*, I'm a gonna flip out of this *darned* contraption, *slow* down *damn* it, *slow* down, I say!"

I took D.L. on a frightening, hair-raising, *white-*

knuckle ride from hell; he was screaming at the top of his lungs as we weaved in and out of other boats, downing skiers and a log or two. *"Paybacks are a bitch,"* I muttered to myself, taking a sharp corner and flipping D.L. off the inner tube. He did a *barrel roll* at least six times, *skidding* across the top of the water. Now I went into my own comedy routine, which I had learned from my former mentor long ago.

"What do you call a man with no legs inner tubing?"

Bronson said, "Skip?"

"Wrong answer . . . that was my first dad, actually, son."

Destiny replied, "Bob?"

"Wrong again, that just happened to be the name of my seventh dad."

"The answer, my friends, is D.L. Kirby, the *Rotund Buffoon.*"

"The Rotund Buffoon? Why do you call him that?" my wife now chimed in.

"It is a name I gave him long ago, when he took me skiing and made me ride on his shoulders. He would scare the snot out of me just for the *sport* of it," I finally recounted these times fully. "He grabbed my hand and made me '*buddy* jump' with him off tall railroad trestles just to show off, and I would scream, *holy crap, I am gonna die.* He wasn't a dad to me—he was the *Rotund Buffoon* and I was the butt end of all his drunken antics as a kid."

I wanted to smile and laugh, but I instead *choked* up and almost started to cry. But I thought better of it; I didn't want my kids to see me *lose it* that day. The inner tubing *ride from hell* was fun, but it hurt me, *touched* me in a way I hadn't anticipated, bringing up all of those boyhood memories to the surface once again. How could a dad do all of those terrible *things* to his own son? Now that I was a father of two great kids of my own, *it* was mind boggling to me.

My kids stared at me—not knowing whether to laugh or give me a big hug. My wife said, "All right, we've had about enough of your *pleasant* little childhood stories for one day, Mark. Pull D.L. in before he drowns out there."

As we pulled the *half*-alive, bloated, sawed-off flounder into the boat, I said, "Hey, *Pard*, you look like you've been eaten by a bear and *shit* over a cliff." My sadness had now suddenly speed-shifted to spite for the old man who once sinisterly posed as my father growing up.

My wife and kids gawked at me in stupefied horror; I turned heartless on this once-friendly family boat trip.

I looked at them all and scoffed, "It's an inside joke, guys, something from my childhood. You had to have been there forty years ago at Loon Lake."

D.L. looked up at me with the timidity of a helpless child as I pulled him in. Chiquita stared at him and started to growl. She wasn't fooled. Her instincts were *spot* on.

It was time to go home for the day, as D.L. toweled his *half*-naked body and we pulled into the dock. Mission accomplished, I thought, as I had given D.L. a taste of his own medicine. Although it did not ease the real troubled emotions I was wrestling with that day.

The following morning, we took D.L. downtown to rent a car. He was off to the McKenzie River to meet some *old* friends. The man at the counter gave D.L. directions to Interstate 5 South and we let him go on his merry way to the land of hillbillies and moonshine.

As Bronson and I got into the car, we spotted D.L.

Kirby going the wrong way on a one-way street in his *Rent-A-Dent* automobile. Fittingly he chose this rental car agency because it was *half* price. It is a sight I'll never forget. My son and I were laughing hysterically. That is the last time I ever saw D.L. alive, and I will maintain with glee, forever etched in memory, that image of D.L. going the wrong way down that busy street.

(7)

D.L. Kirby died five years later. He was driving his motorized home from the grocery store on a cold, dark, December night in Anchorage, Alaska, and crashed headfirst into a snow bank. He wasn't found for several hours and died a week later in a short-term care facility.

Grace said, "He got what he deserved, the drunken old pervert."

My mom said, "I hope he *rots in hell* for what he did, the *dirty* bastard. Oh, by the way Mark, Bob and I are going to Puerto Vallarta next week. We just bought a new time-share there, and it's *absolutely* fabulous." She was as *excited* as a teenage schoolgirl, her mind shifting to more urgent matters in her life.

I was left in charge of his funeral arrangements, being the sole living relative who would actually *claim* him. Thank God for my wife; she handled the arrangements at the funeral home. I just could not *deal* with *it*. He would never tell me that he was *sorry*. D.L. would never *own* his abusive actions in any way. My sister, on the other hand, had *left him for dead* long ago and she would have nothing to do with of any of this situation. I respected her for that.

My wife and I flew to Anchorage to handle D.L.'s meager estate. His small apartment was cleaned out by his landlord and, by the time we got there, his personal belongings were boxed up and moved to a storage room. He owed quite a bit of money to debt collectors, so part of our time was spent selling any items of value on Craigslist and paying off his bills. We sold his car and a few guns. Most of what we had left was just junk he had collected over the years.

As we opened up boxes and boxes of his worthless stuff for hours on end, I found one particular small box that took me aback, and for a moment in time *paralyzed* my actions and my thoughts. In this box, I found a dirty striped pillowcase, tattered and worn, with a *shoe box* in it. This *box*, as I opened it *slowly* and knowingly, contained *those* pictures from long ago. It also had other pictures of boys that D.L. had collected over the years. These were his disgusting *trophies* of what he had either done to little kids, or merely photos of boys that he had fantasized about over the years. Pictures of neighborhood boys from my youth, many snapshots of little Shawn, and me. Wedding pictures of ring bearers and young male wedding participants, snapshots of boys from all the places he had lived, from Korea to Oregon to Klawock, Alaska. It was a scrapbook of *childhood innocence* meets *pure evil,* and I was *trembling.*

At the very bottom of this box was a torn picture of me as a young boy of five in my boxing robe with the name *Kirby* on it. He had kept this picture of me for over forty years, hidden in that box. He wrote on the back, *Pard, May 1965.* For the first time in a very long time, I broke down and cried, sobbing in front of my wife, clutching that small picture in my hand. I felt frustration, anger, and humiliation over my dad the molester, the sexual predator, the pedophile. All of these feelings were unleashed from my body in a single episode of emotional despair. My wife gave me a hug as I sobbed like an abused four-year-old kid in her arms.

I was also *angry* with myself that day. I needed to stop being a victim and own my part in this cycle of child abuse in my family and in our society. I should have been stronger when I was a boy. Should have called the police. I regretted never telling my mom or even Melvin about my abuse. I could have told a teacher or counselor at school. Got DHS involved. This burden that I would bear, was all on *me* now. No more D.L. to blame anymore. I couldn't blame it on my mom, either. Sure, I was *abused*. I know now through counseling *it* wasn't my fault. But that didn't give me the *right* to take other kids down with me. I was a *coward*. A *lost* and *broken* man. I needed to stop drinking.

And I knew at some point, I needed to *share* my story in writing. When I wrote this book, not *one* person in my family (except for my wife) wanted to be mentioned in it by their *real* names. They were afraid of what other people might *think* of *them*. Afraid of *it* affecting their *brand*. Just like I was growing up. We boomers didn't call it our *brand* back then. We just didn't want to get *picked* on at school. This is a *systemic* problem in our society. Maybe they will think you're *gay* was one idiotic comment I got. What does someone's sexual orientation have to do with child abuse? These are *pedophiles* here. A special *brand* of criminal. How naive *we* all are.

At first I was *angry*. Then an ah-ha moment. I realized this is *why* child abuse is such a problem in our society. Seemingly *normal* families, daycares, schools, the clergy.

It happens all the time. Right under people's noses. We just *turn* the other cheek. Don't want to get involved. Don't *ask*. Don't *tell*. No one wants to talk about *it*. *Any* or *all* of *it*. I would make it my mission to write *this* book for *all* of the kids who have been abused moving forward. It was time for *me* to speak. *It's* *Show* and *Tell* time, boys and girls.

I took that box of photos outside to the burn pile that we had been making that day, threw some lighter fluid on that pillowcase and box, chucked my *last* bottle of gin on top and lit it all up, trying to eliminate those images from my mind forever. But you never really can forget *it*. No matter how hard I tried, those many images of innocent kids burn in the back of my mind. Still, I would move forward sober now, realizing that self-medicating *it* would never work. Time to start writing.

D.L. was buried in the Anchorage Veterans Memorial Cemetery with all the honors of having served in the Korean War. It is strange, really—a man who gave to his country, but took so much from his own family. Conflicted is the only way I could make sense of it in my muddled mind. Moving forward, I knew I would have to forgive the man I shared a last name with.

I spoke to his tiny headstone, in that cemetery full of dead war heroes: "D.L., you were a mean old son of a bitch, but I am a better person for having known you. You inspired me to be a good father and an excellent role model for kids as a teacher and coach by being the person I *did not* want to become. Your cutting words will always be in the back of my mind as a challenge for me to do better with my own life. My kids and grandkids will carry on the Kirby name proudly and, from here on out, this family name moving forward will be a great source of pride for generations to come. Not shame, I will see to that. Rest in peace, D.L., rest in peace."

I would move on with my life once again. *He* was *dead* and *I* was still *alive*. You were actually right about one thing though, *Pard* . . .

"Life was indeed a *bitch* and then you died."

(8)

The thought of dying—in that hour of unknowing, waiting for the call from the doctor, I had submitted and became a victim to *it* once again.

I finally got the long-awaited call from urgent care. "Mr. Kirby, I have some good news and some bad news for you."

"Yes?" I slowly answered.

"The *good* news is, your cancer hasn't spread," she said, "In fact, it looks like you currently have *no* cancer at all."

"Thank God, that is *great* news," I replied. "What's the *bad* news?"

"You have some tiny kidney stones that probably account for your lower back pain."

"Thank goodness, just a few kidneys stones! Thank you, doctor."

"Your primary care physician will call you Monday to talk to you about a plan to pass those painful kidney stones. I suggest you get a PSA as well to confirm what we saw on the CAT scan. Have a great weekend, Mr. Kirby."

"Thank you, doctor, you have a great weekend as well."

I hung up the phone, dancing, and screaming for joy

in my boxer shorts and a T-shirt. "I have kidney stones, *only* kidney stones." I laughed and shouted, running around my house like a mad man. "I can't believe it! I *just* have kidney stones!"

To think I was excited by kidney stones. But this is what having cancer is like: one random, drive by scare after another—just like my days spent with D.L. as a young boy. I was beginning to embrace the idea that I needed to stop worrying about my health so damned much. It could always be worse. I could be dead! *Father time* would ultimately win in the end, anyways. He has an undefeated record.

As I sat there alone in the early hours of the morning, leaning back in my leather office chair, a broad smile spurted across my face. Relax. It *ain't* over until the *fat* lady sings.

That Monday, I got a blood test at *Kaiser* to check my PSA level and it registered a .05, below the average level of most grown men my age. This was indeed exciting news. I was for the first time in a long time cancer *free*.

Dr. Johnson told me by phone that week, "We could not have hoped for a better outcome, Mark. I will see you later and have a *happy* life."

(9)

I viewed this news as a second lease on life. I live in the moment now with an eye toward the future. I am finally *happy* in Happy Valley, enthusiastically teaching and coaching high schoolers, eating healthy and exercising every day. I am even taking ballroom dance lessons at Arthur Murray Dance Studios with my wife. We have become excellent dancers, working as a *team*. We take long walks together and play golf in our spare time. We are relaxed, happy and enjoy each other's company every day. My wife and I are taking vacations to new and exciting places, and look forward to growing old *together*. We hope for many birthdays, grandkids' recitals, concerts, and games.

My mom? I haven't seen or talked to her in two years. I wish her the best and understand now that I will never be able to *change* her. She is who she is. Grace and I have stopped the *madness* of our childhood memories by simply being there for our kids. Raising them to the *best* of our abilities. Our kids have always been on the front burner. Taking a backseat to *no* one. We take tremendous pride in being *loving* parents ourselves. We have always had *free will* to make our lives better for our kids and grandchildren. We have *broken* the cycle of family abuse. This is undoubtedly our greatest *accomplishment* in life.

Is my life perfect now? Not by any stretch of the imagination. Besides, there is no such thing as *perfect*. I see a mental health therapist on a weekly basis to *vent* and unpack all that is there. Once I wrote this book, I had a lot of *stuff* from my past that I had to *sort* through and make *sense* of. I was diagnosed with PTSD. I was *frightened* to death. I was *angry* at the world. *Angry* at God. *Mad* at my mom and D.L. And *mad* at myself. The invasive nature of the examinations and the treatments had triggered memories of my childhood *sexual* abuse. Too many *dudes* touching me in all the *wrong* places. I also had to come to *grip* with my cancer. Like my abuse, *it* can always come back. It has been great to talk to someone and I am feeling much better now, but *it's* a process. Just like addiction, *one* day at a time. I am slowly moving forward each day. Baby steps.

My wife got me a rescue dog several months ago, a *comfort* dog. His name is Norman, *Norm* for short. He is a cute, white Maltese/Poodle mix, and more of a Norman Bates from *Psycho* than a Norm from *Cheers*. Norm needed a good *home*. A loving family to live with. Some consistency in his life. A place where he could just be a happy, well-adjusted family *pooch*. Not living in *fear* all of time. As simple as that. Not rocket science, folks. No *smoke* and *mirrors* here.

Norm never got *that* kind of unconditional love in his previous home. He was always living in a state of heightened *fear* and *anxiety*. Worried when **It** would happen next. Like *me* living with D.L. You see, Norm has male trust issues like I once did; we have a lot in common. His previous male owner *abused* him before he was rescued by our family veterinarian. I was lucky enough to have been rescued by Michael Melvin as an *abused* boy. We rescued Norm. How in the world could anyone *abuse* a *helpless* animal? An *innocent* child? It is *beyond* me. But sadly, *it* happens.

When my wife saw Norm, she knew instantly our home would be a perfect *fit* for him. Norman adores my wife and bonded with her immediately. He is really my wife's dog, but Norm and I are bonding—I am gaining his trust each and every day. We are slowly *bonding* with each other. *Trust* takes *time* to build and can easily be broken in *one* negative encounter. *We* should *know*. We survived *it*. Norm is my *boy*. I'm here *to protect* him. He means the *world* to me. I'm giving him the kind of love I *never* got as a kid. Unconditional, *selfless* love.

About Atmosphere Press

Atmosphere Press is an independent, full-service publisher for excellent books in all genres and for all audiences. Learn more about what we do at atmospherepress.com.

We encourage you to check out some of Atmosphere's latest releases, which are available at Amazon.com and via order from your local bookstore:

The Hidden Life, a novel by Robert Castle

Big Beasts, a novel by Patrick Scott

Alvarado, a novel by John W. Horton III

Nothing to Get Nostalgic About, a novel by Eddie Brophy

GROW: A Jack and Lake Creek Book, novel by Chris S McGee

Home is Not This Body, a novel by Karahn Washington

Whose Mary Kate, a novel by Jane Leclere Doyle

Stuck and Drunk in Shadyside, a novel by M. Byerly

These Things Happen, a novel by Chris Caldwell

Vanity: Murder in the Name of Sin, a novel by Rhiannon Garrard

Blood of the True Believer, a novel by Brandann R. Hill-Mann

The Dark Secrets of Barth and Williams College: A Comedy in Two Semesters, a novel by Glen Weissenberger

The Glorious Between, a novel by Doug Reid

An Expectation of Plenty, a novel by Thomas Bazar

Sink or Swim, Brooklyn, a novel by Ron Kemper

About the Author

Mark Kirby has been a lifelong Steelers fan. He earned a bachelor's degree at Oregon State University and a MAT degree at George Fox University. He has taught and coached in public schools for 28 years in the Pacific Northwest. He currently teaches high school Economics. He and his wife of 35 years Barb, raised two children and have been blessed with two grandchildren. He is currently working on his third novel.

CPSIA information can be obtained
at www.ICGtesting.com
Printed in the USA
BVHW031750150321
602572BV00002B/249